Essential Option Strategies

Essential Option Strategies

UNDERSTANDING THE MARKET AND AVOIDING COMMON PITFALLS

JJ Kinahan

WILEY

Published by John Wiley & Sons, Inc., Hoboken, New Jersey.
Published simultaneously in Canada.

Library of Congress Cataloging-in-Publication Data is available.

Names: Kinahan, J. J., 1963- author.
Title: Essential option strategies : understanding the market and avoiding
     common pitfalls / J. J. Kinahan.
Description: Hoboken : Wiley, 2016. | Includes index.
Identifiers: LCCN 2016021570 (print) | LCCN 2016036186 (ebook) | ISBN
     9781119263333 (hardback) | ISBN 9781119291541 (ePDF) | ISBN 9781119291510
     ePub) | ISBN 9781119291541 (epdf) | ISBN 9781119291510 (epub)
Subjects: LCSH: Options (Finance) | Investments. | BISAC: BUSINESS &
     ECONOMICS / Finance.
Classification: LCC HG6024.A3 .K556 2016 (print) | LCC HG6024.A3 (ebook) |
     DDC 332.64/53—dc23
LC record available at https://lccn.loc.gov/2016021570

Cover Design: Wiley
Cover Image: Stock market candle graph © Butsaya/iStockphoto

Printed in the United States of America

10 9 8 7 6 5 4 3 2 1

To Karen, Kaitlin, Kevin, and Kelly. Your love and support make all things possible.

Contents

Foreword

I began trading options on the floor of the CBOE in the early 1980s, just a few years before JJ. Back then, we were trader indifferent, which meant we would trade anything with anybody. Today, we would say the same about our approach to the products and strategies that we choose. These days, the counterparty to our trades is a computer with theoretical algorithm with unlimited funding. Back then, it was some kid just like us—nervous and sweating while trying to make a few eighths.

JJ and I traded together, played together, worked together, and learned together. Luckily, we were among the survivors. We excelled at our craft by managing our egos and not getting caught in the fat tails (volatility) of a few explosive moves. But the business changed as it grew exponentially, and open outcry faced certain extinction around 2000.

Now, the original trader cowboys are gone. Billions of new dollars, lightning-fast servers, and hard-coded theoretical models have taken over. Still, JJ, myself, and a handful of others decided we still had a lot left to learn and to share publicly. The same customers we lived off of were now our partners. And with strong beliefs that options remain the greatest strategic instrument in the world, our new mission was clear: Let's gather the gang together and share our stories. First came the technology to facilitate our mission, and next came the content.

In his first book, JJ reviews, discusses, and critiques almost every progressive strategy available. He puts great context around those ideas, so they are usable in real time. You'll see through his stories that the trader spirit remains in his words and transcends decades and advancements in technology.

Tom Sosnoff

Preface

A lot has changed in the options world since I started my career as a floor trader on the Chicago Board Options Exchange (CBOE) thirty years ago. Obviously, technology has transformed the exchanges, and with one or two exceptions, the live pits with crowds of screaming traders, like in Figure P-1, are largely a thing of the past.

At the same time, options markets are no longer confined to industrial countries or limited to instruments such as stocks and commodities. Contracts are now listed on a wide array of different asset classes, including fixed income, precious metals, energy, and even volatility. In addition, sufficient advances in technology have enabled many emerging economies to offer options as investment opportunities and as tools to manage risk.

My focus in this book is helping you, the retail client, understand some of the more actively traded securities in the U.S. markets, where options on equities and futures trade on more than a dozen different exchanges today, and only two—the Chicago Board Options Exchange and the Chicago Mercantile Exchange—are hybrid markets with both electronic and floor-based pit trading.

Technology is not only driving how instruments are traded, but it has changed how information flows as well. It has leveled the playing field for individual investors. When I started my career, professional traders largely relied on the same sources for price information and financial news. Research was at a premium, and analysts provided reports only to their investment advisers, salespeople, and selected clients.

Today, real-time price quotes are readily available by looking online, through brokerages, and with mobile apps. Wall Street research faces competition from financial websites, blogs, and independent analysts. While information flows freely, social media drives increased interaction among individual investors and encourages the sharing of experiences and ideas.

Figure P-1   Live trading pits like this one are largely extinct
Source: Shutterstock

I have seen the evolution firsthand and from a unique vantage point. Prior to joining TD Ameritrade, I worked for thinkorswim® (TOS), a Chicago-based brokerage firm with a focus on options trading. It was a revolutionary standalone trading platform specifically designed for individual traders. At that time, average daily volume across the listed options market in the United States was about 2 million contracts. Just ten years later, in 2009, that figure had increased to more than 14 million.

That same year, TD Ameritrade acquired thinkorswim and has continued to develop and improve the thinkorswim trading platform. This book includes many charts, examples, and ideas that have been developed over the years by the great team I am on at TD Ameritrade. As the markets change, so do our technology and tools.

Despite the fact that the number of trading instruments has increased exponentially, buying and selling is faster and more efficient, and information is more readily available than ever, some things in the options market are the same today as they were thirty years ago. For example, the determinants of an option price are the same today as in the 1970s. As you will see, there are basic tenets of investing that don't really change, and once you learn them today, they are likely to still apply thirty years from now.

The aim of this book is to share my experiences to help readers better understand the options market and explore the opportunities that exist today. I want to do it in a way that offers a commonsense approach without overwhelming the reader with numbers. But, at the same time, the book won't accomplish its objective unless the reader fully understands key concepts.

In summary, the fundamentals of the investment process don't really change, but the advances in technology have created an environment where individual investors have better information and tools than they did in the past. In fact, there has never been a better time to learn the options strategies that were once the domain of only the smartest professional traders.

The book kicks off with Part 1, appropriately titled "Getting Started in Investing." Chapter 1, "The Opening Bell," begins with very basic information you need prior to investing in stocks or options. For many, this is merely review, but for those of you who are newer to trading options or newer to investing in general, it offers basic information about financial markets today, how to get started, and suggestions for creating a trading plan.

From there, the discussion continues with a list of indicators to track in Chapter 2, "First Days of Trading." Understanding underlying instruments such as stocks, futures, and indexes is important and covered in Chapter 3, "Know the Underlying." I conclude Part I with a discussion about "Avoiding Mistakes," the focus of Chapter 4.

Part II takes a basic understanding of investing to the options market. Chapter 5 covers options basics. Call and put options are defined in Chapters 6 and 7. Chapter 8 explains the determinants of options prices, and the math gets a bit more advanced when I talk about probabilities in Chapter 9. But don't worry, all of the examples are intuitive, and no advanced math is required.

Part III dives into more advanced options strategies. The basic strategies of covered calls and protective puts are covered in Chapters 10 and 11. Then my focus turns to spread trading. Long vertical spreads are the topic of Chapter 12, and short verticals are discussed thoroughly in Chapter 13. Calendar or time spreads are discussed in Chapter 14. Chapters 15 and 16 explore two advanced strategies—butterflies and condors. Chapter 17, "The Close," concludes Part III and covers the important concept of risk management.

For reference, Appendix A offers a look at delta, gamma, and the other Greeks. It offers definitions of each measure and serves as a quick reference. Appendix B shows different charts and basics of technical analysis. It also includes the payoff or risk graphs for the options strategies covered in Chapters 6 through 12. Appendix C is a primer on stock charts and volatility studies. A Glossary is provided at the end of the book as well.

I really hope this book helps you understand the fundamentals of the options market while also providing the confidence and tools you need to begin using strategies as part of a longer-term trading plan. Importantly, while I use real-world examples in this book, they are for educational and illustrative purposes only.

The securities depicted are sometimes real and sometimes hypothetical. They are specifically not solicitations or recommendations to trade a specific security or to engage in a particular trading or investing strategy. In addition, transaction costs, such as commissions and other fees, are important factors that should be considered when evaluating any trading opportunity.

The book starts at a very basic level, and for experienced traders, Part I might seem like a 101 material. But in the end, the reader will come away with a thorough understanding of options, techniques the pros use, and why the industry has experienced exponential growth since I started my career on the trading floor.

Please use this book to help you and your family pursue your investing and trading goals. Keep in mind that options trading entails significant risk and is not appropriate for every investor. Complex options strategies can carry additional risk. And futures and futures options trading is speculative and not suitable for all investors.

For me, the options business is something that I love and am passionate about. Hopefully, after digging through the early chapters, you will share the same appreciation about this business...and how it can provide tremendous opportunities for anyone willing to work hard and learn.

Acknowledgments

I was very happy to be given the opportunity to write a book designed to help retail investors as they embark on their journey into options investing. My goal was to provide information that demystified much of the difficulty by making the approach straightforward, using common sense rather than complicated math. I have been lucky to meet so many of you who are out there day after day working to get better. I admire your desire to learn and your commitment to improving your lives through investing. You are the inspiration for this book, and I hope you find it useful.

This was a large undertaking, and so many TD Ameritrade partners helped make it a success. A big thank you to CEO Fred Tomczyk, President Tim Hockey, and EVP Trader Group Steve Quirk for allowing me to pursue this undertaking. Thank you to the Active Trading Team for letting me work alongside you every day and seeing all your amazing accomplishments. I want to thank the Compliance Team. This took many hours of your time, and I greatly appreciate it. Thanks to the Marketing Team for all the help getting started and the constant guidance along the way. CAPAE Team, you are always a pleasure to work with, and Legal Team, thank you for your trusted counsel.

Fred Ruffy, it was great working with you. Thank you for the insight and suggestions. Thanks to the folks at Wiley. You are wonderful partners who made the process easy.

Thanks to both Zack Fishman and Paul Picchietti for taking a chance on me straight out of college and beginning to teach me the world of options. And also, thanks to Tom Sosnoff, from whom I have learned so much.

Most importantly, I want to thank my family—my late parents who did an amazing job of showing me the meaning of work ethic and sacrifice; my brothers and sisters for helping their youngest sibling every step of the way; and, of course, my wife, Karen, and our children, Kaitlin, Kevin, and Kelly.

About the Author

An options industry veteran, JJ Kinahan started his trading career in 1985 at the Chicago Board Options Exchange (CBOE). As a market maker, he traded primarily on the floor in the S&P 100 (OEX) and S&P 500 (SPX) pits. Later, he worked for ING Bank and Blue Capital. He then became managing director of options trading for Van der Moolen, USA.

In 2006 JJ joined the Chicago-based options trading brokerage firm thinkorswim where he served many roles, including developing educational content and helping build the tools that are integrated into the thinkorswim® platform today. JJ is now chief market strategist for TD Ameritrade, which acquired thinkorswim in 2009.

JJ is a frequent CNBC guest, a *Forbes* contributor, and often quoted in *The Wall Street Journal, Financial Times*, Reuters, and many other respected media outlets. He is on the Advisory Board at the CBOE. When not busy working or trading, he is an avid Chicago sports fan who enjoys reading, fishing, and spending time with his wife and three children.

PART

I

Getting Started in Investing

CHAPTER 1

The Opening Bell

At 9:30 a.m. (EST) on every business day, a bell at the New York Stock Exchange sounds, and trading on the exchange floor begins. Investors buy and sell stocks like jockeys scrambling for positions at the Kentucky Derby. News flow drives the buying and selling decisions from one day to the next.

When the day's news doesn't deviate too much from expectations, the result is typically orderly and normal market action. However, when unexpected events result in dramatic changes in the expectations, large price moves and fast trading ensue. In other words, the day's news events can result in changes in investor sentiment and result in higher or lower levels of market volatility.

It can seem overwhelming. I remember when I left the trading floors after twenty-one years at the Chicago Board Options Exchange (CBOE). My focus shifted from a small number of instruments to a huge universe of different opportunities. I started trading in markets that were unknown to me. The results were horrible. Over time, I realized that it was better to keep a laserlike focus on markets that I understood and believed in. It is simply impossible to track the moves of every different market, much less trade them all effectively.

Moreover, the importance of news events will also vary from one investor to the next. A large pension fund taking positions in a widely held stock like Apple (AAPL) or General Electric (GE) for a longer-term portfolio isn't likely to react to a news report the same way as a stock trader buying and selling stocks for short-term profits. A retiree has a different set of goals than a recent college graduate.

An options market maker on the CBOE is using equity options differently than a financial adviser selling options in an attempt to generate income for a customer's portfolio.

Although we all have different goals and objectives, the millions of participants in the financial markets digest the day's news, and the results move asset prices as the information becomes available. This is not only true of U.S. markets, but of financial instruments around the globe.

My focus in this book is primarily on U.S. Exchange listed equities, options, and equity futures markets that are open during the regular hours of 9:30 a.m. to 4:00 p.m., Monday through Friday, but there are many investments that trade beyond that. In 1985, regular trading hours were expanded beyond these hours. Premarket trading now begins at 4:00 a.m., and the after-hours session runs from 4:00 to 8:00 p.m.

Options, meanwhile, trade on thirteen different exchanges from 9:30 a.m. to 4:00 p.m. currently, and those hours may soon be expanded. Trading hours for futures and futures options vary by product, but more popular instruments like S&P 500 futures now trade nearly around the clock beginning Sunday at 6:00 p.m. and continuing through Friday evening. So when you come home at 2:00 a.m. after a few drinks at a neighborhood party, you can trade S&P 500 futures from your online brokerage account. However, that is not really recommended!

The expansion of trading hours and growth in financial markets is being driven by the exchanges to satisfy investor demand for new investment products and opportunities. At the same time, technology has created better efficiency and linked global markets. News flow travels fast and often results in sudden market moves that ripple from one economy to the next.

Yet, while today's faster and more complex market sometimes seems daunting to investors, the principles of investing have not changed. With a bit of time and effort, the fundamentals are easy to understand. So let's begin.

Probabilities

"How do I get started?"

I hear that question a lot. Many people understand the importance of investing and building wealth but don't know where to turn. Interest rates have been historically low for quite some time, and traditional banking instruments like money markets and savings accounts are not offering much in the way of yields. So what choices exist when seeking returns on one's hard-earned money?

Before I dive into specific instruments, let me introduce the probability concept. There are a myriad of different opportunities available to investors today, and all of them have varying probabilities of success. We can never predict the future with certainty, and so investments decisions are based on expectations about probable outcomes. We might say, based on our expectations, that an outcome is likely, is probable, or has a good chance.

Just like risk and reward, probability and strategy selection are two sides of the same coin. You have no doubt heard the expression, "high risk, high reward." It refers to the fact that investments that offer the highest rewards typically have the greatest risk. Playing the lottery is an example of an extreme high-risk, high-reward endeavor. There is a very high rate of failure, but a winning ticket would mean a big payoff. On the other hand, burying your life's savings in the backyard is probably a low-risk, low-reward scenario (although risks increase if you bury everything near the family dog's bone stash).

In trading options, and remember, options are simply pricing probabilities, a strategy that has a very high probability of success and a low probability of loss is likely to have smaller potential for profit. On the other hand, a strategy with a small probability of profit should generate a larger potential profit when successful.

In later chapters, we will explore simple probability concepts and ways to compute probabilities for various options strategies. The important point to take home for now is that various investments or strategies are more than just good or bad ideas. Each strategy has a quantifiable probability of success.

Getting Started

What investments have the greatest probability of helping you attain your goals? There's no one single right answer, because every individual and institution is different. It's like asking, what's the best car to buy? It really depends on what you're using it for.

The first step to finding appropriate investments is to outline longer-term goals and objectives. Obviously, we all want to build more wealth, but unless we outline a concise plan, we are unlikely to set money aside each month or invest on a regular basis to achieve our objectives. The best investment choices often depend on a person's age, ambitions, and investment time horizon. For instance, as you will see in later chapters, some options contracts exist for a mere week, while others have lives that span many years. What is your investing time horizon, and how much are you putting away each paycheck?

Five Steps in the Investment Process

1. Set longer-term goals and objectives.
2. Develop a trading plan.
3. Identify investment opportunities.
4. Execute (open) trades.
5. Monitor, adjust, and exit open positions.

After the decision to invest has been made, the next step is to develop a plan. How will you try to reach your goals? Can you trade actively during the trading day, or will your investments be made only once per week or per month? Are you investing for five days, five years or fifty years? How much risk are you willing to take? What financial instruments—stocks, futures, bonds, options, commodities—will take part of the trading plan?

Developing a relationship with a brokerage firm is a key part of the trading plan. A brokerage (or broker-dealer) like my firm, holds customer funds and places buy and sell orders as instructed by you, the client. The first step is to open an account and submit any trading approval request forms. For example, investing in options requires applying for options trading approval from your broker.

While many investors focus on brokerage commissions and fees, there are a number of other things to consider besides price. The primary thing to consider is service. For example, does the firm have people that can answer my questions and help me when needed? Make sure they can help you pursue your trading goals. As you read through the chapters of this book, you will likely find the investments and strategies that match your longer-term goals and trading plan.

Research

Believing in your trading plan and your investment choices will lower your stress levels during times of increasing market volatility.

Research is often a key to maintaining that conviction and also to finding attractive investment opportunities. In addition, it often makes sense to research companies or investments that you already know and love.

For example, let's say you own a pizza restaurant and a salesperson from The Pizza Sauce Company stops by your shop with samples of his newest sauce. You like the taste, and the price is $0.10 per can below your current supplier. You agree to sample a few cases and discover your customers love it. Your pies have never tasted better. Mama mia!

Convinced that The Pizza Sauce Company will soon gain substantial market share from its pizza sauce competitors, you check with your broker for any research available on the company. You discover that the stock is trading under the symbol PZZA. Two analysts currently cover the stock, and both agree that the company has a clean balance sheet, and shares are attractive at current levels, according to the research. Both analysts have a twelve-month price target of $26 per share.

At $20 per share, you note on the daily stock chart that the stock hasn't moved much during the past six months, but you believe that is likely to change once it becomes clear that the company is gaining market share over competitors. Your trading plan states that you do not invest more than 5 percent of your $200,000 portfolio, or more than $10,000, on one position. Instead, you place on order on your broker's platform to buy 250 shares of PZZA, for an investment of $5,000, or 2.5 percent of your portfolio.

Fast-forward one year, and as you had anticipated, The Pizza Sauce Company is outperforming its competitors, and the share price has increased to $25. You still hold 250 shares, now worth a total of $6,250, for an unrealized gain of $1,250.

However, a few weeks later, Pepperoni & Mozzarella Inc. says its cheese sales are falling short of previous expectations, and its stock drops 20 percent. The steep decline triggers a ripple effect that is felt across nearly every pizza company, as investors interpret the news as sign that pie sales are falling across the board.

Shares of The Pizza Sauce Company fall back to $22. However, your research continues to indicate that PZZA has strong fundamentals and is still gaining market share. Rather than sell hastily based on the headlines related to Pepperoni & Mozzarella, you are more likely to maintain your conviction in PZZA and possibly even buy more shares on the pullback. And that's exactly what you decide to do.

You place an order electronically to buy another 250 shares of The Pizza Sauce Company for $22 per share. You now own, and you are long, 500 shares at an average cost of $21 per share, for a total investment of $10,500. Assuming you earned 2 percent on the other assets in your account during the past year, the portfolio is now worth $204,150, or $193,650 plus the $10,500 of PZZA.

Long versus Short

- Going *long* is taking a new position as a buyer. If you are long a stock, you want the stock to increase in price so you can sell it at a profit.

- Going *short* is initiating an opening position as a seller. If you are short a stock, you want the stock price to fall so you can buy it back at a lower price. The mechanics of selling stock short are covered in detail in Chapter 3.

Your analysis was correct. Four months later, shares of The Pizza Sauce Company have recovered some losses and now trade for $25. You own 500 shares at a cost basis of $21, and the position is now worth $12,500 for an unrealized profit of $2,000. The total portfolio is now worth $207,700, or $195,200 and $12,500 of PZZA shares.

The stock position now accounts for 6 percent of your portfolio and exceeds the 5 percent threshold dictated by your trading plan. You sell 100 shares at $25 a share and reduce the position in The Pizza Sauce Company to 400 shares. The adjustment leaves you long 400 shares worth $25, or $10,000. You have booked $400 in realized taxable profits and have $1,600 of unrealized gains.

Indeed, as you will see in later chapters, sometimes the best investment opportunities happen when the news headlines seem the worst. At the end of the day, there is no substitute for timely, thoughtful research. Once you have a trading plan and have determined what instruments you will use to pursue your goals, find a broker who offers the type of research that will help you make informed decisions and keep you focused on the bigger picture when short-term events cause momentary setbacks. Research when combined with probability is a powerful combination.

Data

It wasn't that long ago when, outside the trading desks and the professional investment community, most investors relied on printed newspapers to see price changes to their stock positions. Periodicals like *The Wall Street Journal* and *Investor's Business Daily* provided tables of stocks listed alphabetically, and the prices represented the closing prices from the day before.

Five Components of a Stock Quote

- Open: The first price of the trading day.
- Last: The most recent price.
- High: The highest price of the trading day.
- Low: The lowest price of the day.
- Close: The final price of the trading day. It will be the same as the last price at the end of the trading day.

Wow, a lot has changed since that time! Many websites readily offer free delayed intraday prices. Brokerage firms typically offer free real-time quotes to their customers as well. Offerings might include a symbol quote box where you can type in a ticker symbol or tables that include lists of multiple symbols along with relevant information, including last, high, and low prices.

Figure 1-1 is a snapshot of what I watch on the thinkorswim platform each day. It includes indexes like the Dow Jones Industrial Average, the S&P 500, and the NASDAQ Composite, as well as some widely held names like Apple (AAPL), Netflix (NFLX), and General Electric (GE). I also watch some of the action in the futures markets, especially the S&P 500 Futures (/ES), and the US 30 year Treasury Bond Futures (ZB), as well as the Euro/US dollar (EUR/USD) currency pair.

I can also see the price quote for any stock by using the Quick Quote tool. First, identify the ticker symbol of the company you're researching. It's simply an abbreviation to uniquely identify a publicly traded instrument like a stock, index, or fund. For example, the ticker for General Electric is straightforward. It's GE. However, sometimes the ticker is less intuitive and requires a symbol lookup. This is easy to do using most brokerage platforms.

Symbol	Last	Net Chng		High	Low
DJX	178.01	+.03	▥	178.37	177.99
SPX	2090.24	+.13	▥	2093.81	2090.24
/ES[Z5]	2088.25	-1.75	▥	2095.00	2082.25
COMP	5130.8099	+3.2853		5141.3561	5130.7537
VIX	15.73	+.61	▥	15.73	15.52
EUR/USD	1.05799	-.00153		1.05951	1.05636
AAPL	118.35	+.54	▥	118.399	117.75
NFLX	126.11	+.67	▥	126.60	125.61
GE	30.35	-.01	▥	30.40	30.30

Figure 1-1   My Watch List

Quick Quote Main@thinkorswim [build 1880.15]   —   ☐   ✕

Symbol	Last	Net Chng	Bid	Ask
MSFT	54.48	+.55	54.47	54.48

Figure 1-2   Quick Quotes

After the ticker symbol is identified, enter it into the Quick Quote box (Figure 1-2) to see the latest stock prices and the change for the day. In this case, the stock is Microsoft, and the ticker is MSFT. The stock is up $0.55 for the day and last traded at $54.48 per share.

The default setting for Quick Quotes on the thinkorswim plat- form also includes two other important pieces of information—the bid price and the ask price. The bid price is currently the best bid price by a buyer. If an investor wants to sell in the current market, he can expect to receive $54.47 per share. On the other hand, a buyer pays the asking price or $54.48 per share.

Bid versus Ask

Bid and ask reflects the current quotes to buy or sell a stock, option, or futures contract. The bid reflects a willingness to buy, and there- fore a seller can expect to receive the bid price at the time of sale. The ask, or offering price, is a level that a seller or sellers are willing to receive for the security. A buyer typically pays the asking price.

Bids and asks are constantly changing, and there is no guarantee that you can buy or sell at the quoted prices. In addition, less actively traded names can see fairly large differences between bids and asks, which is also called the *bid-ask spread*. In later chapters we explore the mechanics of order entry and explore bids, asks, and bid-ask spreads in more detail. For now, the point to take away is that the last price is not necessarily an indication of the current market price to buy or sell. Bids and asks provide the latest market prices available to sellers and buyers.

Charts

A stock chart is simply a graph that shows price changes over time. In this book, I use two types. The first is a chart that shows the price of the underlying instrument, like stock, future, or index, over a period of time. The second is a payoff chart, or risk graph, and shows the potential risks and rewards of an options strategy. It is covered in more detail in later chapters. For now, let's discuss the basics of stock charting.

The simplest chart type is a line chart. For instance, it's easy to plot a line chart in a spreadsheet using data like date and price. Figure 1-3 shows a daily chart of hypothetical oil prices over twelve months. The line connects the twelve points where price and date intersect on the graph. It starts at $50 per barrel in January and ends at $53 in December.

Traders plot charts for instruments like stocks, interest rates, or commodities to see trends over time. Obviously, few create the charts

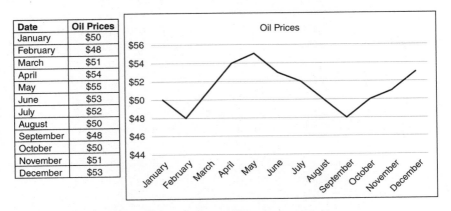

Date	Oil Prices
January	$50
February	$48
March	$51
April	$54
May	$55
June	$53
July	$52
August	$50
September	$48
October	$50
November	$51
December	$53

Figure 1-3   Line Chart of Monthly Oil Prices

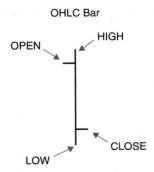

Figure 1-4   OHLC Bar

by hand or in spreadsheets. Charts are readily available on financial websites like StockCharts.com or Google Finance and also through online brokerage firms.

A second, more widely used chart is the open-high-low-close, or OHLC, chart. While the line chart is plotted using just the closing price, an OHLC chart includes bars that contain four pieces of price information.

Figure 1-4 shows an individual bar of an open-high-low-close chart. The small horizontal lines are the opening and closing prices. In this example, the stock opened at one price and closed at a lower price. The length of the vertical line represents the trading range of the day, because the top of the bar is the highest price and the bottom is the lowest.

Like the price chart, the horizontal axis (or bottom) of the OHLC chart represents time, such as days, weeks, or months. The vertical axis (or side) indicates price per unit, such as shares or contracts. Figure 1-5 shows an OHLC chart for a three-month period ended 11/30/2015. The time frame is plotted across the horizontal axis, and the change in price is depicted along the vertical axis.

Notice that the OHLC bars are not all the same length. Longer ones suggest greater distances between highs and lows, and therefore increasing volatility in the security. Shorter ones suggest narrow trading, smaller daily moves, and periods of lower volatility or narrow trading ranges.

The time frame of an OHLC chart can be changed to weekly or monthly. If so, each bar represents the change over one week or one month. Short-term traders sometimes watch intraday bar charts at five-, ten-, or fifteen-minute intervals. Most of the examples throughout this book use daily OHLC charts.

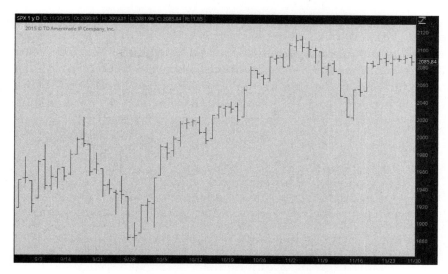

Figure 1-5   Daily Chart of S&P 500 Index (8/31/2015–11/30/2015)

More advanced charting tools are covered in Appendix B. If you have no previous experience with charting, take some time to learn how to identify areas of support and resistance with indicators like trend lines and moving averages. In addition, because the focus of later chapters is on options strategies, volatility studies are also useful. Those are covered in Appendix B as well.

Commissions and Fees

Brokerage firms vary in what they charge their customers. The costs associated with traditional brokerage activities like executing buy and sell orders have been somewhat commoditized, and costs are significantly lower today than they were twenty years ago. The growth of discount and online brokerages is a big reason.

But costs are relative to service. That is, brokerage services can range from very personal to simply taking orders online. Costs typically relate to service level and tools being offered. In short, you can expect to pay higher costs at some firms relative to others, and in an ideal world, the higher costs reflect the value being added.

At the end of the day, the investor's trading plan is a determining factor in broker selection. Are you trading once per month or five times per day? Some firms offer lower rates to active traders, and some charge more for broker-assisted trades.

Also, what types of investments are you buying and selling? Some firms offer certain products that others do not. In fact, futures are regulated under a different umbrella and require different account approvals compared to equities and equity options accounts.

Pattern Day Trader?

Certain rules apply to investors who trade frequently. A pattern day trader is defined as someone who buys and sells a security in the same trading day (intraday) and does it four or more times during a rolling five-business-day period. In order to pattern day trade, the investor must maintain a minimum of $25,000 in a margin account.

Lastly, what kind of technology does the firm offer? Not long ago, charting software, quotes, and live news were expensive. Some firms still charge for these services, and some don't. Other firms also offer premium subscriptions to newsletters, research, and other analytics. Lastly, the costs of trading vary by firm as well. Some of the fees active traders are likely to encounter include:

- **Stock trading costs.** Brokerage firms typically charge a commission to execute stock trades. Some charge a flat commission per trade, some a commission per share, and some a combination of flat plus per share. The rates vary quite a bit across the industry, and many firms will charge more for broker-assisted trades or phone trades compared to online orders.
- **Options trading costs.** The commission and/or fees on options trades vary from one firm to the next. Some firms charge a flat fee or commission plus a per-contract fee. Others might charge only a flat commission or only a per-contract charge. Some offer a combination of both and let the customer decide.
- **Futures trading costs.** As you progress in your trading, you may want to consider using futures to help hedge your portfolio. Similar to stocks and options, these costs may vary.

Virtual Trading Platforms

Over the years, brokerage firms have developed platforms to help individual investors better understand financial markets and how to buy or sell investment securities. The idea is not new, but the technology is. Virtual platforms offer an advanced way to paper trade, which simply means to write down and track your ideas on paper rather than implementing them with real money in the live market. Paper trading makes a lot of sense when attempting to learn new strategies and ideas.

In essence, a virtual trading platform lets you test-drive ideas without risking a dime. The goal is to help you develop an understanding of various financial instruments and the process of investing, which will help you build confidence as a trader.

Keep in mind that successful virtual trading during one period does not guarantee successful investing of actual funds during a later period, as market conditions are always changing. Backtesting is great for learning but has its limits. As you have probably heard many times, past performance is not an indicator of future results.

Many of the examples throughout this book are pulled from TD Ameritrade's paperMoney® virtual trading platform, and therefore, the bells and whistles will be duly highlighted in later chapters.

Summary

The first step in the process is to establish longer-term goals and objectives. Develop a trading plan that considers how much time you have available to trade, your risk tolerance, and the types of investments that might best help you to achieve your longer-term goals. Find a broker who offers the research and tools that meet your objectives. Identify potential trading ideas and test them on paper. Once new positions are opened, monitor, adjust, and exit them accordingly.

There has never been a better time to take a proactive approach to investing. Technology has resulted in better efficiency in financial markets and has substantially reduced trading costs. Research, data, and charts are readily available at little or no cost. Confidence in your plan, strategy selection, and risk management are important elements to long-term success. A virtual trading platform can help by offering a realistic tool to practice trading before going live.

References

CBOE Extended Trading Hours for VIX and SPX www.cboe.com/micro/ eth/pdf/ethfactsheet.pdf

CME Futures Trading Hours www.cmegroup.com/trading-hours.html#
    equityIndex
finance.yahoo.com/
finance.yahoo.com/lookup
www.google.com/finance
NASDAQ Trading Schedule www.nasdaq.com/about/trading-schedule
    .aspx
www.thinkorswim.com/t/pm-registration.html

CHAPTER 2

First Days of Trading

I am interested in the stock market because it really is a fascinating and exciting world to me. Each day, millions of investors make decisions to buy or sell shares of companies based on the latest news and information. Whether it's economic data, earnings, a merger story, geopolitical headlines, or some other event, it's often reflected in the stock market before it even makes the rounds in the news outlets. It's truly an amazing and efficient process.

While stock prices can react rapidly to incoming information, trends often develop over time as well. In bull markets, for instance, stocks are moving broadly higher, and investor sentiment is typically upbeat. In bear markets, shares trend lower, and the overall mood can sour. In addition, there are periods of quiet and uneventful trading, while at other times prices swing wildly in volatile fashion.

But when we say *stock market*, what exactly do we mean, and how do we gauge it from one day to the next? Is it the New York Stock Exchange? Are we referring to the Dow Jones Industrial Average or the NASDAQ? How do we measure the stock market, track its performance from one day to the next, and trade it? Those questions are answered in this chapter. Let's first begin with a brief history of stock market averages and then focus our attention on the key barometer the pros use: the S&P 500 Index.

Brief History of Stock Market Averages

In 1896, Charles Dow computed the average share price of twelve leading companies of the day and started printing the number daily in *The Wall Street Journal*, a publication founded by Dow, Charles Bergstresser, and statistician Edward Jones. Outside of the railroads, the included companies were considered to have the most economic importance at that time. He called his index the Dow Jones Industrial Average, and the index is still a widely watched barometer for economic activity today.

The Dow has since expanded to include thirty different companies; General Electric is the only component of the first average that is still a member today. In fact, the term *industrial average* is a bit deceiving, because the index now includes health care names such as Pfizer and Johnson & Johnson; tech companies such as Apple and Microsoft; food companies such as Coke and Procter & Gamble; and financial companies such as American Express, Goldman Sachs, and Travelers. Table 2-1 shows the Dow Jones Industrial Average, then and now.

The Dow Jones Industrial Average is one of the benchmarks for the stock market (the Dow Transports date back to 1884 when Charles Dow first created the Dow Jones Railroad Average) and is still mentioned daily when the media discusses day-to-date happenings. For instance, if reporters say, "Stocks were up two hundred points," or, "The market lost sixty points," they're likely talking about the industrials. However, the Dow tracks the average performance of just thirty names, and thousands of stocks are trading on the U.S. exchanges.

Table 2-1   The Original Dow Twelve and the Dow Thirty Today

1896	2016	
American Cotton Oil	Apple Inc.	Coca-Cola
American Sugar	American Express	McDonald's
American Tobacco	Boeing	3M
Chicago Gas	Caterpillar	Merck
Distilling & Cattle Feeding	Cisco	Microsoft
General Electric	Chevron Texaco	Nike
Laclede Gas	DuPont	Pfizer
National Lead	Disney	Procter & Gamble
North American	General Electric	Travelers
Tennessee Coal & Iron and Railroad Company	Goldman Sachs	United Healthcare
US Leather	Home Depot	United Tech
US Rubber	IBM	Visa
	Intel	Verizon
	Johnson & Johnson	Wal-Mart Stores
	JP Morgan	Exxon Mobile

Key Market Indexes Today

While the Dow tracks the share price action of thirty leading companies and is considered a "cool" market indicator for television, it is not what professional traders rely on day-to-day. Instead, the S&P 500 is an index that includes five hundred of the largest names traded on the U.S. stock exchanges and represents roughly 80 percent of the total value of the U.S. stock market.

The S&P 500 is not only viewed as a barometer for the performance of the U.S. equities market, but it is often used to benchmark the performance of portfolio managers from one year to the next as well. That is, the relative performance of many money managers is measured against the S&P 500. When your livelihood depends on something, you will watch it very closely!

According to Standard & Poor's, the index represents a total of $2.2 trillion in assets today. The companies are included within the index not because they are the largest, but because they are considered leading companies in key industries within the U.S. economy. In addition, although you cannot buy or sell the index itself, there are many ways individual investors can trade the S&P 500, including options on the S&P 500 Index (SPX); S&P 500 Futures (/ES); and the exchange-traded fund (ETF) SPDR 500 Trust (SPY), or Spiders.

The Index Effect

With a history dating back to 1923, the S&P 500 is now the most widely watched barometer for the performance of the U.S. equity market. In addition, nearly $8 trillion is benchmarked to its performance. Therefore, when a stock is added or removed from the S&P 500, the adjustment triggers strong buying or selling by the mutual funds and portfolios that attempt to mimic the index's performance. The rise or fall of shares of the individual companies being added to or ousted from the S&P 500 is known as the *index effect*.

While the S&P 500 covers far more companies and is a more widely used index than the Dow, the methodology used to compute the S&P 500 is different as well. The industrial average is price weighted, and stocks with higher prices within the index exert more influence than low-priced ones. On the other hand, the S&P 500 is a market-value-weighted average.

Table 2-2   Largest S&P 500 Companies as of April 29, 2016

Company	Ticker	Market Cap (in billions of dollars)
Apple Inc.	AAPL	520
Microsoft Corp	MSFT	394
Exxon Mobil Corp	XOM	367
Berkshire Hathaway B	BRK.B	359
Amazon.com	AMZN	311
Johnson & Johnson	JNJ	309
General Electric Co	GE	287
Facebook	FB	270
Wells Fargo & Co	WFC	254
Alphabet	GOOG	239
AT&T	T	239
JP Morgan Chase & Co	JPM	232
Wal-Mart Stores	WMT	214
Procter & Gamble	PG	213
Verizon Communications	VZ	208
Alphabet	GOOGL	207
Pfizer	PFE	198
Coca-Cola Co	KO	194
Chevron Corp	CVX	192
Home Depot	HD	170

Source: CBOE.com

The top twenty S&P 500 companies account for just 4 percent of the five hundred stocks, but as of this writing, they represent nearly 30 percent of the market value. Table 2-2 shows the largest companies, which include Apple, Microsoft, and Exxon in the top three spots. Because market value is computed as shares outstanding multiplied by share price, it's the biggest companies that dominate the S&P 500 and drive its performance from one day to the next.

The Dow and S&P 500 are not the only two indexes that track the performance of large-cap stocks. The NASDAQ Composite Index represents share prices of companies that trade on the NASDAQ Stock Market. While the NASDAQ Composite does not have listed options, the NASDAQ 100 Index (.NDX) is a separate index that does have puts and calls linked to its performance. The index includes the top one hundred nonfinancial names that trade on the NASDAQ, and large-cap tech names like Apple, Microsoft, and Oracle dominate the index.

Thinking Caps

Capitalization, or cap, refers to the size of a publicly traded company and is computed as the number of shares of the company outstanding multiplied by the current market price. So if a company has 10 million shares outstanding and a $20 stock price, the market cap is $200 million.

Beyond the large-cap Dow, S&P 500, and NASDAQ, a number of mid- and small-cap indexes exist as well. There are, in fact, too many to list here. Table 2-3 summarizes some of the more popular ones. Note that not all of them have listed futures or options contracts.

The Volatility Index

Launched in 1993 by the Chicago Board Options Exchange (CBOE), the CBOE Volatility Index (VIX) was created to offer a real-time gauge of market volatility. Computed using an options pricing model and calculated as a percentage, the index reflects the expected or implied volatility (IV) priced into a strip of short-term S&P 500 Index options. The term *IV* will be defined and discussed in more detail in later chapters.

Table 2-3   Large-, Mid-, and Small-Cap Indexes

Index	Ticker	Description
S&P 500 Index	$SPX	The big daddy of all indexes. It includes 500 stocks and 80 percent of the market cap of the U.S. equities market.
Dow Jones Industrial Average	$INDU, $DJI	With its roots dating back to 1896, it holds 30 large companies from a diverse set of industries.
NASDAQ Composite	$COMP $COMPQ	Along with the Dow and S&P, it is one of the most followed indexes for the U.S. stock market. It includes only names listed for trading on the NASDAQ stock market. No options.
NASDAQ 100 Index	$NDX	Includes the 100 biggest, nonfinancial stocks trading on the NASDAQ stock market.
Russell 2000 Small-Cap Index	$RUT	Sometimes called The Russell, the 2000 is one of many indexes created by Russell Investments. It is arguably the most widely watched barometer for small caps.

For now, let's view VIX as a gauge of investor sentiment and a measure of overall levels of market volatility. It is sometimes called the market's fear gauge, because it typically moves inverse to the S&P 500 and spikes during periods of market uncertainty. The reason for this is that as the market goes down, people are willing to pay more for protection. As the market goes higher, we typically see security-based options become cheaper, and as the market goes down, options usually become more expensive. As I will talk about later, the changes in S&P 500 volatility are also built into options pricing through a concept referred to as *skew*.

For example, the volatility index rose to its highest levels in three years in August 2015 after the S&P 500 suffered a series of setbacks and dropped to 2015 lows. Figure 2-1 shows how a spike in VIX typically happens as the S&P 500 suffers losses.

Over the years, the VIX has become not just the most widely watched gauge for market volatility but also a tradable asset, because it has listed options and futures. The VIX pit at the CBOE is one of only two remaining live trading pits at the exchange. (SPX is the other.) The volatility index has listed futures contracts as well.

Futures

Trading of futures and futures options isn't covered in great detail in this book, but a basic understanding of the instrument can help

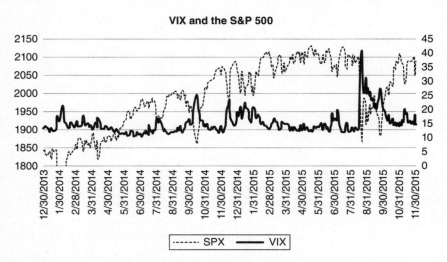

Figure 2-1   Inverse relationship between VIX and the S&P 500

you stay on top of market trends. On the one hand, futures are available on a wide array of instruments, including stocks, bonds, metals, foreign exchange, gold, oil, and a substantial number of agricultural commodities. At the same time, many futures trade outside of normal market hours for the equities markets and can help get a sense of what markets are moving and why.

Futures are typically used to either hedge risk or to speculate. A hedger typically looks to manage risk by taking a position in a futures contract that is opposite to a current position. For example, a soybean farmer might sell soybean futures today to lock in a desired price and hedge the risk of falling prices at a later time. A speculator, on the other hand, trades futures to potentially profit on the direction of the underlying asset. For instance, an investor might buy, or go long, gold futures if he expects strength and rising prices in the metals market.

As the name suggests, a futures contract represents an agreement to buy or sell a commodity or instrument at a later date at a certain price. The futures contract will trade at a different level from the present price (also known as the cash or spot price) due to interest rates and carrying charges. For example, grain futures are priced to reflect charges associated with storage and insurance of the physical commodity.

S&P 500 futures are often a starting point for individual investors, because the product is a natural extension of the equity products that they are already familiar with. An important difference, however, is that futures prices are not the same as the price of a spot or cash market. S&P 500 futures are also priced to reflect dividends paid by S&P 500 components and interest rates. In the current market, S&P futures trade for less than the cash index. As time passes and the futures contract approaches expiration, the cash and futures prices converge.

To arrive at the fair-value price, one must consider that with interest rates near zero today, it is more attractive to own S&P 500 stocks and collect dividends than it is to hold a futures contract. In the past when interest rates were higher than the yield from S&P 500 dividends, the relationship was reversed. That is, the fair value of the futures contract was greater than the cash price.

Although understanding fair value can be beneficial, there is no need to dwell on it here. The only time it gets way out of line is after stocks close at 4:00 p.m. (EST) each day, and the futures keep trading overnight. The relationship will be put to fair value again as soon as all stocks in the index open the next morning. One important point is that the options strategies discussed in this book are applicable to options on equity-based futures.

Futures Price Formula

Futures price = Spot price × (1 + Risk-free rate–Dividend yield)

A detailed discussion of futures pricing lies outside the scope of this book. (For further reference, the Chicago Mercantile Exchange offers a comprehensive discussion of the futures that trade on the exchange, including product specifications and educational material.) The point to take home is that S&P 500 futures trade nearly around the clock, and while the prices will differ from the spot index due to the cost of carry, the futures offer a way to monitor market moves outside of normal market hours in the United States. Many investors, including myself, use S&P 500 indicators as a good movement barometer throughout the trading day.

Within the futures market, commodities are also among the most actively traded contracts, and their price changes can reflect important economic trends. Crude oil, for instance, is sometimes viewed as a gauge of economic strength or weakness. Gold is typically considered a safety hedge during periods of market uncertainty or when inflation fears arise. Some of the futures I track, along with their ticker symbols, are included in Table 2-4.

Table 2-4   Actively Traded Futures Contracts

E-Mini S&P 500 Futures	/ES	Futures contract equal to one-fifth the standard S&P 500 contract
E-Mini Dow Futures	/YM	Based on the Dow Jones Industrial Average
E-Mini NASDAQ	/NQ	Futures based on the NASDAQ 100 Index
Treasury Note Futures	/ZN	Futures on the 10-year U.S. Treasury
30-Year Futures	/ZB	Called the long bond; trading on the U.S. Treasury 30-year bond
VIX Futures	/VX	Trading on the CFE, a futures contract based on forward values of the VIX
Gold Futures	/GC	Futures contracts listed on the yellow metal
Crude Oil Futures	/CL	1,000 barrels of crude traded as a futures contract
Corn Futures	/ZC	5,000 bushels of corn in a futures contract

The Bond Market

Fixed-income securities, or bonds, are actively traded like stocks and come in many different forms. Bonds issued by states and cities are known as municipal bonds. Private companies issue corporate bonds. The fixed-income market that gets the most media attention, however, is the Treasury bond market.

A Treasury bill, note, or bond represents debt issued by the U.S. government. Each bond has a principal amount that is returned at the end of the bond's life, known as maturity. Maturities can vary from months (bills) to many years (notes and bonds). Figure 2-2 shows Treasury yields across various maturities in the first few days of December 2015. Longer-dated bonds have higher yields compared to shorter-term bonds.

Yields move opposite to price. Therefore, if bonds are being sold and prices fall, yields rise. On the other hand, if bonds are drawing interest and prices move higher, yields will decline. The different yields across maturities are known as the yield curve. If longer-term yields move higher relative to short-term rates, the curve is growing steeper. A flatter yield curve happens when short-term rates tick higher vis-à-vis longer-term yields.

The CBOE Ten-Year Index (TNX) is an index worth watching to monitor movement in the Treasury bond market. It is simply the yield on the ten-year Treasury, which is considered the benchmark for the market, multiplied by a factor of ten. If it's at 23.2, then ten-year yields are 2.32 percent. As it rises, TNX indicates that Treasuries are falling, and yields are rising. A drop in the index reflects higher bond prices and declining yields.

While there are no options listed on the TNX index, ten-year note futures and thirty-year bond futures are actively traded

Date	1 Mo	3 Mo	6 Mo	1 Yr	2 Yr	3 Yr	5 Yr	7 Yr	10 Yr	20 Yr	30 Yr
12/01/15	0.19	0.21	0.42	0.51	0.91	1.19	1.59	1.93	2.15	2.55	2.91
12/02/15	0.19	0.21	0.42	0.52	0.94	1.23	1.63	1.97	2.18	2.55	2.91
12/03/15	0.18	0.21	0.45	0.57	0.96	1.27	1.74	2.10	2.33	2.72	3.07
12/04/15	0.17	0.23	0.49	0.60	0.96	1.25	1.71	2.28	2.28	2.65	3.01

Figure 2-2   Treasury Bond Yields, December 2015
Source: Treasury.gov

instruments. For example, an investor with an approved futures account might go long on TY futures (ten-year notes) when bonds are expected to rise and yields fall. On the other hand, going short on ten-year or thirty-year Treasury bonds reflects expectations for lower, longer-term bond prices and higher yields.

Fed Watch

Bond traders spend a lot of time and effort attempting to anticipate changes in interest rates, and the Federal Reserve is sometimes an important part of the equation. As the world's largest central bank, the Fed holds periodic meetings (eight times a year roughly six weeks apart) to discuss the economic outlook and initiate changes to monetary policy. It has several tools at its disposal to do so:

The federal funds rate: The fed funds rate is the rate that banks and credit unions charge each other for overnight loans. The Fed sets a target for this rate—lower when it wants to promote more lending and higher to tighten lending.

The discount rate: The rate at which eligible financial institutions can borrow from the Federal Reserve. The Fed raises and lowers the discount rate to control the supply of available funds, which can influence economic activity and inflation.

Quantitative easing: A relatively new, and sometimes controversial, strategy used by Fed officials is quantitative easing (or QE). It is an effort to hold longer-term rates steady by purchasing billions of Treasury bonds and other securities. The first easing happened from December 2008 to March 2010. QE2 spanned from November 2010 to June 2011. QE3 was announced in September 2012 and ended roughly two years later.

Historically, expectations for looser monetary policy through either rate cuts or QE programs are well received by the equity market, because the moves are intended to stimulate the economy, which is typically good for corporate earnings. Some worry that these efforts can also create asset bubbles in housing or equities, which may eventually pop and create a different set of economic problems. We saw the first Fed tightening of credit in many years in December of 2015.

Three Steps and a Stumble

There is an old adage called "three steps and a stumble," which states that stock and bond prices are to likely fall if the Federal Reserve raises the discount rate three times. The idea is that the higher rates will drive up borrowing costs for companies and increase the attractiveness of money market funds, CDs, and other short-term interest-bearing securities relative to stocks and bonds. However, the saying gained popularity in the 1970s and 1980s when officials were more aggressive in raising rates—a percentage point at a time. More recent rate hikes have been relatively small and incremental.

On the other hand, tighter monetary policy, or the initiating of higher rates, is typically viewed as a negative for the equity markets because it can slow the economy and also increase the attractiveness of interest-bearing securities. Importantly, however, the Federal Reserve is only inclined to raise rates during times when the economy is strengthening and inflationary pressures begin to mount. Therefore, rate hikes are often initiated during periods of economic expansion and when corporate profits are likely improving.

Economic Indicators

Stocks and bonds move because new information arrives to the market and alters investor expectations, triggering buying and selling from one day to the next. Important market-moving news events are sometimes referred to as *catalysts*, and economic releases are chief among them. Most of the reports are scheduled out ahead of time, and the market impact typically varies based on (1) the perceived importance of the data and (2) how far the numbers deviate from economist estimates.

For instance, monthly jobs reports are released on the first Friday of each month and can have important implications for both stocks and bonds, especially if the numbers are significantly better or worse than economist projections. Other reports with broad market significance include manufacturing, inflation, retail sales, and housing. The numbers often shape expectations for future economic activity and Federal Reserve policy.

Earnings

Earnings—it's like when you brought home your quarterly report card from grade school. Your parents had certain expectations. Maybe they expected to see mostly As and a couple of Bs. If you brought home all As, they were pleasantly surprised, and you might have been rewarded in some way, like with a new toy or video game. On the other hand, if the report card was littered with Cs and Ds, you might have been asked to spend more time doing homework in the next term or perhaps take on a few more chores. We all know the consequences of bad grades are never good.

Similarly, analysts and shareholders have certain expectations from the corporations about their potential profits from one quarter to the next. These are captured in analyst estimates. Analysts spend a lot of time attempting to forecast corporate profits, especially for more widely followed names.

For most companies, fiscal quarters end in March, June, September, and December, and peak earnings reporting periods begin roughly two weeks after the end of the quarter and span several weeks. For example, investors can expect a flood of first earnings reports from mid-January to mid-February.

Dividends Defined

A dividend is a payment by a company to a shareholder. It represents a percentage of profits that is being returned to shareholder. Younger growth companies typically don't pay dividends, and some industries that have heavy cash flows, like utilities and Real Estate Investment Trusts, often pay hefty dividends. The percentage of dividends relative to the share price (or dividend/share price) is known as the dividend yield.

Earnings reporting seasons are significant, because in the long run, shareholders are rewarded from company profits. Strong profit growth typically drives share prices higher. In addition, in the absence of profits, a company can't pay dividends. Therefore, periods of strong profit growth are likely to be accompanied by rising share prices, and when earnings growth is lackluster and falls short of expectations, the result is falling stocks and higher volatility.

Find Your Niche

After years of successfully trading S&P 100 and S&P 500 Index options, I decided to use my same strategies on the Russell 2000 Index. While the two instruments are similar, there are important differences. The most important is that while the S&P 500 is a barometer for the performance of large companies, the Russell is designed to track two thousand of the smallest listed stocks on the US exchanges.

For some still unknown reason, I simply couldn't achieve the same results trading options on the small-cap index. I lost money on my strategies, until I shifted my focus back to the large-cap S&P 500 contract.

Don't get me wrong. There are many traders who find success with strategies on the Russell 2000. There is nothing wrong with the product itself. It just wasn't the best trading vehicle for me. So, while I consider it a valuable indicator for tracking the performance of the small-cap asset class, it is no longer a name I trade.

Summary

Many of the indexes, stocks, futures, and indicators mentioned in this book can find a place on your trading screen, but it's very difficult to track and trade them all. Instead, experience will teach you to focus on a handful of instruments that you will come to know well and that you can trade with confidence.

VIX and other indicators have been mentioned in this chapter. In addition, when looking for trading opportunities, stay tuned to the pulse of the markets by paying attention to Federal Reserve policy updates, watching economic releases, and observing how shares react to earnings results from one quarter to the next.

My focus turns to the analysis of single stocks in Chapter 3. The information there serves as building blocks to better understand the strategies using equity options in later chapters. Keep in mind that all investing involves risk, including loss of principal. Certain complex options strategies carry additional risk. Know your risk tolerance and fully understand the product before you begin trading. Focus on a few key markets rather than trying to trade them all. Now let's talk stocks!

References

Malkiel, *A Random Walk Down Wall Street*
www.bankrate.com/rates/interest-rates/federal-discount-rate.aspx
www.djaverages.com/
insidefutures.com/
us.spindices.com/indices/equity/sp-500
tickertape.tdameritrade.com/marketupdate
www.treasury.gov/resource-center/data-chart-center/interest-rates/
    Pages/TextView.aspx?data=yield

CHAPTER 3

Know the Underlying

The global financial crisis of 2007–2008 is considered by many economists as the worst financial catastrophe since the Great Depression of the 1930s. A number of large global financial institutions were near the brink of collapsing before national governments offered bailouts. The housing market collapsed, and equity markets around the globe were left reeling. When the dust settled, experts scrambled to find reasons to explain the course of events. Some partially blamed the financial debacle on complex financial products called *derivatives*.

It's important to note, however, that the types of derivatives that created problems for financial institutions during the crisis are very different than those I trade, or that most brokerages would allow you to trade, and the ones I cover throughout this book. The typical definition of a derivative is any instrument that has its value *derived* from another asset. It covers a wide range of different types of instruments.

A futures contract is a derivative because its price is driven by the value of the commodity, index, or equity. For instance, S&P 500 futures derive their values from the S&P 500 Index. The futures are the derivatives, and the S&P 500 Index is the underlying index.

Relatively new instruments, including credit default swaps, were among the derivatives that sent shock waves through financial institutions in 2007–2008. They were structured by a handful of firms and traded over-the-counter between major banks. Swaps, structured notes, and other over-the-counter (OTC) derivatives are not discussed in the pages of this book.

Instead, the focus is on exchange-traded options that have existed for more than forty years in the United States. My examples use puts and calls that are standardized contracts and listed on a number of different exchanges. The underlying instruments of these contracts are equities and indexes. Similar strategies can be applied to options on futures and exchange-traded funds (ETFs) as well, but those underlying instruments are for an entirely different book.

Where Do Options Trade?

The listed options market is a vibrant, largely electronic venue where buyers and sellers trade puts and calls for a variety of different reasons. An investor might be writing (selling) call options against positions in a stock portfolio to potentially generate additional income. A fund manager is possibly buying puts on the S&P 500 to hedge risk. An aggressive trader might be taking a position in options on a technology company to participate if shares move higher during the next few months.

Regardless of the objective, all customer orders to buy and sell options are directed to a brokerage firm, and those orders are delivered to the exchanges. As of this writing, thirteen different options exchanges exist in the United States, and additional ones are expected in the years ahead.

The Options Clearing Corporation (OCC) processes the options transactions that happen across all exchanges. The OCC is a clearinghouse and also the entity responsible for ensuring that obligations of individual contracts are fulfilled.

The role of the OCC is extremely important. Any investor who enters into a contract to buy or sell an underlying asset wants to be confident that the terms are honored by the counterparty. A buyer wants to make sure a seller can pay, and a seller needs to know that the buyer can deliver.

When a listed options contract is traded on an exchange, there is no direct link between the buyers and sellers. The exchanges establish a clearing firm—in this case the OCC—to process trades and also guarantee that any contract listed on the exchanges is fulfilled. If a firm or individual runs into trouble, the terms of the contracts are still honored and fulfilled. No clearinghouse in the United States has ever failed.

Dialing into Volume

Volume refers to the number of units traded in a particular security. In options and futures markets, volume is measured in contracts. Stock volume is equal to the number of shares traded.

Of the current thirteen equity options exchanges, the Chicago Board Options Exchange (CBOE) is the oldest options exchange and is today perhaps best known for its trading pits of two products. The S&P 500 Index (SPX) and the CBOE Volatility Index (VIX) are exclusively listed on the CBOE and still trade in live, auction-style markets.

Beyond VIX and SPX options, however, the majority of options contracts are multiply listed across all options exchanges. Market makers update options quotes as needed, and prices are typically uniform across all exchanges; otherwise, a risk-free arbitrage opportunity would exist. That is, an investor could buy on one exchange if a lower price existed and then sell on the competing exchange where a lower price was present.

The Options Pricing Reporting Authority (OPRA) provides the latest options quotes and sales information to market vendors, as reported by the various exchanges. Those quotes are then distributed to market participants. In later chapters, I will show how options data on volume and open positions can be used to gauge the liquidity of specific contracts.

Figure 3-1 shows an example of volume by exchange for a typical trading day in late 2015. In addition to the CBOE, the International Securities Exchange (ISE), the Philadelphia Stock Exchange (PHLX), NYSE-AMEX, NYSE-ARCA, NASDAQ, and BATS see substantial market share. Relatively new players include the Boston Options Exchange (BOX), C2, ISE Gemini, Miami Options Exchange, and EDGX Options.

There is one important reason why there are thirteen exchanges and the list is likely to grow: technology. Some of the newer exchanges emerge with new technology designed to appeal to specific trading firms and institutional investors. Each exchange has its own bells and whistles that are designed to capture market share and order flow.

Options

Exchange	Equity	
	Volume	Market Share
AMEX	1,464,187	11.50%
ARCA	1,238,401	9.73%
BATS	1,277,720	10.04%
BOX	431,110	3.39%
C2	248,393	1.95%
COBE	1,724,062	13.54%
EDGX	48,513	0.38%
GEM	399,530	3.14%
ISE	1,830,508	14.38%
MIAX	921,702	7.24%
NOBO	135,399	1.06%
NSDQ	858,043	6.74%
PHLX	2,154,883	16.92%
OCC Totals	12,732,451	100.00%

Figure 3-1   Daily Market Shares by Exchange, December 8, 2015
Source: Optionsclearing.org

Futures and futures options, meanwhile, trade primarily on the Chicago Board of Trade (CBOT), Chicago Mercantile Exchange (CME), and the New York Mercantile (NYMEX), which, due to various mergers and acquisitions over the years, are all under the umbrella of the CME Group. Their primary competitor is the ICE group.

Regardless of the number of futures and options exchanges, once the order to buy or sell an option is directed to the brokerage firm, it is then sent for execution at the best price possible. The individual investor doesn't need to specify to which exchange the order is delivered.

After the order is executed, positions are updated in the investor's account, all within fractions of a second. In the next chapter, we explore a few different order types when placing trades. For now, my focus turns to the underlying. Key indexes were already discussed in Chapter 2, so now I will address individual stocks.

Stock Talk

Equity or single stock options represent roughly half of the total listed options volume in the United States today. Index, ETF, and futures options make up the other half. Many of the strategies in later chapters will use stock options as examples; therefore, an understanding of the underlying instrument is important as well. So, what is a stock or equity?

A stock (or common stock) represents a slice of ownership interest in a publicly traded company. In order to have shares publicly listed, a company must issue stock through an initial public offering (IPO). After the IPO, shares begin trading on the stock exchanges, and investors can buy and sell through their brokers.

Where Do Stocks Trade?

While options are typically listed across all the exchanges, most stocks are listed on either the New York Stock Exchange (NYSE), BATS or the NASDAQ. While the NYSE still maintains a live trading floor in the financial district of Manhattan, the NASDAQ is all electronic.

As an example, you have opened an account with a brokerage firm and deposited cash into the account. You have identified company XYZ as a suitable longer-term investment for your portfolio and placed an order to buy two hundred shares for $25 per share. Your brokerage firm executes the order on your behalf. You pay $5,000 ($25 × 200 shares) for the stock from the cash in your account and now have a long position in two hundred XYZ shares.

As a shareholder, or stockholder, you legally own stock in the publicly traded company XYZ. Because they are listed on the exchange, you can sell the shares at any time as well. If you sell the stock for more than what you paid, the sale generates a (typically taxable) profit. On the other hand, if you sell for less than what you paid, you book a loss.

Until the shares are sold, you are a shareholder and have certain rights and privileges, which include:

- The right to dividends, if any are declared
- The right to purchase new shares if issued by the company
- The right to vote on directors nominated by the board

The market price of a stock can change from one minute to the next due to general market conditions or company-specific news.

For instance, shares of energy-related companies are sensitive to changes in the price of crude oil, and a financial services stock might see gyrations if there are sudden changes in interest rates.

Quarterly earnings reports and any midquarter guidance can also trigger rapid changes in stock prices. While some names see very fast price changes from one minute to the next, others can seem to grind in ranges for weeks, months, or even years. The speed of price changes is sometimes referred to as volatility, and because it's a very important concept for options traders, it is covered in great detail in later chapters.

When buying and selling stocks during market hours, there are three key pieces of price information to consider: last price, bid price, and asking price. As an example, using TD Ameritrade's paperMoney® platform, we can get the latest information for U.S. Steel by typing the stock's easy-to-remember ticker symbol, X, into the Quick Quote box or on the Trade screen (Figure 3-2).

In this example, the best bid is $8.18 per share, and that's the best price a buyer is willing to pay for shares at that time. If an investor enters an order to buy three hundred shares for $8.20, that price becomes the best bid and will replace the $8.18. Note that the size (as seen in Figure 3-3) will also change from 2 to 3, reflecting the fact

X	▼	3	UNITED STATES STEEL CORP COM	**8.25**
✓ Underlying				
✓	Last X	Net Chng	Bid X	Ask X
	8.25 N	-.58	8.18 K	8.23 K

Figure 3-2   Stock Price—Last, Change, Bid, Ask

✓ Underlying					
Last X	Net Chng	Bid X	Ask X	Size	Volume
8.25 N	-.58	8.18 K	8.23 K	2 x 11	11,860,194

> Trade Grid			BUY	
✓ Option Chain	Filter: **Off** Spread: **Single** Layout: V		SELL	
	CALLS		Buy custom	▶
	Volume Open.Int Bid X Ask X		Sell custom	▶
> DEC 15	(6) 100		🔔 Create alert...	
> DEC4 15	(12) 100 (**Weeklys**)			
> DEC5 15	(19) 100		Analyze	▶

Figure 3-3   Example of a Stock Quote with Order Entry Screen

that the best bid is now $8.20 for three hundred shares. (You multiply 3 × 100 when looking at quote sizes.) It is an industry standard that the bid or ask price shown should be multiplied by one hundred.

The opposite is true if an investor places a sell order for three hundred shares at $8.20 per share. The best asking price, or the price an investor is willing to sell the stock, updates to $8.20, and the size changes from 11 to 3. In many trading platforms, you can simply click the bid or ask price in order to place a trade (Figure 3-3).

Obviously, the bids and asks change as investors place buy and sell orders for different sized blocks of shares. It is the market makers' or specialists' job to maintain steady quotes in the equities market, and most of this is done electronically today. In addition, as shares are bought and sold, the total volume traded for the day also changes. In the case of the U.S. Steel example, as we can see in Figure 3-4, the stock dropped $0.58, and the last price was $8.25 on 11.9 million shares traded for the day.

Click the arrow by the last price to get to know the stock a bit better. In the U.S. Steel example in Figure 3-4:

- The stock offers a 2.4 percent *dividend yield*, which means that the total dividends paid ($0.05 per quarter) in the past twelve months equals 2.4 percent of the current stock price.
- The *price-to-earnings ratio* is negative because the company has been posting *earnings per share* (EPS) losses.
- The *high* and *low* prices for the most recent trading day were $8.59 and $8.08, and for the past year (fifty-two weeks), they were $29.62 and $6.80.
- The company has 146 million shares outstanding and a $1.2 billion market cap ($8.25 × 146 million).
- The *beta* of 1.97 suggests that the stock is nearly two times more volatile than the broader market. An expanded definition of *beta* follows.
- Click Company Profile to see more detailed stats and other information.

X		UNITED STATES STEEL CORP COM	8.25	-.58 -6.57%	B: 8.18 A: 8.23	ETB	↕ ±0.365		⬢ Company Profile
∨ Underlying									
∨	Last X	Net Chng	Bid X	Ask X	Size	Volume	Open	High	Low
	8.25 N	-.58	8.18 K	8.23 K	2 x 11	11,860,194	8.53	8.59	8.08
	Yield	PE	EPS	Div	Div.Freq	Ex Div.Date	52High	52Low	Shares	Beta ⬢
	2.42%	-5.145	-1.604	.05	Q	11/10/15	29.62	6.80	146,273,790	1.969

Figure 3-4   Quote Detail

Brief Note on Beta

A stock's beta is a measure of the volatility of the underlying instrument. Based on the capital asset pricing model (CAPM), it captures the systematic risk of the security compared to the overall market. While useful for stock investors, options traders typically gauge the volatility of a security using other measures such as historical and implied volatility, which are covered in more detail in later chapters.

Charts can also be helpful tools for becoming familiar with a stock and how it behaves from one day to the next. In many charting applications, time frames can be changed to daily, weekly, and monthly to see trends over time. Shorter time frames, including minute-by-minute, can be charted to see how the stock is trading throughout the trading day (or intraday).

Charts typically also show times when the company reported earnings, held conference calls, and paid dividends, as illustrated in Figure 3-5 with blue, red, and green circles. Charts will often include share volume along the bottom. We can see in Figure 3-5 that some obvious volume spikes in U.S. Steel occur around earnings reports. Numerous other studies can be displayed on charts as well. As an example, a thirty-day moving average is included on the U.S. Steel chart in Figure 3-5. Moving averages and other studies are explained in more detail in Appendix B.

Breaking news can also impact stock prices, and remaining aware of the current news on a stock is important. Many modern platforms import news from various third-party providers. Some might even display news related to a given stock near the stock chart. As illustrated in Figure 3-5, news from Dow Jones Newswires, CNBC, PR Newswires, and tastytrade are displayed.

Exchange-Traded Funds

Exchange-traded funds (or ETFs) represent a substantial percentage of activity in the U.S. equities and options market today. As the name suggests, an ETF is simply a fund that trades on the stock exchanges. Investors can buy and sell shares as they do shares of common stock.

The SPDR 500 Depository Trust (SPY), or Spiders, is among the most actively traded among them. Launched on the American Stock

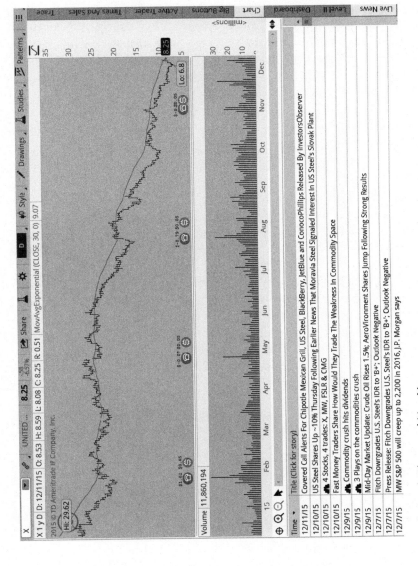

Figure 3-5   Daily Stock Chart and Live News

Exchange in 1993, the fund was created to offer investors a way to trade the entire S&P 500 with just one instrument. It has very actively traded options as well.

Since the launch of Spiders, a number of other ETFs have been launched. Some hold equities, while others have been created to hold bonds, commodities, and even volatility futures. ETFs are an important part of the options market today and account for more than a third of the daily trading activity from one day to the next. The examples in this book, however, include stocks and indexes as underlying instruments.

Short Selling

A short seller typically takes a position when the investor expects a stock's price to fall. The idea is to sell now and buy back (or cover the short) later at a lower price. In most short-selling situations, the investor does not own shares of the company in question. Instead, the stock is borrowed from the brokerage firm before it is sold. This is possible because some investors, particularly big institutions, are willing to lend shares out, and the brokerage firm has permission to do so.

Not all stock is available for short selling, however. When a stock becomes hard to borrow, it is difficult to find for the purpose of short selling. A hard-to-borrow stock might even be impossible to borrow or very expensive to short, because borrowing rates (fees charged by brokerage firms to lend shares out) typically increase. In addition, exchanges can place short-selling restrictions on certain names during periods of increasing volatility.

Don't Squeeze Me

A short squeeze happens when a stock with heavy short interest moves higher and short sellers scramble to cover positions. This can happen when a heavily shorted name surprises investors with better-than-expected earnings or other news.

In many cases, however, the stock is available for shorting, and some more advanced options strategies use short stock. Keep in mind that the short seller borrows the stock and is also responsible to pay out any dividends declared by the company while shares are held short. Additionally, the risks to an unhedged short position can be considerable if the stock makes a sudden move higher. Theoretically, there is no limit to how high a stock price can go; therefore, there is no limit to the potential losses to the short seller.

On the Margin

An investor can borrow money from a brokerage firm to buy or sell shares if a margin account is opened. In essence, buying on margin involves the purchase of a stock by paying a portion of the total cost (the *margin*) and borrowing the balance from the brokerage firm. The brokerage firm will charge you interest on the amount that you borrow. For stock trading, the amount of margin required is set industry-wide by the Federal Reserve Board, but amounts and margin rates can vary from one broker to the next as well.

Meanwhile, in the futures market, the futures exchange states a minimum amount of margin to deposit in the account to enter a futures contract. Called the initial margin, it is typically 5 to 10 percent of the futures contract and will vary based on the value and volatility of the product. Lastly, in the options market, contracts are paid for immediately and in full. Margin requirements for more complex strategies are based on the amount of risk involved.

Some investors, based on clearly defined approvals and account balances, can also use portfolio margin when trading multiple securities or strategies at once. Rather than computing margin based on the risk of the individual securities or strategies within an account, portfolio margining is computed using the portfolio's overall risk considering the net exposure of all positions. It can lower margin requirements and increase account leverage and the associated risks as well.

At the end of the day, each investor must decide if margin and leverage align with financial objectives and should be included as part of their long-term trading plan. The first step is to understand the underlying and the risks. This chapter and the previous one covered underlying stocks and indexes. The next chapter considers risk.

Summary

Listed options in the United States started trading on the CBOE in 1973. Since that time, the number of exchanges has increased to more than a dozen, and tens of millions of contracts change hands each day. Each option derives its value from another asset known as the underlying security.

Knowing the underlying is therefore essential when trading options contracts. Indexes were covered in detail in the previous chapter. This chapter offered a background on stock trading. Futures and ETFs are an important part of the options industry as well but are not covered throughout the remainder of this book. Instead, the focus is on stock and index options.

References

The Options Clearing Corporation, OCC, optionsclearing.org
futuresfundamentals.cmegroup.com
www.opradata.com
online.wsj.com/ad/focusonetfs/history.html

4

Avoiding Mistakes

My early experiences on the trading floor taught me a lot. After being given the opportunity to pursue a career as a floor trader, I was excited and convinced that I could be very successful trading options if given a chance. It was, therefore, surprising to me that the two gentlemen who served as my early financial backers said they'd hire me on only one condition: I could keep the job if, after a six-month trial period, I had learned how to reach breakeven.

Their experience taught them that the key to longer-term success when trading options is not shooting for the stars. The important thing is not losing. Maintaining breakeven was obviously not a long-term goal, because the ultimate goal is to generate revenues from trading. But risk management and avoiding large losses were seen as the keys to longer-term viability.

I did a bit better than breakeven after my first six months, and after a few years of successful trading, I bought the other two gentlemen out and started trading for my own account. Forming the good habits in the early years helped me tremendously, and I spent a total of twenty-one years on the Chicago Board Options Exchange (CBOE) floor.

If I can avoid losing, my chances of winning improve. That's the philosophy that still drives my trading approach today. So, how do investors avoid losing, especially in the early days of their trading pursuits? What are the mistakes people sometimes make that set them back and limit their success? Let's dig into that now.

Position Size

You have already heard it a million times, and common sense tells us that if an investment idea seems too good to be true, it probably is. Yet, there have been times in my career when I have been so confident on a position that I have bitten off more than I could chew and suffered the consequences.

What I learned: There are absolutely no free lunches in investing. You can never know how other people will interpret news or how markets will react. A sure thing doesn't exist, and the all-in attitude with respect to an investment or position is simply dangerous.

Instead, position sizes should be consistent with one's overall portfolio, risk tolerance, and trading plan. An investor should be able to withstand a series of losing trades, and one bad trade should not decimate an entire trading account.

I suggest starting small while you're learning the ropes. As your knowledge, experience, and skills develop, consider bigger trades. However, be sure the trades are commensurate with your risk appetite and trading plan. Market conditions change all the time, so you want to avoid an all-in attitude, even if you have scored a series of winning trades using a strategy or methodology.

Think in terms of partials. That is, if I want to buy 1000 shares of stock, I set a target for an average buy price and might start by purchasing 300. That way, if things move against me, I have the opportunity to buy more at a better price. If it moves against me again, I can purchase more at an even better price. But if it moves my way immediately, it's winner, winner, chicken dinner! On the other hand, the stock price could continue to fall and result in additional losses. Also, a dollar-cost–averaging strategy like this will incur additional commission charges.

Remember though, it's typically better to try to hit singles and doubles over time rather than try to hit a home run once every season. Swinging for the fences typically leads to a lot of strikeouts. I will demonstrate in later chapters how an understanding of probabilities can help identify the types of strategies that have served me well over the years.

Volume and Liquidity

Not all stocks or options see the same amount of activity or *volume* from one day to the next. In stock trading, volume is measured in the number of shares traded. A name with robust volume typically has lots of bids and offers, because there are more orders to buy and sell. A stock like this would be considered very liquid. On the other hand, a stock with relatively little trading activity from one week to the next sees fewer bids and offers. Some might call it thin or illiquid.

Don't Fall for Slippage

Slippage refers to the amount paid to enter or exit a trade due to the difference between the bid-ask spread. Trading very active names with narrow spreads can help reduce the impact of slippage. Wide spreads, particularly in less active options, can result in noticeable slippage.

The difference between the bid and asking price is called the *spread.* In 2016, Apple Inc. is a popular and actively traded name. It has a lot of trading activity, and a substantial number of investors buy and sell from one day to the next. It typically has a very narrow (or tight) one-penny spread. In Figure 4-1, for example, the last price it traded at was $111 per share with the bid-ask at $111 to $111.01.

Narrow spreads are important to all traders, because they reduce the amount of slippage associated with buying and selling. In the Apple example, for instance, there is virtually no slippage to consider, because price quotes are a penny apart. However, brokerage firms typically charge a fee or commission for each transaction, and that, in turn, should be factored in to the cost of trading as well.

Obviously, to an investor only trading once or twice per month and holding positions for many months or years, the impact from bid-ask spreads or commissions is less significant compared to an active trader placing frequent orders to buy and sell. Using a virtual trading platform to practice trading can help you get a better sense of how much slippage can impact results.

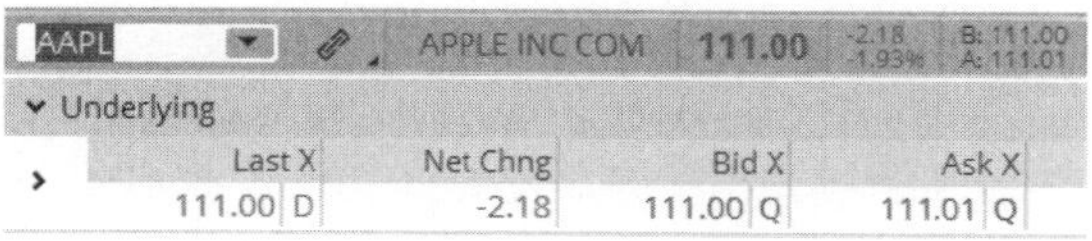

AAPL	▼	🔗	APPLE INC COM	**111.00**	-2.18 1.93%	B: 111.00 A: 111.01
✓ Underlying						
›	Last X	Net Chng	Bid X	Ask X		
	111.00 D	-2.18	111.00 Q	111.01 Q		

Figure 4-1   Apple Stock Quote

For this book, I tried to focus on names that are relatively actively traded with ample liquidity in both stocks and options contracts. Too much slippage from wide spreads can negatively impact results. It's also important to consider transaction costs from commissions and other fees.

Order Entry Techniques

Savvy traders know the importance of using different order types in different situations. As an analogy, if you're a bass fisherman like me, you know that some lures or baits work in different locations, times of day, or weather. When you head out to the lake, you bring along an entire tackle box, because you want to be prepared for any possible condition.

Must-have order types for your trading tackle box include:

- **Market orders:** An order to buy or sell at the next available price.
- **Limit orders:** An order to buy or sell at a specific price or better.
- **Stop market:** An order that is triggered when a stock hits a certain price. Once the stop is hit, the order becomes a market order, seeking a fill at the next available price.
- **Stop limit:** A stop limit is similar to a stop market order. However, once the stop price is hit, the order becomes a limit order.
- **Market on close:** MOC is an order to buy or sell at the close of the trading day at the best price possible.
- **Limit on close:** An LOC order is triggered at the close of trading at a specific price or better.

Market orders and limit orders are used more than any other type. A market order is simply an instruction to buy or sell the security at the next available price. It seeks immediate execution, but the investor has no control of the price being paid (if buying) or received (if selling).

In fast-moving markets, bids and asks can change rapidly, and an investor placing a market order might pay a higher or lower price than the last price at the time the order was entered. Be very careful with market orders as you quickly lose control of your fate.

For instance, let's say the current market for XYZ shares is $50 bid to $51 ask, and the investor wants to sell one hundred shares at $50.

The stock is moving lower, and after the market order was entered, it had dropped $1 to a bid-ask of $49 to $50. The order is executed at $49 per share, or $1 less than the investor had hoped for.

Limit orders can only be filled at a specific price or better. For instance, if the current bid-ask for a stock is $50 to $50.10, an investor might enter a limit price at $50.05 to buy one hundred shares. The bid-ask now becomes $50.05 to $50.10, and the order might or might not be executed depending on overall market conditions. Compared to market orders, limit orders sometimes have less likelihood of quick execution but will not be executed at a price worse than the amount specified on the order ticket. In other words, a limit order guarantees a price but not an execution.

Meanwhile, stop orders are often used to exit or enter positions when certain conditions are met. A stop market order to sell, for example, is triggered when a stock falls to a certain level, and then the order becomes a market order. If an investor has concluded that she wants to exit a stock if it drops from $50 to $48, a stop market sell order can be placed at $48, and then the shares are sold at the next available price if the stock falls to that level. That level could be higher or lower than $48. The stop limit is similar, but once triggered, it becomes a limit buy (or sell order).

Stop the Madness

Setting the right stops is a skill that takes time to learn. While they are useful tools, you will see later that option strategies can offer important advantages, such as clearly defining risks when the trade is first placed.

Lastly, some active traders use trailing stops to help protect gains or limit losses as shares move in one direction or another. A trailing stop can be set as a percentage or a dollar amount higher than or lower than the market price. For instance, a trailing sell stop might be set $2 lower than the current stock price. If shares are at $50, the position will be stopped at $48, but if it moves to $52, the stop order moves to the $50 level.

Whether to use market orders, limits, or stops depends on the objectives of the trade, market conditions, and the level or risk you are comfortable with. If time is of the essence and a position needs to be covered quickly, market orders are typically used. However, limit orders can be placed between bids and asks to potentially limit the impact of slippage. Stop orders especially make sense as risk-management tools for active traders. In later chapters, you will see how certain option strategies can produce results similar to stop or limit orders.

Understand Risk

A perfect investment for one person is not necessarily the best idea for the next. For example, eighty-year-old Aunt Gertrude from Wichita probably has different risk tolerance than twenty-five-year-old Tony from Toledo. Aunt Gertrude is concerned about protecting her nest egg, generating income from her investments, and estate planning. Tony wants to invest part of his paycheck each month and build a portfolio over the longer term. Because of Tony's youth he is able to take on more risk.

To determine if a strategy or investment aligns with your financial objectives and risk tolerance, it makes sense to consider the risks and rewards of the idea. That is, does the opportunity offer enough reward to compensate for the risks? Is there too much risk and not enough potential gain? Or are there insufficient rewards given the level of risk?

Just like a stock chart can help you see changes in price over time, a risk graph (or risk curve) can help you visualize the potential risks and rewards of an idea or strategy. It shows the profits and losses of a position as the price of an underlying changes. Figure 4-2 shows a simple example of a risk graph for owning or going long a stock.

The first thing to note on the risk graph is that it includes two axes. The y-axis is the vertical axis and represents the potential profits and losses of the strategy. The x-axis is the horizontal axis and represents the change in the stock price (futures, index, or whatever other underlying security is being analyzed).

Because a stock price can't be negative, the x-axis is never less than zero. As the stock price moves higher, the position increases in value, and as the stock price moves lower, the value decreases. Anything on the y-axis above the x-axis is in the profit area. Anything on the y-axis below the x-axis suggests a loss.

Risk graphs are useful because they show how various strategies might perform as the price of the underlying changes. In Figure 4-2,

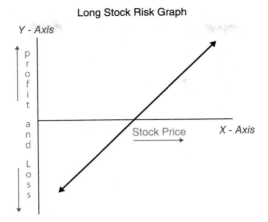

Figure 4-2   Long Stock Risk Graph

it's easy to see that the profits of a long stock position increase as share prices move higher and lose value as share prices fall. Intuitively, this makes sense. If you buy a stock, you want it to move higher, not lower. However, the simple risk graph in Figure 4-2 doesn't show the dollar amount of profit or losses.

While it's possible to draw risk graphs by hand, trading software makes the task a whole lot easier. For example, in Figure 4-3 we see that eBay is currently trading for $28 per share. By clicking on the ask price, the drop-down menu in this software package includes the word *Analyze*. To the right of that, we select "Buy trade." We can then analyze the risks and rewards of buying one hundred shares of EBAY at $28 per share.

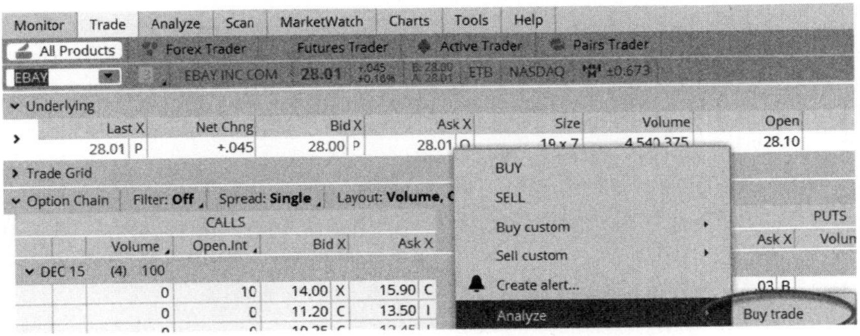

Figure 4-3   Analyzing a Stock Trade

Obviously, if an investor buys shares of eBay, he wants the price to move higher. For instance, if one hundred shares of stock are bought for $28 per share and sold for $30, the net profit is $2 per share, or $200 on one hundred shares. The investor bought one hundred shares for a total of $2,800 and sold one hundred shares for $3,000. On the other hand, if the stock drops to $25 and is sold at that price, the loss is $300 on the trade. The investor paid $2,800 for the purchase and collected only $2,500 for the sale.

Figure 4-4 shows a risk graph for buying one hundred shares of eBay for $28 per share using an analyze tool. Notice that the x-axis is the stock price, and the y-axis represents the profit or losses. At the point where the stock price equals $28, the profit and loss equals zero. On the other hand, if shares climb to $30, the profit is $200. The position loses $300 if shares drop to $25. Figure 4-5 expresses the same information in spreadsheet format. In many trading platforms, the numbers update in real time during the trading day, which is especially useful when plotting out more advanced option strategies that include multiple contracts.

Risk graphs of options positions can also be useful, because some of the more complex strategies actually get their names from the way

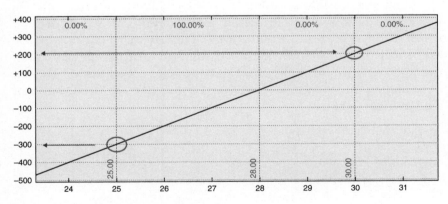

Figure 4-4   Buy Stock for $28 Risk Graph

| ▾ Price Slices | | | | | | | |
Stk Price	Offset	Delta	Gamma	Theta	Vega	P/L Open	P/L Day
30.00		100.00	.00	.00	.00	$200.00	$200.00
32.00		100.00	.00	.00	.00	$400.00	$400.00
25.00		100.00	.00	.00	.00	($300.00)	($300.00)
28.00		100.00	.00	.00	.00	$0.00	$0.00

Figure 4-5   Profit/Loss (P/L) Table for Long 100 Shares Purchased at $28

the risk profile graphs are shaped. Butterfly and condor spreads, discussed in Chapters 15 and 16, are two examples. Their risk graphs, as well as all of the other strategies covered in this book, are also included in Appendix B for quick reference.

Summary

New investors and options traders sometimes focus a lot on the prospect of making money in stocks or options but don't give adequate consideration to the risk of losing. I was fortunate, because I learned the importance of not losing money early in my career when I was working on the exchange floor. I learned good habits, and I'm confident that if you can focus on managing risk, your chances of winning can improve.

In this chapter I addressed some important factors to consider, including how volume and liquidity can affect slippage and how order entry techniques can help mitigate the impact of slippage. Some orders, like stops, can also be used as tools to manage risk. In addition, spreading your risk can help you avoid taking on positions that are too large, and you definitely don't want an all-in mindset when looking at new investment opportunities. Obviously, you also want to know the product and how it trades. Lastly, risk graphs are valuable tools when considering the risks and rewards of both simple and complex option strategies.

Now let's start talking options!

References

www.tdameritrade.com/tools-and-platforms/trader-offering/stock-order-types.page

www.optionseducation.org/documents/literature/files/understanding-profit-loss-graphs.pdf

PART

II

The Options Market

CHAPTER 5

Options Basics

You wrote your first novel, and the book is an amazing success. Titled *The Final Last Option*, this 250-page thriller is selling more copies than you ever imagined. Readers can't get enough, and there is even talk of making the story into a feature film.

A producer approaches you about the book rights for a movie deal. However, he isn't yet sure if he can get approval for a budget from the production company. Nevertheless, the producer wants to retain the right to the story for a specified period of time while he tries to obtain the necessary financial backing.

You and the producer agree to a fixed, one-time payment of $10,000 for the right to buy the story from you for $1 million for a movie scenario. You agree that at the end of a six-month term, the agreement ends, and you are free to sell to a different movie production company if the producer has not paid you $1 million within that time frame. You keep the one-time payment of $10,000 regardless of whether the producer moves forward with the movie.

Five months later, you get a different offer of $1.5 million from another movie producer. You are hoping the first producer doesn't ask for the rights, because his initial $1 million offer is $500,000 less than the latest one. Unfortunately, he says he wants to move forward with the film deal. You are now obligated to sell him the rights based on the agreed upon terms. He is buying the story from you for $1 million, and you also keep the initial payment of $10,000.

Using options terminology, you sold a call on your story, and the producer bought the option to purchase it. The producer paid a premium of $10,000 for the contract and had a fixed period of time to exercise the terms of the contract. While the producer had the right to the story through a fixed date, he was not obligated to buy it from you. On the other hand, you were obligated to fulfill the agreed upon terms—even if the story increased substantially in value, and another buyer was willing to pay more.

Now, fast-forward twelve months. After you receive your one-time payment for *The Final Last Option* thriller, you do what many people do when they receive a big lump of cash: You buy a hot new car! Naturally, you also buy car insurance to protect it.

The next day, a garbage truck slams into your new car as you're drafting a second novel while at a neighborhood coffee shop. You run outside, and to your dismay, the car is a total loss. You file a claim, and the insurance company pays you a lump sum amount to replace your vehicle.

The insurance policy is a lot like a put option. You paid a premium to the insurance company but were under no obligation to exercise the terms of the agreement unless you needed to. However, once you exercised that right, your insurance company was obligated to deliver the money to replace your car.

The insurance company collected the premium, and if nothing had happened, then the policy would expire at the end of the term. In order to maintain insurance, the old policy must be replaced with a new policy. Any premiums paid during the life of the insurance contract belong to the insurance company, even in the event of a claim. The insurance policy is for a fixed amount of time and must be renewed (by paying a premium) to continue to do so.

In the world of options trading, contracts are obviously not based on movie rights or auto insurance. Instead, underlying assets are stocks, exchange-traded funds (ETFs), indexes, futures, and other financial instruments. The idea is similar, however.

A call option gives the owner the right to buy (or call) a specific instrument for a fixed period of time (expiration date) and for a set price (strike price). The seller (writer) of the option collects a premium from the buyer and, in exchange, is obligated to honor the terms of the contract and deliver the product if asked to do so.

A put option gives the owner the right to sell (or put) the underlying asset at a strike price through an expiration date. The seller collects a premium and is obligated to buy (have put to them) the underlying asset per the terms of the contract until it expires.

Once the expiration date is reached, options contracts cease to exist. As you will see, options contracts can be closed or offset at any time prior to the expiration as well.

Stock Options

A stock or equity option is a contract to buy or sell shares of an individual company. A standard contract controls one hundred shares. In other words, the underlying asset of one stock option is one hundred shares. One call option gives the holder the right to buy one hundred shares, and a put option is the right to sell one hundred shares.

In addition to the underlying stock, the options contract is defined by three other variables. Is it a put or a call? What is the strike price? What is the expiration date? These four variables define an options series. For instance, an Apple call breaks down to the following:

Stock symbol: AAPL

Expiration: December 18, 2015 (121815)

Type: Call (C)

Strike price: $115

In the trading world, this would be abbreviated to AAPL December 115 call.

Quick Take on Options Tickers

Just as stocks have tickers, so do options. They include several pieces of information: stock ticker, expiration date, put or call, and strike price. For instance, an options ticker for Apple December 115 call option is AAPL121815C115. Fortunately, most trading platforms make it easy to find individual options simply by knowing the underlying security's symbol.

To purchase an options contract, an investor pays a premium, which is determined by several factors. As you will see in later chapters, the price of the underlying stock and the option's volatility are typically the most important determinant of an option's price, but certainly not the only ones.

For now, I will focus only on the mechanics of buying and selling options and not the determinant of options prices (which is the subject of Chapter 8). The price of each contract is quoted in dollars and cents, and the premium is multiplied by one hundred to arrive at the total cost of the contract. This makes sense intuitively, because one contract controls one hundred shares. [Note: Sometimes options contracts are adjusted due to events like splits or special dividends and become nonstandard. Always double-check to confirm you understand the underlying and what it represents.]

Option type: Put or call

Option class: All puts or calls on an underlying are an options "class." For instance, all puts and calls on XYZ are called a class of options.

Option series: All options contracts of a given type with the same strike price and expiration date. An XYZ March 110 call is an options series, as is a ZYX June 100 put.

As an example, your neighbor across the street likes to talk about his investments at the neighborhood barbecue. One Saturday afternoon, he mentions to you that he recently bought one hundred shares of General Electric for $30 per share and is considering also buying two January 30 call options for $2 per contract. How much would he have invested total?

Answer: $3,400. He bought $3,000 GE in shares (100 shares × $30 per share) and $400 in options (2 × $2 × 100). Each call option for $2 costs $200 when you factor in the multiplier. Transaction costs (commissions and other fees) are not included in the example but are important factors to consider when evaluating any trade.

The premium is $2 per contract and totals $200 per contract because of the multiplier. In the options market, a purchase is also referred to as a *debit transaction*. The trade or purchase costs money, and that amount is debited from the account when the order is executed. On the other hand, the sale of an options contract is a credit transaction, as cash is credited to the account when the order is executed. When I cover more advanced strategies later, some will be initiated for debits and others for credits.

Don't Forget the Multiplier

Stock options contracts are quoted in dollars and cents, but the quotes are not the total premium. The premium is the quote multiplied by one hundred. That is, the multiplier for standard stock options is one hundred.

Obviously, the amount of time left until the expiration is an important determinant for the value of an options contract. Naturally, a contract that expires a year from now is worth more than one that expires in the next few days.

Importantly, not all options contracts follow the same expiration cycles. More popular and actively traded names often have very short-term options, known as weeklys, as well as longer-term contracts listed for trading. Less actively traded stocks might have no options listed at all or maybe only options with monthly expirations. In addition to standard monthly expirations, other expiration terms on an underlying might also include:

- **Weeklys:** Options that are typically listed on Thursdays and expire on Fridays of the following week.
- **Quarterlys:** Options that expire at the end of each fiscal quarter—March, June, September, and December.
- **LEAPS:** Long-term Equity Anticipation Securities are options that are listed with expiration dates up to three years in the future.

The options chain is the easiest way to see the options, expirations, and strike prices currently listed on a specific stock. A chain is just a table that sorts contracts by expiration date and strike prices. Calls typically appear on one side of a chain and puts on the other. The options then appear sorted by expiration term and strike prices.

Figure 5-1 shows (for illustrative purposes only) an options chain for Apple Inc. The stock trades under ticker symbol AAPL, and on that particular trading day, it was down a dime to $107.23 per share. The bid-ask to buy and sell shares was $107.28 to $107.34, and 32.8 million shares traded. The high and low for the day were $107.72 and $106.45.

	CALLS					Strikes: 6			PUTS			
	Volume	Open.Int	Bid X	Ask X	Exp		Strike	Bid X	Ask X	Volume	Open.Int	
▼ DEC4 15	(2) 100 (Weeklys)										20.86% (±1.509)	
	3,765	2,982	2.31 X	2.38 Q	DEC4 15		105	.13 Z	.14 C	10,672	16,476	
	7,203	5,436	1.44 M	1.49 C	DEC4 15		106	.25 Z	.26 N	13,313	6,600	
	18,837	10,313	.75 Q	.78 Q	DEC4 15		107	.54 Z	.57 C	17,927	6,524	
	15,546	10,543	.29 Z	.31 N	DEC4 15		108	1.06 C	1.12 E	6,622	4,273	
	8,449	11,175	.09 Z	.10 Z	DEC4 15		109	1.84 T	1.96 A	550	6,348	
	11,094	23,530	.04 Z	.05 A	DEC4 15		110	2.80 Z	2.95 X	1,102	7,464	
▶ DEC5 15	(9) 100										24.18% (±3.358)	
▶ JAN2 16	(17) 100 (Weeklys)										25.89% (±4.87)	
▶ JAN 16	(24) 100										26.65% (±5.93)	

Figure 5-1   Apple Inc. Options Chain

The options chain starts with December weekly options that had two days left until expiration. There were options that also expired the following week and, after that, January weeklys that expired in seventeen days. The January monthly options were expiring in three-and-a-half weeks.

If you noticed in Figure 5-1 that not all of these expirations were seven days apart, bravo! That's because expiration Fridays for December 25, 2015, and January 1, 2016, were exchange holidays. Therefore, the expirations were on Thursday, December 24, and Thursday, December 31. That explains why there are eight days between the last expiration in December and the first one in January on the Apple chain.

When all is said and done, options chains are probably the best and easiest way to see all available expiration terms. There is no need to guess what expirations might or might not exist. In the case of Apple, as of this writing, the expirations range two days to options expiring to more than two years. Chapter 9, which is on probabilities, will dig a bit deeper into expiration months and strike prices.

The strike prices are in the middle of Figure 5-1 and are arranged from lowest to highest. In this example, the six strikes nearest the stock prices were added to the chain. With shares near $107, it included 105-, 106-, 107-, 108-, 109-, and 110-strike calls and puts. More strikes were listed, but they would take up an entire page to show them all here.

In this case, the stock had contracts listed in $1 strike increments, but other stocks might have larger or smaller intervals, depending on the current share price and the amount of interest in the name.

> ### Expect the Expiration
>
> When do options expire? Prior to February 2015, the expiration date on standard monthly contracts was the Saturday following the third Friday of the expiration month. After February 2015, the expiration date for equity options is the third Friday of the expiration month. Expiration Friday is also the last day to trade expiring stock options. When trading index options, pay close attention to the last day to trade. It can vary by index, and some index options cease trading on the Thursday before expiration Friday. As weeklies are now expanding to different days of the week, there can be many different expiration days.

Stocks with more active options tend to boast greater numbers of individual contracts, which include additional strikes and expiration terms. As options expire or share prices move higher or lower, the exchanges add new expiration months and/or strike prices as needed.

Option Value

Each option contract includes a strike price that might be greater than, equal to, or less than the current underlying share price. Whether it is a put or call, an option that has a strike price that is equal to the price of the underlying is said to be at-the-money (ATM). A call option that has a strike price lower than the underlying price, or a put option that has a strike price above the stock price, is in-the-money (ITM). A call with a strike price higher than the price of the underlying, or a put with a strike below the stock price, is out-of-the-money (OTM). Another way to think about value is that an ITM option has intrinsic value, but ATM or OTM contracts do not.

To compute the intrinsic value of a call option, one can use the following simple formula:

$$\text{Stock price} - \text{Strike price} = \text{Intrinsic value}$$

And for puts:

$$\text{Strike price} - \text{Stock price} = \text{Intrinsic value}$$

For example, if a stock is trading for $15, a call option with a 10 strike has $5 of intrinsic value. An investor can exercise the option and call the stock for $10 and then immediately sell it for $15.

It is $5 ITM. On the other hand, if the stock is trading for $5, the 10-strike put has $5 of intrinsic value. The stock can be bought in the market for $5 and put (or sold) at $10. The contract is $5 in-the-money.

Note that intrinsic value can never be a negative number. When it equals zero, the option consists only of time value or extrinsic value. In-the-money options have intrinsic value, while out-of-the-money and at-the-money options consist only of extrinsic or time value. To recap:

At-the-money (ATM): Strike price = Stock price

In-the-money (ITM): Call strike price < Stock price or put strike price > Stock price

Out-of-the-money (OTM): Call strike price > Stock price or put strike price < Stock price

Note that an option's intrinsic value is independent of the expiration date and relates only to the strike price versus the price of the underlying. The June 90 call on an $85 stock has the same $5 of intrinsic value as the March 90 call. However, the June 90 call will have a higher premium compared to the March option due to higher extrinsic or time value.

The extrinsic value (or time value) of an option is the additional premium beyond intrinsic value that investors are willing to pay for the contract. The price of an ATM or OTM option consists only of time premium.

Exercise and Assignment

All options transactions are either opening or closing. An investor can buy or sell an option to open or to close. If, for instance, a new position is initiated as a purchase, it is an opening buy. That position can later be closed (or covered) through an offsetting sell-to-close transaction. Options can also be sold-to-open and bought-to-close. The four order types are therefore: buy-to-open, sell-to-open, buy-to-close, and sell-to-close.

An options contract can be closed at any time prior to the expiration. For instance, if an investor buys five XYZ January 30 call options for $1 to open, and the contract increased in value by $0.50, she can cover the position by selling five XYZ January 30 calls at $1.50 to close.

On the other hand, if an investor sells ten XYZ January 30 puts at $1 and the value decreases by $0.50, she can cover the position by buying ten XYZ January 30 puts for $0.50 to close. The investor might also close out part of a trade by, for instance, buying half (five) of the XYZ January 30 puts to close. I will discuss the mechanics of this later.

If a position is not closed prior to expiration, two things can happen. First, if a contract is ATM or OTM at expiration, it has no intrinsic value and will likely expire worthless and will no longer exist. For instance, a call option with a $50 strike is not worth anything at expiration if shares are trading for $45. An investor would not call a stock for $50 that he can buy in the market for $45. (Note that in rare instances an investor might exercise an OTM or ATM options contract. Whether by error or for other reasons, it can happen, but this is a rare occurrence to be discussed on another day.)

On the other hand, when an options contract is ITM, it has intrinsic value and is subject to automatic exercise. According to Options Clearing Corporation (OCC) rules, any contract that is ITM at expiration is subject to auto-exercise. For example, a long put with a $40 strike will be automatically exercised if shares are trading for $39 at expiration. The contract has $1 of intrinsic value that would be lost if not exercised. Chapter 7, which discusses put options, offers some examples of the exercise of put options.

OCC auto-exercise rules are designed to protect investors from leaving money on the table. However, an investor can also instruct the brokerage firm not to exercise the option in some very unusual situations. Ultimately, the investor wants to be aware of what options are ITM at the expiration and take the appropriate action by either closing the position through an offsetting transaction or by anticipating assignment if they are short the option. Open interest will also decrease if options are exercised or assigned.

American Style

Stock and ETF options are American-style and can be exercised any time prior to expiration. Most index options, on the other hand, settle European-style and can only be exercised at expiration.

Additionally, a stock option can be exercised any time prior to the expiration as well. It rarely makes economic sense to exercise an options contract that has extrinsic value (or time value), because, if exercised, the time value is lost. However, as expiration approaches and time premium approaches zero, the possibility of assignment increases. So if you're short options, you should be aware of any options you have that, due to dividend or other circumstances, can be subject to early exercise. Once the contract is assigned, it is too late to close it through an offsetting transaction.

Volume and Open Interest

Options chains can also be used to see the amount of trading activity associated with an individual options contract. On the options chain for Lululemon (Figure 5-2), volume and open interest are provided in addition to the bid-ask prices for each strike.

Volume represents the number of contracts traded during that particular trading session. This is merely a screenshot of what happened one day and is for illustrative purposes only. Note that the December 49.5 puts were the most active, with 227 contracts changing hands.

Volume is reset each day and equals zero at the open. As more contracts are traded, the volume will increase for that particular day. It doesn't matter if the trade was initiated by a buyer or seller, opening or closing. As more contracts change hands, volume increases.

Some names see thousands of contracts traded daily, while others see only a few. Typically, the more volume associated with the contract, the greater the number of buyers and sellers, as well as the higher number of bids and offers.

LULU ▾		LULULEMON ATHLETICA INC COM	**50.00** +.03 +0.06%	Bi 49.99 A: 50.01	ETB NASDAQ			≜ Company Profile	☰

▾ Underlying								
>	Last X	Net Chng	Bid X	Ask X	Size	Volume	Open	High	Low
	50.00 D	+.03	49.99 P	50.01 K	2 x 2	1,948,965	50.55	51.24	49.75

> Trade Grid

▾ Option Chain   Filter: **Off**,   Spread: **Single**,   Layout: **Volume, Open Interest**,

		CALLS			Strikes: 5 ▾		PUTS			
	Volume	Open.Int	Bid X	Ask X	Exp	Strike	Bid X	Ask X	Volume	Open.Int
▾ DEC 15	(1) 100									40.13% (±1.126)
	11	4,065	1.09 X	1.27 Q	DEC 15	49	.16 Z	.19 Q	33	784
	91	437	.78 Q	.88 N	DEC 15	49.5	.30 Q	.33 Q	227	195
	125	3,351	.49 Q	.55 Z	DEC 15	50	.50 N	.54 Q	62	1,908
	38	1,508	.29 X	.33 N	DEC 15	50.5	.78 N	.85 Q	20	173
	96	1,054	.16 A	.20 Q	DEC 15	51	1.07 X	1.26 C	33	722
	7	1,011	.10 Q	.13 C	DEC 15	51.5	1.44 X	1.94 C	0	3,017
> DEC4 15	(7) 100 (Weeklys)									40.92% (±2.39)
> DEC5 15	(14) 100									40.89% (±3.293)
> JAN2 16	(22) 100 (Weeklys)									41.70% (±4.173)
▾ JAN 16	(29) 100									52.60% (±6.042)

Figure 5-2   LULU Options Chain with Volume and Open Interest

Open interest is another gauge to measure an options contract's liquidity. It represents the number of contracts that have been opened by all market participants and not yet closed out. For instance, if you buy ten XYZ January 30 puts to open, then open interest increases by ten contracts. If you later cover those ten contracts by selling-to-close, open interest decreases by ten contracts. Open interest is updated just once per day, and like with volume, some names have substantially more than others.

Index Options

While a stock represents shares of just one company, an index represents the price action of shares of many different companies. The first index options made their debut in 1983 when Chicago Board Options Exchange (CBOE) listed puts and calls on the S&P 100 Index (OEX). Puts on the index resonated particularly well with portfolio managers looking for a tool to hedge portfolios with one instrument.

Over the years, the S&P 500 Index (SPX) has gained in popularity, and the options are much more actively traded than OEX options. The examples in this book going forward use SPX options, but other optionable indexes were mentioned in Chapter 1 as well.

Index options differ from equity options in several important ways. The first distinction is that an index is cash settled. Recall that one single stock option represents the right to buy or sell one hundred shares of stock. Exercise, therefore, involves the delivery of one hundred shares at the strike price.

The S&P 500 Index is a cash index. While trillions of dollars are tied to its performance through various financial instruments, the index itself does not have listed shares. There is nothing to buy or sell.

Instead, if an option is ITM and exercised at expiration, cash is transferred from one party to the other. The cash is equal to the difference between the strike price of the option and the value of the index at expiration, or its settlement value. Later chapters on puts and calls will explore the settlement process of both stocks and indexes in greater detail.

Another important difference between single stock options and index options is that most (but not all) indexes settle European-style. This means that exercise and assignment only takes place at expiration. There is no risk of early assignment on S&P 500 Index European-style options.

A Quick Note about Notionals

Notional value is computed as the units in one contract multiplied by the spot price of the underlying. For instance, one call option on the S&P 500 has a notional value of $190,000 if the index is trading at 1900.

A third fact to keep in mind when looking at index options is that notional values and premiums are often much higher when compared to equity options. The multiplier for an S&P 500 Index option is also one hundred. Therefore, if the S&P 500 is trading at the 2000-level, one contract controls $200,000 in notional values, and one S&P 500 Index contract that last traded for $50 represents $5,000 in premium. The higher notional values and premiums on some index products are important to consider when initiating various options strategies.

Summary

Welcome to the world of options. If you understand everything through this chapter, you are familiar with the basics of where options trade, the difference between puts and calls, and what their prices represent. With this information, it is possible to structure a number of strategies with different risks and rewards. I will cover them in more detail in later chapters, but keep in mind that each of the examples is for illustrative purposes only. They are not recommendations to buy or sell particular securities.

Other important points to take home for now are:

- Each option is a contract to buy or sell a security and can be defined by its underlying security, type (put or call), expiration, and strike price.
- A contract is ITM if it has intrinsic value and OTM if it consists only of time value.
- As expiration approaches, options lose time value. Options that are OTM or ATM at expiration will expire worthless.
- ITM options that are not covered at expiration are automatically exercised.

- Index options differ from equity options in several important ways, including notional values and cash settlement rather than physical delivery of shares.

The next two chapters start to explore basic option strategies using puts and calls. Then the focus turns to the determinants of options prices before diving into the final section in Part II: "Probabilities."

References

McMillan, L. 2012. *Options as a Strategic Investment*, 5th ed., Prentice Hall.

Natenberg, S. 2015. *Option Volatility and Pricing: Advanced Trading Strategies and Techniques*, 2nd ed. McGraw Hill.

www.cboe.com/micro/weeklys/introduction.aspx

www.cboe.com/micro/spx-stock-index-options.aspx

CHAPTER 6

Introduction to Call Options

A call option represents the right to buy an underlying asset for a specific price through an expiration period. One single stock call option, for example, is the right to buy one hundred shares of stock. The premium paid for the calls is often a fraction of the cost of the actual shares. This is known as leverage.

Another analogy can help demonstrate the important concept of leverage. Let's say you have $500 of your own money and borrow $4,500 from Uncle Bill to invest in a sailboat you intend on fixing and selling next summer. Bill expects some sort of compensation for the loan and agrees to give you the money if you repay him $4,700 once the boat is sold.

Twelve months later, you have completed the necessary improvements and repairs. You sell the boat for $5,500, and total profit is the sale price ($5,500) minus the money you invested ($5,000), or $500. Of that, Uncle Bill received $200 (on his $4,500 investment), while you received $300 (on a $500 investment). Stated differently, you earned a 60 percent return on your $500 and did much better than the 4.4 percent return Bill earned on his $4,500. The leverage ratio in this case is nine-to-one, because you borrowed $9 for every $1 you invested of your money.

Now what happens if the boat sells for less than expected? For instance, at the end of twelve months, let's say the best you can get for the boat is $4,700. In this case, you repay Bill $4,700, according to the agreed upon terms. Yet, you invested $500 and have nothing to show for it. Although the sale of the boat was a total loss of $300

($5,000 invested minus the $4,700 sale price), you lost your entire investment, and Bill earned 4.4 percent on his $4,500.

As you will see in the next two chapters on calls and puts, leverage is a double-edged sword that can amplify returns but also result in large percentage losses, depending on changes in the underlying. This chapter begins with a focus on single-stock call options and then looks at some examples using indexes. The next chapter covers equity puts and index puts.

The examples, some using real tickers and some hypothetical, are for illustrative purposes only and are not a recommendation to buy or sell any individual securities. At the end of the chapter, you should understand the risks and rewards associated with being long or short call options. These are certainly not recommendations, as options trading is not suitable for everyone. As we all know, market conditions constantly change, and just because a strategy may have worked in the past, there is no guarantee it will work in the future.

Call Options versus Stock

Many investors see options trading as a natural extension of stock trading. Consequently, buying calls often makes the most sense intuitively. That is, rather than buying shares of a stock outright today and hoping to sell them at a higher price at a later time, one strategy is to buy calls in anticipation that the premiums will increase and then sell the calls later at a higher price. It's the old adage "buy low, sell high" that you have heard many times.

As you will see, however, there are a number of important differences between owning shares of stock and owning call options. The owner of calls doesn't receive dividends and doesn't have the same rights as a stockholder. Additionally, if a stock moves up $1, the options might move up smaller amounts or maybe not at all. (This is explored in more detail in Chapter 8, "Components of

> ### Rights versus Obligations
>
> The owner of an equity call option has the right to buy the underlying stock per the terms of the contract. It is his choice. A call option seller (or writer) on the other hand, has the obligation to sell the underlying stock per the terms of the options contract.

Options Prices.") As we will see in this and later chapters, one of the primary differences is that call options are decaying assets. This time decay is due to the way options premiums are priced, which will be made clear in later chapters as well.

As you probably already know, bullish options traders buy calls when they expect the stock price to go up. The concept is similar to simply buying shares of stock, but call options will have different risks and rewards due to the leverage involved. The amount of leverage will depend on the amount paid to enter the trade (the debit), as well as the number of contracts traded, the time left until expiration, and the relationship between the strike price and the underlying share price. All of this will become clearer as we work through some examples.

Risk and Reward of Long Call

All investments carry some degree of risk, and the most an investor can lose on a long call purchase is the amount of money paid to enter the contract (the options premium plus any associated brokerage commissions and fees). In most cases, the desired outcome is for the stock to move higher in price and the calls to increase in value. However, if shares fall, the call will likely decrease in value and might even expire worthless.

When a Call Doesn't Fall

There are times when the call or put option might not behave as anticipated because it is far out of the money (OTM) or other factors, like time or volatility, are affecting premiums. The reasons this happens will be made clearer in Chapter 8 when I discuss the components of options prices.

To better illustrate, Figure 6-1 shows the simple risk graph of owning a long call option. Recall from Chapter 4 that a risk (or profit/loss) graph shows the profit and loss of a trade on the y-axis (vertical) and the changes in the underlying stock price along the x-axis (horizontal). The upward to the right shape of the long call risk curve is due to the fact that calls increase in value as the underlying stock moves higher. The expiration breakeven is at zero, where the diagonal line moves through the x-axis.

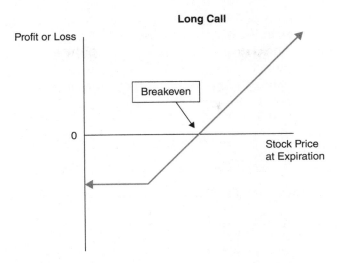

Figure 6-1   Long Call Risk Graph

Mathematically, the breakeven of a long call purchase at expiration is equal to the strike price plus the debit paid for the calls. A call that is bought for $1 with a 20-strike price, for example, has an expiration breakeven at $21 per share. At that price, the calls are $1 in-the-money (ITM). That $1 of intrinsic value at expiration covers the $1 that was paid for the options, and the position breaks even, excluding transaction costs.

Breaking Even

Options traders talk a lot about the *breakeven* (BE) of a trade. It's an important concept, because the BE is the level at which the strategy has no gains or losses. In this book, I refer to the breakeven at the expiration of the options and explain how to compute breakeven levels for various strategies. Trading software can be used to compute breakeven levels as well.

Returning to the 20-strike call bought for a $1 debit, any share price above $21 at expiration results in profits, and anything below that price level translates into losses. However, the calls can be sold-to-close at any time prior to expiration as well. The profit or loss if the position is sold-to-close will depend on the price of the options prior to the expiration. If the options are sold at the same price as the purchase price, the position breaks even. Of course, the call buyer wants the option to increase in value and either sell it at a higher price or exercise the option and call the stock.

To summarize the long call purchase:

Strategy: Buy calls

Direction: Bullish

Debit or credit: Debit

Risk: Premium paid + Transaction costs

Breakeven: Strike price + Debit

Potential profits: Theoretically unlimited

If the call is not sold-to-close prior to expiration, several things can happen, depending on where the stock price is relative to the strike price of the option. If a call is ITM and has intrinsic value of a penny or more, it will be subject to auto-exercise. That means the long call holder will call (or buy) one hundred shares of the stock per contract at the strike price of the call option. If exercise is not the desired outcome, then it is important to either close the position before expiration or express do-not-exercise instructions to the broker. Out-of-the-money options have no intrinsic value and, in most cases, expire worthless.

Real-World Example

At this point, the idea of buying a call option should be well understood. It's time to go through some real-world examples using actual prices. The examples are for educational and illustrative purposes only and are not solicitations or recommendations to trade a specific security or use a specific strategy.

Facebook (FB) was trading for roughly $90 per share at the end of September 2015. Looking at the option chain in Figure 6-2, you can see a couple of options strikes and that the January 85 call options on the social media company were trading for $9.65 to $10.05 per contract.

I will use round numbers throughout the strategy discussions as much as possible to simplify the math. For example, with Facebook trading for $90, the 85-strike call is $5 ITM and trading

| FB | ▼ | 🖊 | FACEBOOK INC COM | **89.90** | | CTB | +0.505 | | | 🔒 Company Profile | 09/30/2015 | 🗔 | 🖩 | ≡ |

▾ Underlying

	Last	Net Chng	Volume	Open	High	Low
	89.90	+3.23	36,169,146	88.44	90.02	88.01

▾ Option Chain | Filter: **Off** | Spread: **Single** | Layout: **Last, Mark**

			CALLS		Strikes: ALL				PUTS		
	Last	Mark	Bid	Ask	Exp	Strike	Bid	Ask	Last	Mark	38.86% (±15.346)
▾ JAN 16	(107) 100										
	9.65	9.850	9.65	10.05	JAN 16	85	4.75	5.05	4.98	4.900	
	8.30	8.275	8.15	8.40	JAN 16	87.5	5.75	6.05	6.00	5.900	

Figure 6-2   Facebook Options Chain (9/30/2015)

for $10 per contract. Because the multiplier is one hundred, one contract costs $1,000.

> ## Buy Value, Sell Junk
>
> I often see new investors focus their call buying on OTM options, but this is opposite to what I teach. I prefer to buy ITM options and sell extrinsic value. My motto is "buy value, sell junk."

A buyer takes a long position in one FB January 85 call for $10 on expectations that Facebook shares will advance in the months ahead. It is a debit transaction of $1,000, and that, plus transaction costs, represents the risk to the trade. If shares fall below $85, don't recover, and the position is left open through the expiration, the options expire, and the entire premium is lost. The breakeven is at $95 per share (strike plus debit), and potential profits accumulate as shares move higher.

Strategy: Buy 1 FB January 85 call for $10 per contract

Direction: Bullish

Debit or credit: $1,000 debit

Risk: $1,000

Breakeven: $95

Potential profits: Theoretically unlimited

Figure 6-3 shows the P/L graph of one January 85 long call on Facebook for $10. It restates what was already noted, but in a graph. That is, the potential loss is $1,000, and the profits happen above the $95 breakeven. As the stock climbs, the profits increase and are

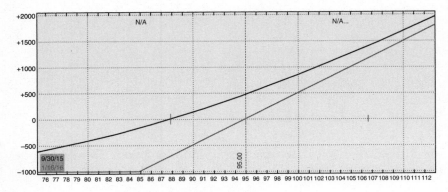

Figure 6-3   Facebook Long Jan 85 Call Graph

theoretically unlimited, because there is no limit to how far a stock can climb.

Note that, in addition to the expiration profit and loss curve, the risk graph also shows the potential P/L at the time the position is opened. The breakeven shows only the profits and losses at expiration when time value has reached zero. However, the position will show gains or losses prior to that time, depending on the movement in the underlying. For instance, looking at the risk graph, if shares saw a sudden spike to $95, the profit is expected to be roughly $500 per contract.

Fast-forward three months. It is the end of December and three weeks before the January expiration. Facebook shares have advanced and now trade for $105 per share. The January 85 call is $20 ITM, and the bid-ask to sell or buy the option is $21 to $22. The investor wants to monetize the gain in the options after the nearly 25 percent rally in the stock.

If the calls are sold-to-close at $21 minus the $10 debit, the profit is $11 per contract, or $1,100 on one contract. Had the investor bought one hundred shares for $85 and sold at $105 instead, the gain would have been $2,000. So in dollar terms, owning shares yields greater profits. However, the return (of more than 100 percent) on the long calls is obviously much greater. While the shareholder saw a 23.5 percent increase in his holdings, the option holder more than doubled his money. There's the leverage.

What happens if the options are exercised? For instance, the investor can call the stock for $85 and sell it at market price for $105 per share. In that case, the investor records a profit of $20 by exercising, minus the $10 that was paid for the options. The profit is $10 per contract (representing one hundred shares) and less than the $11 profit received for selling the calls. The reason? Time value. At $21 per contract, the calls had $20 of intrinsic value and $1 of time value. If the calls are exercised rather than sold-to-close, any time value remaining is lost.

Sometimes exercise is the optimal play, but it also depends on whether the investor wants to take delivery of shares. Other times, an investor might exercise options to take delivery of shares, even when a contract is slightly OTM. That's why a short call might be assigned, even if it has no intrinsic value. This is rare, but it does happen.

Transaction costs such as commissions, exercise charges, and other fees should be considered as well. In cases where the contract has remaining time value, it rarely makes sense to exercise to monetize the gain. Instead, it makes more sense to sell-to-close the contract. If you are unsure, ask your brokerage firm for guidance.

Rolling, Rolling, Rolling

Rather than selling or exercising an option, another approach to is to roll a position. That is, if a stock has moved higher and a long call is now deep ITM, the investor can adjust the position by selling-to-close the call and buying-to-open a call at a higher strike price. The adjustment is called a roll and will be covered in more detail in Chapter 17, "The Close."

In summary, long calls are often used when an investor expects the underlying stock to move higher. The options lock in the right to buy shares at a later time, and the premiums paid to enter the position are often a fraction of the cost of buying the underlying shares. The greater leverage can lead to larger percentage gains, but also big losses, including the loss of 100 percent of the premium. At the same time, the potential risk or loss of a long call position are also clearly defined beforehand.

Short Calls

Selling calls without a position in the underlying is a strategy that offers limited rewards but can theoretically carry unlimited risks.

Because a call option gives the owner the right to buy the underlying, the writer is under an obligation to deliver (sell) the shares at a fixed price regardless of how high the price of the underlying climbs.

For example, if an investor writes ten XYZ January 50 calls at $1 per contract with shares near $50 and the stock rallies to $70 before the expiration, the intrinsic value of the calls is suddenly $20, or a $19 loss per contract, excluding any remaining time value and transaction costs. On ten contracts, the investor collected $1,000 in premium but suffered more than $19,000 in losses.

Figure 6-4 is the simple risk graph for the short-call strategy. The maximum gain is limited to the premium received. The breakeven equals the strike price plus the credit received for selling the calls. Losses increase as shares move beyond the breakeven. The potential losses are theoretically unlimited, because there is no cap to how far a stock can climb.

Until the short call position is closed, assigned, or exercised, any gains or losses due to changes in premiums are unrealized. So, if the position is not closed or exercised, what happens when an investor is short ITM calls at expiration? You already saw how the buyer can exercise the right to buy (or call) shares at the strike price. The call writer, on the other hand, is obligated to sell the stock at the strike price.

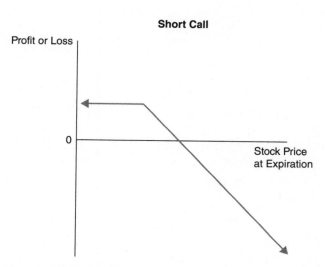

Figure 6-4   Short Call Risk Graph

Strategy: Sell calls

Direction: Bearish or neutral

Debit or credit: Credit

Risk: Unlimited

Breakeven: Strike price + Credit

Potential profits: Limited to credit received

There is no way to know for certain when assignment will happen. In addition, assignment might involve all contracts at once, or it might be one or a few contracts at a time. The Options Clearing Corporation (OCC) allocates assignment randomly, and as already noted, the chances of assignment increase as expiration approaches. It also increases just before an ex-dividend date.

Once assignment happens, it's too late to close the position, and a call writer is obligated to deliver one hundred shares per contract at the strike of the option. If the shares are not held in the account, the investor must have sufficient funds to meet the margin requirement for being short the stock.

Using another real-world example, an investor expects Apple Inc. shares to see limited upside in the next six months and is looking to sell calls. With the stock around $108 per share, the options chain shows July 130 calls trading at $1 even. Ten contracts are sold at $1 each, and a total of $1,000 in premium is collected, less transaction costs.

Figure 6-5 shows the risk graph for shorting 10 July 130 calls on Apple at $1 per contract. The potential profit is limited to the premium collected, or $1,000. The potential loss is unlimited. The breakeven equals the strike plus the credit, or at 130, strike plus the $1 debit, equals $131 per share. At that point, if the calls are assigned, the investor sells (has the stock called) at $130 per share. The difference between the market price ($131) and the strike price ($130) is offset by the $1 premium collected for the calls, and the trade breaks even.

Losses begin to mount as shares rally and, as you can see from the graph, can be considerable in the event of a major move higher in the underlying. The short call can also be closed before the expiration through a buy-to-close transaction. If the calls are bought for less than the sale price, the investor monetizes a gain. If the purchase price at the time of closing is higher than the sale price, the result is a loss.

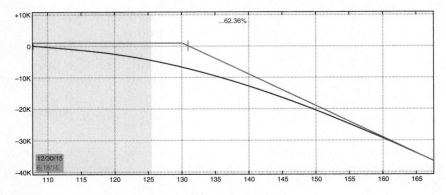

Figure 6-5   Short Apple July 130 Calls Risk Graph

Strategy: Sell 10 Apple July 130 calls at $1

Direction: Bearish or neutral

Debit or credit: $1,000 credit

Risk: Unlimited

Breakeven: $131 (plus transaction costs)

Potential profits: $1,000

The short call strategy offers limited profit potential, and the best profits happen if shares hold below the strike price through the expiration. At that point, the maximum profit has been achieved, because the options expire worthless. The risks are theoretically unlimited due to the fact that a stock can continue climbing to infinity. Therefore, this is not a strategy that is appropriate for novice investors.

Later chapters on covered calls, calendar spreads, and vertical spreads will introduce other strategies that can be initiated when an investor is bearish or neutral on the underlying stock. The key, and a theme that you will see over and over again in the strategies section of this book, is that it's really all about clearly defining and understanding your risks.

Index Call Options

While a single stock option represents control of shares in just one company, an index option offers exposure to a basket of different companies. Several indexes were discussed in Chapter 2, "First Days of Trading," including the S&P 500 Index. Unlike shares of individual companies, an index itself can't be bought or sold. However, the S&P 500 Index and many others do have listed options.

Like the purchase of a long call on a stock, buying call options on the S&P 500 Index is typically a strategy used when an investor is bullish on the stock market and expects it to move higher. In this case, the underlying reflects roughly 80 percent of the U.S. stock market. The investor pays a premium to enter the contract, which has a fixed strike price and a set expiration date.

Selling or Writing Index Options

Selling index options is a strategy that requires significant capital and advanced options account approvals. Later, I will show some examples that involve selling index options as part of spreads. However, naked (or uncovered) writing of index options is not among the strategies discussed within this book, because the risks can be substantial and I am very focused on defining risks.

For example, a self-directed investor is looking to position a portion of her portfolio for a possible turnaround in the U.S. equities market. After a volatile month of August and September, she wants exposure for the final few months of the year, because her portfolio has been underinvested in stocks and she also expects the market to rebound through year-end. She is also starting a new job with a retirement plan and higher salary at the beginning of the year.

In order to get exposure to equities, she looks at various opportunities and thinks S&P 500 Index call options are the best way to express her bullish view. Her goal in buying S&P 500 Index calls is to obtain upside exposure to the equity market through the remainder of this year before proactively making changes to the portfolio at the beginning of next year when other life changes are taking place.

ITM versus OTM Call Buying

This example is using OTM calls and is to demonstrate the mechanics of call buying on an index. My approach is typically to purchase ITM calls when looking for upside exposure to long stock or calls. I like options that have some value already when I purchase them. This will become clearer as I work through more advanced strategy examples.

It's the end of September, and the S&P 500 Index (SPX) has listed December quarterly options that expire at the end of the year. With the index near 1,920, the 1950-strike calls are trading for $50 per contract. Four contracts at $50 apiece are purchased for the portfolio. She is now long four SPX December quarterly 1950 call options for $50 each, costing her a total premium of $20,000, plus transaction costs.

The maximum risk to buying calls is the premium paid, or, in this case, $20,000. If the S&P 500 stays below 1,950 and the position is left open through the expiration, the options expire worthless, and the premium paid is lost. The expiration breakeven is equal to the strike price plus the debit, or the 2,000 level for the S&P 500. Potential profits are above the breakeven.

Strategy: Buy four SPX December QTRLY 1950 calls for $50

Direction: Bullish

Debit or credit: $20,000 debit

Risk: $20,000

Breakeven: $2,000

Potential profits: Unlimited

You can see two profit and loss curves on Figure 6-6. One is the expiration P/L, and one is the potential profit or loss at the time the calls were purchased. The difference between the two lines reflects the fact that the expiration risk line shows only the profit and loss at expiry, when there is no time value remaining in the options. The other line is an estimate using options pricing models and will factor

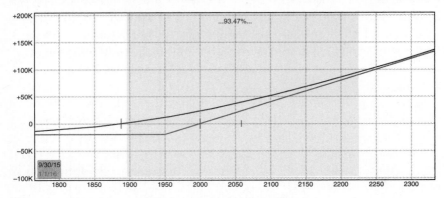

Figure 6-6   Long SPX December 1950 Call Risk Graph

in the time value that remains in the contract. Notice that the two lines get closer together as the contract moves either deep ITM or far OTM. The two lines will also converge at the expiration.

After two months, it's the end of November, and the equity market has performed better than the investor had expected. In fact, the S&P 500 has risen 130 points, or 6.7 percent, to 2080 during that time. The December quarterly 1950 calls are 130 points ITM and trading for $130 per contract. The investor exits the position to monetize the gain by selling-to-close four SPX December quarterly 1950 calls at $130 per contract, for a gain of $80 per contract, or $32,000 on four contracts.

Could the investor have exercised the contract rather than selling-to-close the position? In the case of S&P 500 Index options, the answer is no. Because it is a European-style index, the options can only be exercised at expiration.

At expiration, the settlement of the options involves the transfer of cash. Say, for example, the S&P 500 settled at 2050 at expiration (settlement value was $2,050), the 1950-strike calls are 100 points ITM. If the investor exercises the calls, she gets a cash deposit equal to the difference between the settlement value and the strike price, or (2050 – 1950) × 100 multiplier, minus any transaction costs for handling the exercise.

Now suppose, instead, that the market had turned against the call buyer in the S&P Index example. For example, if she bought the same December quarterly 1950 calls for $50 and the market dropped 5 percent the following week, there would be two options: sell-to-close the options contract after the market decline or hold the options and hope for a rebound. If, for instance, she covered the calls at $25, the loss would be $10,000 on four contracts ($25 × 100 × 4), or 50 percent of the initial investment. On the other hand, if the options were left open and the S&P 500 remained below 1950, the calls expire worthless, and the loss is 100 percent of the initial investment.

In sum, the premium levels and dollar value of the S&P 500 Index are much larger than most single stock options. The index is also cash settled, and options can only be exercised at the expiration. In addition to transaction costs, the risks to buying puts and calls is the total premium and can result in losing all of one's investment. Selling (or writing) index options involves different risks of losing additional money beyond that. This is a much more advanced strategy.

Summary

The mechanics of selling calls along with stock positions (or covered calls) are explored in detail in Chapter 11. Other than that, short calls are not mentioned again in this book, because it is not a strategy that I personally find interesting from a risk-reward perspective. However, later chapters explore spread trades that can be considered over straight call buying, or selling, in some situations.

To recap, long calls on single stocks offer upside exposure to the underlying with less capital than buying shares outright. The strategy makes sense when an investor has a bullish view on the underlying but doesn't want to buy the shares at the current time. Instead, he is locking in the right to buy the shares at a specific price at a later time. The result is leverage that can lead to large percentage gains and losses.

Index call options can offer upside exposure to the broader market. Dollar values and premiums on index products are typically higher than single stock options. There are differences in how the options settle at expiration as well. These nuances are important to understand going into the next chapter on put options, protective puts, and hedging strategies using equity and index options.

Reference

www.optionseducation.org/content/oic/en/tools/faq/general
    _information.html

Introduction to Put Options

Insurance is an important part of the world today. I buy auto insurance for my car in case there is an accident. I have life insurance to protect my family financially. My home is insured against fire or weather-related damage. I have health insurance to cover medical expenses.

Yet, given all the insurance that we buy from one year to the next, it's surprising to me how many people never consider buying insurance for their stock portfolios. There are tools available to do so, and one of them is called the put option.

Put options are not exactly like insurance, and some important differences will be addressed in this chapter. Nevertheless, a put option is a tool that can be used to hedge (or protect) an individual stock position from a price drop for a limited period of time. Index put options are often used to hedge entire stock portfolios.

Put options are also used in other ways. For example, an investor can sell puts as a way to collect a premium if she is willing to buy the shares (have the shares put to her) at the strike price of the option at a later date. Selling puts as part of a cash-secured put strategy is covered in Chapter 12.

Meanwhile, a long put is sometimes used when an investor is expecting shares of a stock to decline in price and wants to participate in the move lower or as a temporary hedging strategy to help protect a long position without selling it out. Specific examples of long puts on single stocks and indexes are presented for readers over the next few pages.

Like short selling, the long put is a strategy initiated when the short-term outlook is bearish on the underlying security. However, long puts along with a stock position is actually a bullish trade and somewhat similar to the long call. Let's see how all this works.

Long Puts versus Short Selling

An investor might sell a stock short when the price is expected to fall. As was duly noted in Chapter 3, the idea is to sell the stock now, wait for a drop in the price, and then buy back shares (or cover the short) at a later time. Of course, the stock price could instead rise, exposing the investor to unlimited risk.

A long put can also offer exposure to a stock when the investor expects the price to fall. However, instead of selling now and buying later, the investor is buying the put (or going long) when he expects the stock price to drop. This is sometimes confusing in the beginning, but with puts, you are actually buying to take a short position in the underlying stock or index. If the underlying falls as expected, the puts can typically be sold later at a higher price.

Recall that if you buy the put, you are locking in the right to sell the underlying security. One equity put option, for example, represents the right to sell one hundred shares of the underlying stock. In most cases, the investor is buying the put, anticipating a move lower in shares, and either selling-to-close the put or exercising the put. The put can also expire worthless if left open through the expiration or, if in-the-money (ITM) by a penny or more at the expiration, subject to auto-exercise (as explained in Chapter 5, "Options Basics").

The point to take home for now is that, like short selling, buying a put is a bearish view on the underlying. Being long the put (unless used in a protective manner for hedging) reflects expectations that the stock will move lower. However, while shorting stock involves selling now and buying later, the opposite is true of long puts. In addition, long puts can be sold-to-close, exercised, or left open through the expiration.

Risk and Reward

Like buying call options, buying puts has limited risks. The risk is losing part or all of the premium paid—that is, the debit. If an investor expects a move lower in shares, he might buy the put. If he's wrong, that option might expire worthless, because if the contract is out of the money (OTM) or at the money (ATM) at expiration, it has no intrinsic value. It expires worthless, and 100 percent of the premium paid to buy the put is lost. That's the worst-case scenario, and the good thing is that this risk is something you can define upfront.

Risk of Auto-Exercise

Any options contract that is ITM at expiration is subject to auto-exercise per Options Clearing Corporation (OCC) rules. This means a long put holder with an ITM contract would end up with a short stock position (or selling shares if she already owns them), and that, in turn, could increase the risk of buying puts beyond the premium paid. Importantly, if auto-exercise is not desired, the investor wants to communicate the instructions to his broker.

Figure 7-1 shows the risks and rewards of a long put with a simple graph. Losses happen below the expiration breakeven (BE) line as shares move higher. Profits build as the share price moves lower. The potential gains to owning a put on a single stock option are limited because an equity cannot fall below zero.

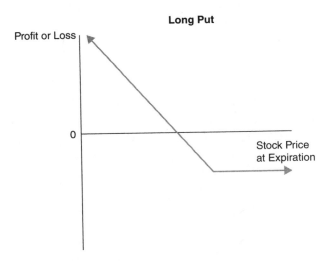

Figure 7-1   Long Put Risk Curve

Like the BE for a long call, the BE for a long put is easy to compute. It equals the strike price of the option minus the debit. If an investor pays $0.50 for a 20-strike put, the trade breaks even if shares fall to $19.50 (excluding transaction costs). At that point, the puts have $0.50 of intrinsic value, which equals the debit paid to open the position. Profits accrue as shares fall below the breakeven.

To recap the long put position:

Strategy: Buy puts

Bias: Bearish

Debit or credit: Debit

Risk: Premium paid

Breakeven: Strike price – Debit

Potential profits: Strike price – premium paid – current price of the underlying

While the risk to buying puts is limited to the premium paid, selling (or writing) puts can carry significant risk, especially on a high-priced stock or index. By selling the put, the writer is taking on the obligation to purchase shares of the underlying at the strike price (or deliver cash for index option) regardless of how far the price of the underlying falls.

In some cases, put writing is an attractive alternative to owning stock, or as we will see in Chapter 11, a way to position yourself to purchase stock through the cash covered put. For now, let's keep the focus on long puts and then consider the protective put strategy.

Real-World Example

As a reminder, options trading involves risks and is not suitable for everyone. Examples presented in this book are for educational and illustrative purposes only. The securities depicted are real but are specifically not solicitations or recommendations to trade a specific security or to engage in a particular trading or investing strategy. Market conditions do change, and just because a strategy has worked in the past, there are no guarantees it will work in the future.

Twitter (TWTR) shares had a rough time in the social media company's first two years as a publicly traded company. After hitting a high of almost $75 per share shortly after the initial public offering in late 2013, the stock moved lower throughout much of 2014 and by the end of 2015 fetched less than $25 per share. April 28, 2015, proved to be a particularly volatile trading day after the stock lost more than 18.1 percent in one day when the company reported earnings that missed analyst estimates.

With expectations the stock would suffer another setback when earnings are reported again at the end of July, an investor is looking at put options on Twitter with the stock near $36. On July 15, a January 37 put on the stock is offered at $5 per contract (Figure 7-2). The investor buys one contract for $5 for a net outlay of $500 per contract plus commissions.

The risk to buying a put is clearly defined as the debit paid (or $500 plus transaction costs) for one January 37 put on Twitter, and the maximum loss happens if the option expires worthless. The BE is equal to the strike price minus the debit, or $32 per share. The potential profits accumulate below the BE and are only limited to the stock falling to zero. In other words, the potential profits are equal to the strike price minus the premium minus the stock price.

Strategy: Buy 1 TWTR January 37 put for $5

Bias: Bearish

Debit or credit: $500 debit

Risk: $500

Breakeven: $32

Maximum potential profit: $3,200

The risk graph of the long Twitter January 37 puts (Figure 7-3) confirms that the position has a bearish bias. It breaks even if shares are at $32 at the expiration. If shares close at $22 at expiration,

TWTR		TWITTER INC C...	35.66	-1.06 2.89%	NASDAQ	≌ ±0.494	≙ Company Profile	07/15/2015		
⌄ Underlying										
		Last	Net Chng		Volume		Open	High		Low
		35.66	-1.06		18,296,837		36.66	37.09		35.55
⌄ Option Chain	Filter: **Off**	Spread: **Single**	Layout: **Last, Mark**							
		CALLS			Strikes: 4			PUTS		
		Last	Mark	Bid	Ask	Exp	Strike	Bid	Ask	Last	Mark
> DEC 15	(156)	100								44.59% (±8.545)
⌄ JAN 16	(184)	100								43.74% (±9.136)
		5.26	5.250	5.20	5.30	JAN 16	34	3.30	3.45	3.31	3.375
		4.75	4.750	4.70	4.80	JAN 16	35	3.80	3.90	3.83	3.850
		4.27	4.250	4.20	4.30	JAN 16	36	4.30	4.45	4.10	4.375
		3.85	3.825	3.75	3.90	JAN 16	37	4.90	5.00	4.52	4.950

Figure 7-2   Twitter Options Chain (7/15/2015)

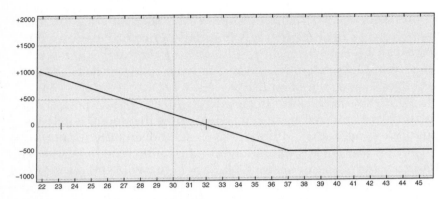

Figure 7-3   Risk Graph for TWTR January 37 Put

for example, the profit is $10, because the contract is $15 ITM ($37 – $22), and that minus the $5 debit is the profit (times the one hundred multiplier).

Twitter shares slipped on earnings again in late July and fell toward $27 per share on September 30. At that point, the January 37 puts were trading for almost $11, or $10 in intrinsic value and $1 in extrinsic value (or time value). To monetize the gain, the investor would sell-to-close one TWTR January 37 put at $11. The profit is $6 per contract, or $600. So while Twitter shares lost $9, or 25 percent, the puts more than doubled in value. There, again, is an example of leverage.

Because equity options are American-style, the investor could also exercise the puts at any time. Continuing with the scenario above, if the investor buys one hundred shares of Twitter at $27 per share, he can then sell (or put it) at the $37 strike price for a profit of $10 per share on the stock sale minus the $5 paid for buying the put. In that case, the stock sale produces $1,000 in gains and $500 profits on the trade after subtracting out the initial $500 paid for the puts. However, a profit of $500 is less than the $6 gain for selling-to-close the puts. The difference is the $1 in time value, as there were more than one hundred days remaining until the January options expired. In this case, exercise is not the optimal way to monetize the profit.

Obviously, the risk to the long put is that the underlying may move higher instead of lower. If, for example, the stock moved higher than $37 and the position was left open, the entire premium paid is lost. The position can also be sold-to-close prior to the expiration, and the gain or loss will depend on whether the sale price (credit) is greater or less than the initial $5 purchase price or debit plus transaction costs.

Protective Puts

Because puts increase in value when shares of the underlying fall, the options can be used to hedge (or protect) individual stock positions for a limited time. For example, one put can be bought against one hundred shares of stock, and if the share price falls, the investor can sell (or put) the stock at a fixed strike price upon exercise of the options contract. Buying puts against a position in the underlying is known as a protective put.

The risk graph for the protective put (Figure 7-4) shows that the directional bias of the position is bullish. That is, although she bought puts, the investor wants shares of the underlying stock to move higher. If the stock falls instead, the put purchase can help limit losses. The strike price will determine the degree of protection.

The BE of the protective put is equal to the purchase price of the stock plus the premium for the options (minus any dividends received plus transaction costs). The risk is defined by the put option strike price and, mathematically, equals the cost of the stock plus the

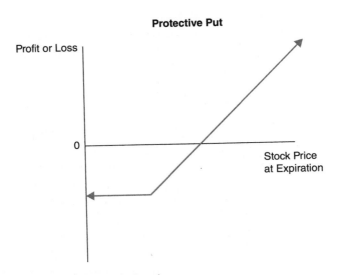

Figure 7-4   Protective Put Risk Graph

option premium minus the strike price—or, simply, the BE minus the strike price of the put.

Strategy: Long stock + Long puts

Direction: Bullish

Debit or credit: Debit

Risk: Stock price paid + Option premium – Strike price

Breakeven: Stock price + Debit

Potential profits: No limit

You might have noticed that the risk graph of the protective put and the long call are the same shape. In fact, the protective put is sometimes referred to as a *synthetic call* because their risk profiles are equivalent. In both strategies, the shareholder is looking for share prices to move higher. While the long call buyer pays a premium, the investor with the protective put position is long stock and paying a premium for an option to hedge shares for a period of time. Therefore, like the long call, the strategy is a bullish play on the underlying, but the investor is buying put to define the risk.

Married Puts

The term *married put* is used to describe a strategy when the investor buys shares and puts simultaneously. It is the same as a protective put, but the stock shares and options are purchased at the same time. The term *protective put* refers to buying puts against shares that are already in the portfolio.

Returning to the Twitter example, in this case, the investor is long one hundred shares of Twitter for $36 per share and buys one January 37 put for $5 to help hedge the risks of a potential drop in the price of the shares. The total cost of the position is now $36 per share plus the $5 premium for the puts (ignoring transaction costs). The BE of the position is equal to the total cost and is at $41 per share, as you can see from Figure 7-5.

The protective put caps the downside risk by locking in the right to sell (or put) the shares at the $37 strike price. Because $41 was paid to enter the position, the potential loss is $4, or $400 on one

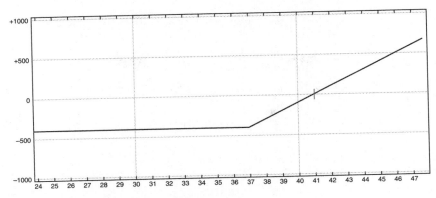

Figure 7-5   Twitter January 37 Protective Put

protective put. For example, if the stock is trading for $25 at the expiration, the investor can sell (or put) shares at $37 each. That, in turn, is better than the loss suffered if shares are sold at $25 in the market and suffering an $11 loss without the protective put.

Strategy: Long 100 shares for $36 and 1 January 37 put for $5

Direction: Bullish

Debit or credit: Debit

Risk: ($36 + 5 − 37) × Multiplier = $400

Breakeven: $36 + $5 = $41

Potential profits: No limit (because there's no limit to how high the price of the stock can climb)

Of course, the investor can also sell-to-close the puts while maintaining a position in shares if the stock is expected to rebound. Or, vice versa, the shares can be sold and the puts left open if the stock is expected to see additional losses. Transaction costs and tax consequences associated with selling the shares or options should not be overlooked when breaking apart or adjusting the protective put.

The protective put strategy makes sense if the investor wants to hedge an existing stock position for a period of time, but when seeking upside exposure in an underlying, it sometimes costs less up front to buy a long call. The risks and rewards are the same, but the transaction costs differ. It typically costs less to buy calls compared to buying long shares and long puts. Of course, the protective put position will collect any dividends paid by the underlying stock, because the investor is a shareholder. The call holder is not entitled to dividends paid.

Now what if the investor wants to not just hedge one stock but an entire portfolio?

Index Put Options

An index put option typically increases in value as the underlying moves lower in price. Therefore, puts on the S&P 500 Index (SPX) will increase as the stock market falls, because the S&P is a barometer for the performance of the total stock market, representing more than 80 percent of the total value of equities traded. For that reason, portfolio managers often turn to S&P 500 puts when looking to hedge their stock portfolios.

Recall from Chapter 6 that SPX options are cash settled and are European-style. Therefore, the options can only be exercised at the expiration, and when exercised, the settlement involves the delivery of cash. However, an investor can typically open and close SPX options contracts prior to the expiration as well.

Let's consider an example pulled from the options chain of S&P 500 Index options. The quotes in Figure 7-6 are from the end of July 2015 and just before the U.S. stock market suffered a nasty spill throughout the month of August. The example is for illustrative purposes and not a recommendation. Market conditions can and often do change, and the example here was picked due to the volatility seen at that time. Simply because a trade worked in the past, there is no guarantee it will work in the future.

With the S&P 500 near 2100, a self-directed investor is concerned about the potential for an 8 percent to 10 percent market decline during the next few weeks and wants to purchase downside protection in case it is significantly more than that. His portfolio includes large-cap U.S. equities that closely mirror the S&P 500. Meanwhile, September 2000 puts on the index, expiring in

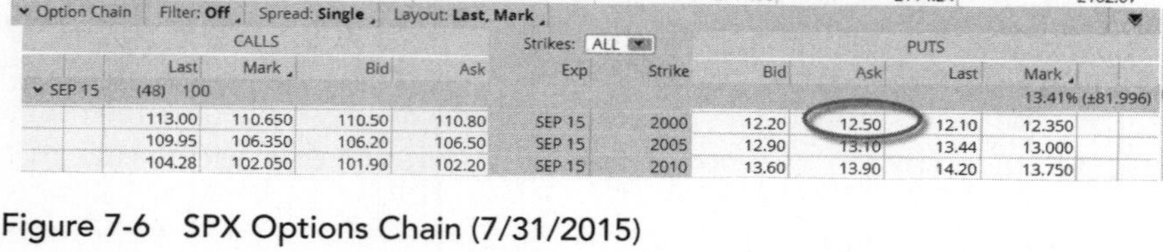

SPX | S&P 500 INDEX 2103.84 | 07/31/2015

Underlying

Last	Net Chng	Volume	Open	High	Low
2103.84	-4.79	0	2111.60	2114.24	2102.07

Option Chain Filter: Off Spread: Single Layout: Last, Mark

SEP 15 (48) 100 — 13.41% (±81.996)

CALLS Last	CALLS Mark	CALLS Bid	CALLS Ask	Exp	Strike	PUTS Bid	PUTS Ask	PUTS Last	PUTS Mark
113.00	110.650	110.50	110.80	SEP 15	2000	12.20	12.50	12.10	12.350
109.95	106.350	106.20	106.50	SEP 15	2005	12.90	13.10	13.44	13.000
104.28	102.050	101.90	102.20	SEP 15	2010	13.60	13.90	14.20	13.750

Figure 7-6 SPX Options Chain (7/31/2015)

forty-eight days, are currently trading for $12.50 per contract. The investor takes a position in ten contracts for a cash outlay of $12,500 plus transaction costs.

Strategy: Buy 10 SPX September 2000 puts for $12.50

Direction: Bearish

Debit or credit: $12,500 debit

Risk: $12,500

Breakeven: $1,987.50

Potential profit: $1,987.50

Ignoring the investor's other positions, the risk to buying the SPX September 2000 puts is equal to the premium paid, or, in this case, $12,500. The BE is equal to the strike price minus the debit, or $1,987.50. At that level, the 2000-strike puts are worth $12.50, and that, excluding transaction costs, covers the debit. The potential profits on a long put are limited to the underlying falling to zero, or the strike price minus the debit minus the value of the index.

The S&P 500 had fallen sharply through August and early September. It settled at 1970.10 at the September expiration. The investor holding 10 September 2000 puts could exercise the contract and collect a total of $29.90 per contract (2000-strike minus $1,970.10 settlement value), or $29,900 on ten contracts. That's $17,400 in profits, because the initial debit was $12,500.

The $17,400 in profits on the puts, in turn, would likely help offset some of the losses suffered in the investor's stock portfolio, as the overall market had declined 6.2 percent since that time. The puts could have been sold-to-close prior to the expiration as well, and the profit or loss on the options would depend on how much was collected on the sale. For example, selling at $25 would result in a profit of $12.50 per contract, or $12,500.

The example here included ten contracts, but more or less might be needed to hedge a different stock portfolio of a different size. In order to determine how many, one must consider the overall value of the portfolio and the notional value of the index at the time. The following formula can offer a rough estimate for the number of contracts to buy:

Portfolio % value to be hedged/Notional value of the index

If, for instance, the S&P 500 is trading at 2000, the notional value is $200,000 because of the one hundred multiplier. An investor with a $600,000 portfolio would buy at least three SPX 2000 strike put options to adequately hedge ($600,000/200,000 = 3 contracts).

The amount of protection offered by S&P 500 Index options will depend on other factors, including the strike price, the expiration month, and the nature of the portfolio that is being hedged. For instance, portfolios heavily concentrated in specific stocks or industries (such as energy, technology, or biotech) might not be fully hedged by S&P 500 Index options, which holds five hundred names across ten broad economic sectors. There might be other indexes that track the portfolio better than the S&P 500.

Still, SPX options are among the most actively traded index products, and many institutions rely on them for portfolio hedging strategies. In the next chapter, I dig deeper into the components of options prices, and you will see how increasing levels of volatility, which sometimes occur when the S&P 500 moves lower, can have a significant impact on the prices of put options as well. This increase in volatility can give SPX puts an added kick when the market falters but can also cause premiums to lose value when it rebounds.

Summary

Insurance is around us everywhere, but not every investor has considered insuring stock portfolios. Yet, for a premium, the purchase of a put option can help hedge against potential losses in stocks or entire portfolios for a short period of time. The amount of protection will vary based on number of contracts purchased, the selection of strike prices, the expiration term, and the nature of the underlying asset.

Like short selling, puts can also be used to speculate when an investor expects a downward move in the share price and wants bearish exposure to the underlying. The long put is a relatively simple strategy, and the risk involved is limited to the premium paid. Spread trading techniques using puts are explored in later chapters.

Risks are all around us. Puts can help us manage risks, including the loss of principal. However, options trading is not suitable for all investors, and certain complex strategies carry additional risks. In addition, transaction costs (commissions and other fees) are important factors and should be considered when evaluating any trade. Other important factors to consider are how time decay and changes in volatility affect options prices, which is the focus of the next chapter.

References

www.optionseducation.org/strategies_advanced_concepts/strategies/
    protective_put.html?prt=mx
www.cboe.com/strategies/indexoptions/buyindexputstohedge/part6
    .aspx

CHAPTER

8

Components of Options Prices

An insurance company looks at many things when setting rates for an auto policy. The insured's driving record, age, and vehicle are all factors that are considered. Some companies might give discounts to students with good grades. Others charge more for convertibles or sports cars. If you have several speeding tickets, you can expect to pay more in auto insurance as well.

Similarly, share prices of companies that move very fast typically have higher options premiums than slow-moving ones. This is similar to how volatility works. Why? Consider two stocks: XYZ and ZYX. While XYZ has been trading in a range between $30 and $40 per share during the past twelve months, ZYX has been in a range between $20 and $90. If both stocks are currently trading for $35, which one is more likely to move to $60 during the next twelve months?

All else being equal, a volatile stock will have higher options premiums because the options have a higher probability of being in the money (ITM) at expiration. That is, a 60-strike call on ZYX has a higher probability of being ITM at expiration, because the stock has been trading between $20 and $90 during the past year, and XYZ has been in a range between $30 and $40.

In addition to the speed or volatility of the underlying, other determinants of options prices include the price of the stock, the strike price of the option, the time left until expiration, dividends paid, and current interest rates. These components are covered in this chapter, and I will also talk about the important mathematical relationship between the prices of puts and calls known as put-call parity.

Table 8-1   Stocks Up, Calls Up, Puts Down

If Underlying Price	Call Prices	Put Prices
Increases	*Increase*	*Decrease*
Decreases	*Decrease*	*Increase*

Delta and Other Greeks

Most people understand that the value of a put or call option is driven by changes in the price of the underlying asset. If XYZ moves higher, we expect call options on XYZ to increase, and if XYZ falls, we expect to see the value of its put options to move higher. Indeed, while there are five other determinants of an option's price, the price of the underlying security is hands down the most important. Table 8-1 summarizes how calls and puts typically react to changes in the underlying security.

Sometimes, however, call options or put options don't increase or decrease as much as expected. As we will see as we go through this chapter, premiums might not move at all or even move opposite to what we expected because changes in other determinants, such as time and volatility, offset the changes in premiums that resulted from the move in the underlying. For now, our focus is on the changes in the price of the underlying and how it drives premiums in the options market.

Delta, one of the Greeks I mentioned in the introduction, can help us determine how much changes in the price of the underlying could affect an option's premium. Computed using an options pricing model, delta measures the expected price change in a contract for every point move in the underlying. Therefore, calls have positive deltas ranging from 0 to 1, and puts have negative deltas ranging from 0 to -1. In addition, short calls have negative deltas, and short puts have positive ones.

The Greeks

In the world of options, delta, gamma, vega, theta, and rho are known as the Greeks (even though vega is not actually a Greek letter). Each measure helps us better understand and anticipate how changes in variables such as time and volatility might affect our options positions. While I mention the Greeks briefly in this chapter, readers can find a more in-depth discussion in Appendix A.

A call option with a delta of 0.75, for instance, can be expected to increase in value by \$0.75 for every \$1 move higher in the underlying. Delta is constantly changing as prices move higher or lower, and the change in delta for every move in the underlying is measured by another Greek, called *gamma*. (See more on gamma in Appendix A.)

Call options with deltas of 1 and put options with deltas of –1 will move one for one with the changes in the underlying share price. However, options with deltas approaching 0 are going to see smaller changes for each \$1 move in the underlying. The amount of delta of each options contract is very dependent on where the strike price is relative to the underlying price.

Delta can also be used to estimate the probability of an option expiring ITM at expiration. For instance, an at-the-money (ATM) option, where the strike price equals the price of the underlying, typically has a delta of 0.50. That ATM option also has a 50 percent probability of expiring ITM, because there is an equal chance of it moving higher or moving lower.

Keep in mind that if a stock is trading at \$20, we do not know whether the next tick will be up or down. It is reasonable to assume that if it ticks up, the delta of \$20 call might tick up to 0.51 and the put delta to 0.49. On the other hand, if it ticks down, the put becomes 0.51 and call 0.49.

The relationship between delta and probabilities is explored in more detail in Chapter 9. The point here is that the price of an underlying asset is one of the components of an option's price, and delta helps us see how much the options price might change for each one-point move in the underlying.

Strike Price

As we saw in Chapter 5, the value of an option can be described by the relationship between its strike price and the underlying asset price. Whether it is a put or call, the contract is in-the-money, at-the-money, or out-of-the-money. To recap:

- **In-the-money (ITM):** A call option with a strike price below the current stock price or a put option with a strike price above the current stock price. An ITM option always has intrinsic value and can have extrinsic value (or time value) as well.

- **At-the-money (ATM):** A put or call where the strike price equals or is near the stock price. It has little or no intrinsic value, only extrinsic (or time) value.
- **Out-of-the-money (OTM):** A call option with a strike price above the stock price or a put with a strike below the stock price. There is no intrinsic value in OTM options, only extrinsic (or time) value.

Delta and value of the option are related. Deep ITM call options are more likely to have deltas approaching 1, and deep ITM puts will have deltas approaching −1. On the other hand, deep OTM calls and puts have very low deltas. ATM options typically have deltas of 0.50.

Figure 8-1 shows an options chain for Apple call options with strikes ranging from 100 to 115. The stock was near $109 per share at the time. Notice that the ATM options have a delta approaching 0.50. Lower strike ITM call options are on the top half of the chain and have deltas that decrease as the strike prices increase. The highest strike 115 calls have the lowest delta of 0.05. The same pattern holds

AAPL			APPLE INC COM	**108.74**	+1.92 +1.80%	B: 108.75 A: 108.77	ETB	NASDAQ

∨ Underlying

	Last X	Net Chng	Bid X	Ask X	Size
>	108.74 Q	+1.92	108.75 K	108.77 Q	17 x 1

∨ Option Chain Filter: **Off** Spread: **Single** Layout: **Delta, Gamma, Theta, Vega**

CALLS   Strikes: ALL ▼

	Delta	Ga...	Theta	Vega	Bid X	Ask X	Exp	Strike
∨ JAN2 16	**(10)**	**100 (Weeklys)**						
	.93	.02	−.03	.02	8.75 X	8.95 X	JAN2 16	100
	.93	.02	−.03	.03	7.75 A	8.00 A	JAN2 16	101
	.91	.03	−.03	.03	6.80 M	7.00 M	JAN2 16	102
	.89	.04	−.04	.03	5.85 T	6.05 M	JAN2 16	103
	.86	.05	−.04	.04	4.95 E	5.10 C	JAN2 16	104
	.82	.06	−.05	.05	4.05 X	4.20 M	JAN2 16	105
	.76	.08	−.05	.06	3.20 T	3.35 T	JAN2 16	106
	.68	.09	−.06	.07	2.47 W	2.59 W	JAN2 16	107
	.58	.11	−.06	.07	1.80 M	1.86 M	JAN2 16	108
	.47	.11	−.06	.08	1.24 W	1.29 A	JAN2 16	109
	.36	.11	−.06	.07	.80 W	.84 C	JAN2 16	110
	.25	.10	−.05	.06	.48 M	.52 W	JAN2 16	111
	.17	.08	−.04	.05	.28 W	.31 X	JAN2 16	112
	.11	.05	−.03	.03	.16 M	.18 W	JAN2 16	113
	.07	.04	−.02	.03	.09 M	.11 Q	JAN2 16	114
	.05	.03	−.02	.02	.07 Q	.08 C	JAN2 16	115

Figure 8-1   Options Chain with Delta, Gamma, Theta, and Vega

for puts, but flipped upside down, as (negative) deltas increase, moving up to higher strikes. In this case, if AAPL moves up $1, we should expect the 109 call should move up by $0.47 (0.47 delta), but if AAPL moves down $1, the option should move down by $0.47.

Theta and Time Decay

"Time Is on My Side" was a popular song in the 1960s, and it sometimes rings true in options trading, especially if you are short options. Recall that puts and calls are often called *wasting assets* due to the fact that, all else being equal, the contracts lose value over time. This time decay is beneficial for holders of short options positions but typically works against long-only options strategies.

Three Things

Options traders sometimes joke that there are only three certainties in life: death, taxes, and time decay. The amount of premium lost with each passing day can be estimated with the Greek theta. Whether looking at puts or calls, all options have negative thetas. Referring back to the options chain in Figure 8-1, Apple options had thetas ranging from −.06 to −.02, and the highest ones were in the ATM or nearly at-the-money (near-the-money) contracts. That's where the most time value is lost each day.

Time decay is also nonlinear, because short-term options lose value at a faster rate compared to longer-term ones. This means that the rate of premium loss picks up as the expiration approaches, especially in the final days and hours. Strategies, like calendar spreads, that seek to benefit from the nonlinear nature of time decay are discussed in Part III of this book.

Vega and Implied Volatility

Have you ever bought a call option and seen it lose value despite a move higher in the price of the underlying? Implied volatility is probably the reason. In fact, one of the most important determinants of an options price is volatility, and it can have a dramatic impact on premiums in the options market.

Each underlying instrument trades differently. Some asset classes, such as bonds or currencies, can typically see very small percentage moves from one day to the next. However, shares of individual companies can often see quite dramatic moves in short periods of time.

Options premiums will reflect expectations about the future volatility of the underlying instrument, and the estimate is captured in an options pricing component called implied volatility (IV). Each options contract will have a unique level of IV that can be constantly changing.

Finding Implied Volatility

Expressed as a percentage, IV can range from low values in the single digits for low volatility instruments to the triple digits for some securities that are seeing fast price moves. While options calculators can be used to compute IV, many trading platforms and options-related websites offer the information today. Appendix C, "Charts and Volatility Studies," offers a few resources for finding IV information.

CBOE Volatility Index (VIX) is the most widely watched implied volatility indicator. Computed and disseminated throughout the trading day by the Chicago Board Options Exchange, VIX offers a look at the IV currently priced into a strip of short-term S&P 500 Index ($SPX) options. When VIX moves higher, it indicates that the expected volatility of the S&P 500, and its options premiums, are becoming more expensive. Falling VIX is a sign that IV is easing, and short-term SPX options are getting cheaper (see Figure 8-2).

Just as VIX tracks the IV of S&P 500 Index options, each underlying asset has an average level of implied volatility that can be computed from one minute to the next. Importantly, the average volatility is not necessarily an indicator of the implied volatility in an individual contract, because each option has its own implied volatility that can be computed using an options pricing model.

In fact, two options on the same underlying security can have very different levels of implied volatility. When this happens, it is known as an *implied volatility skew,* and there are two types:

- **Time skew:** When two options in different expiration terms have different levels of IV.
- **Price skew:** When options with different strike prices have different IV levels.

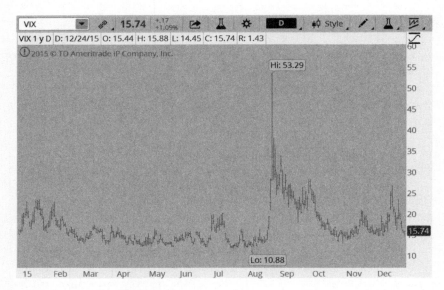

Figure 8-2   VIX as of 12/24/15

Later chapters will explore spread strategies that attempt to take advantage of skews, because when two options on the same underlying have different levels of implied volatility, it can prove to be an opportunity to buy the lower IV cheaper contract and sell the higher IV contract.

Many options trading platforms available today integrate implied volatility information for users. For example, I use the thinkorswim trading platform to see how implied volatility has changed over time. Specifically, the implied volatility percentile tool allows me to see how current levels compare to the past. It is found at the bottom of an options chain where it says Today's Options Statistics.

In Figure 8-3, we can see that the current implied volatility for the stock is 30.7 percent. That, in turn, compares to a one-year range of 15.1 percent and 34.4 percent, which places it in the eighty-first percentile of the range. Anything greater than 75 percent is considered high IV for the name and anything below 25 percent would be viewed as the lower end of the range.

There are sometimes important reasons why implied volatility might be higher in one expiration term or strike price relative to others, and those reasons are worth noting. In the equity options market, for example, one of the more common time skews arises before a company reports earnings.

▾ Today's Options Statistics	
52 week IV High:	0.344
52 week IV Low:	0.151
Current IV Percentile:	81%
52 week HV High:	0.332
52 week HV Low:	0.092
Current HV Percentile:	28%
Implied Volatility:	30.69%
VWAP:	116.593

Figure 8-3   Volatility Percentiles

Because earnings reports sometimes send shares moving sharply higher or lower, the short-term premiums typically see an increase in implied volatility ahead of the numbers. Short-term options see the biggest increase in IV, and the result is a time skew that typically doesn't last very long because IV will fall, or revert back to normal levels, after the earnings are out and the stock has reacted to the results.

Not Your Average Crush

When the implied volatility falls sharply in the wake of earnings or other one-time events, traders refer to the drop as *volatility crush.*

Vega is the Greek of the options world that offers estimates about the potential changes in options prices for each one-point move in the volatility of the underlying asset. The number, which is expressed in volatility, is always a positive number regardless of whether the option is a put or call. Vega is typically higher for ATM or near-the-money options and declining in the ITM and OTM strikes. Longer-dated options can often have substantially higher levels compared to short-term ones as well. Some of the strategies outlined in Part III will discuss options strategies that seek to take advantage of implied volatility skews.

Dividends

An important difference between a stock and a call option is that, while shareholders have the right to dividends, the owner of a call option contract does not. Therefore, when comparing the benefits of owning shares versus options prices, any dividends paid by the company are worth noting. In addition, options premiums will sometimes see a small but measurable change due to increasing and decreasing dividends.

Special Dividends

In addition to quarterly dividends, companies occasionally pay out one-time cash distributions to shareholders. Depending on the size of the dividend, the result is sometimes an adjustment to the options contract. The same is true of stock splits and spin-offs. When it happens, the options contracts will be adjusted to reflect the change in the underlying security.

In most cases, dividends cause call options to decrease in value and the puts to increase in value around the ex-dividend date as the dividend amount is commonly taken out of the stock price. But the puts don't suddenly leap in value if the company pays a dividend. While the stock price normally corrects on the ex-dividend date, the options can swing in the weeks or even months before the dividend payout. When the dividend is the same from one quarter to the next, those payouts are likely priced into the options already. This also explains why some longer-dated options on higher-dividend-paying stocks might have seemingly very rich put premiums compared to calls at similar strikes.

Rho and Interest Rates

The true impact of interest rates on options has been the subject of some academic debate, but it does seem to exist. Rho is the Greek that estimates the changes in an options price for each point increase in interest rates. The rho for a call is positive, and the contract price should increase as rates rise. That's because some investors use deep in-the-money calls as stock substitutes. So, when rates are higher, there is more theoretical demand for call options and, all else being equal, higher premiums. Puts have negative rho.

An options-pricing calculator is the best way to see how the changes in rates, and the other variables for that matter, can affect premiums of puts and calls. Rho is considered to have the least impact on options of the Greeks and is less critical to options traders than delta, vega, gamma, and theta. A more detailed discussion of the Greeks, along with an example of an options-pricing calculator, is provided in Appendix A.

Put-Call Parity

You were introduced to the concept of synthetics in Chapter 7 when the protective put strategy was discussed. It was noted then that the protective put is sometimes called a synthetic call due to the fact that the payoffs from being long calls and protective puts (long stock plus long puts) are similar. Synthetics are particularly important to market makers and professional traders who need to continually price and hedge options positions.

For example, the synthetic equivalent of being short a stock is to sell calls and buy puts at the same strike price with the same expiration date. Intuitively, this should make sense, because puts increase in value and calls lose value as the underlying stock falls, and vice versa. Buying puts and selling calls at the same strike at same expiration month is sometimes called a *combo*. Selling puts and buying calls is another combo.

Let's put some numbers to it. If you sell an ATM call, you become short fifty deltas; if you buy an ATM put, you are short fifty deltas. Together, the combo is short one hundred deltas and the equivalent of short one hundred shares of stock, because one hundred shares is the underlying in a standard stock option.

If an investor buys stock and a bearish combo, the net position is not likely to yield profits or losses, because the long stock position is the exact opposite of the synthetic short position. On the other hand, a bullish options combo can be created to replicate being long stock. A bullish combo and short stock is a neutral position as well.

Let's consider a hypothetical example to better understand some important relationships between puts and calls. XYZ stock is now trading for $49 per share; a 50-strike put trades at $2, and a 50-strike call trades at $1. The investor creates a synthetic long stock position by selling a put at $2 and buying a call for $1. The synthetic long stock is opened at a $1 credit ($2 for the put minus $1 for the call), and one combo controls one hundred shares.

If the stock remains below $50 and the investor is assigned on the put, one hundred shares are bought (put to them) for $50 per share, or $5,000. Because the call expires worthless, that's $1 per share more than the $49 per share at the time the options combo was initiated. However, the investor sold the put at $2 ($1 more than the call). Therefore, he collected $100 on the combo, and the net cost is $4,900 for the shares, or the same as the market price at the time the synthetic position was opened.

Anticipating Assignment

Keep in mind, if you are short an ITM American-style option, assignment can happen at any time prior to the expiration. Therefore, if an ITM put is sold, as in the example, it could potentially be assigned as early as the next day. If so, one hundred shares of stock are put at the strike price of the options contract.

On the other hand, if the stock moves higher, the shares can be called for $50. Again, the shares are purchased for $50 each, and minus the $1 credit for the options combo, the purchase price is $49 per share. Because the puts expire worthless, the price is the same as the market price when the synthetic was opened. The payoff from going long on the stock for $49 per share or selling the 50-strike combo at $1 were equivalent. The put-call parity relationship in this example can be expressed as follows:

$$XYZ = \$49 \text{ per share}$$

$$XYZ \text{ 50-strike put} = \$2$$

$$XYZ \text{ 50-strike call} = \$1$$

And:

$$\text{Call} - \text{Put} = \text{Stock price} - \text{Strike price}$$

Or:

$$\$1 - \$2 = \$49 - \$50$$

Understanding put-call parity and the concept of synthetics can help in a few ways. First, synthetics help us better see how options can be used to replicate or replace stock positions. Table 8-2 shows that long calls and short puts are synthetic equivalents to being long stock. The table summarizes other important relationships as well. Second, there are times when two strategies (like protective puts versus long calls) are synthetically equivalent, but one strategy might have an advantage of lower transaction costs. Third, synthetics can

Table 8-2   Synthetic Equivalents of
Long and Short Stock, Calls, and Puts

Strategy	=	Synthetic Equivalent
Long stock	=	Long call + Short put
Short stock	=	Short call + Long put
Long call	=	Long stock + Long put
Short call	=	Short stock + Short put
Long put	=	Short stock + Long call
Short put	=	Long stock + Short call

>	Last X	Net Chng	Bid X	Ask X	Size	Volume	Open	High	Low
	30.01 Q	-.37	27.82 Q	32.05 Q	0 x 7	1,052,051	30.00	30.49	29.85

> Trade Grid

✓ Option Chain   Filter: **Off** ,   Spread: **Single** ,   Layout: **Volume, Open Interest** ,

		CALLS			Strikes: 4 ▾			PUTS			
	Volume ,	Open.Int ,	Bid X	Ask X	Exp	Strike	Bid X	Ask X	Volume ,	Open.Int ,	
✓ JAN2 16 (7) 100 **(Weeklys)**										47.59% (±1.674)	
	0	0	1.04 Z	1.26 X	JAN2 16	29.5	.54 Q	.62 Q	4	14	
	27	68	.76 M	.84 N	JAN2 16	30	.76 Q	.84 M	34	46	
	19	29	.52 X	.59 N	JAN2 16	30.5	1.01 N	1.18 C	10	5	
	268	65	.35 Z	.42 N	JAN2 16	31	1.29 Z	1.59 X	0	0	

Figure 8-4   Near-the-Money Options on a $30 Stock

be a great topic of conversation at family dinner. (Okay, not really, but it's nice to have three reasons for everything.)

Bid-ask spreads and transaction costs will impact the put-call parity relationship and sometimes make it seem as if options are mispriced. For example, Figure 8-4 shows an options chain for a handful of short-term, near-the-money options for a stock trading for $30 per share. Notice that the bid-asks for the puts and calls are equivalent because the market in both is $0.76 to $0.84.

Using put-call parity, the synthetic equivalent of buying one hundred shares of the stock for $30 is to sell puts and buy calls. Using the info in Figure 8-4, we buy one January 30 call at the offer of $0.84 and sell one January 30 put at the bid of $0.76. At market prices, the investor is paying $0.84 for the call and collecting $0.76 for put. The combo appears to be $0.08 more expensive than the underlying (or $30 + $0.84 − $0.76).

If a synthetic long or stock position seems mispriced, it might create an arbitrage opportunity. For example, if the combo is expensive, an investor can buy the stock and sell the synthetic (short calls and long puts). This is a strategy known as a *conversion*. On the other hand, when the synthetic portion is cheaper, an investor can sell the underlying and buy the synthetic equivalent, which is known as a *reversal conversion.* Due to costs and complexity, these are professional strategies, but it is good to be familiar with them.

In this example, however, the difference in the price paid for the call and the price received for the put is really due to the bid-ask spread. Using the same formula but using midmarket prices shows that put-call parity holds. That is, because midmarket (midway between the bid and ask) is $0.80 in both the puts and calls, while the stock is at $30, the synthetic long call and short put is equivalent to taking a position in shares (or short puts, long calls is same as selling the stock short). The put-call parity relationship holds using midmarket prices but not if we sell on the bid and buy on the offer.

In rare events where the synthetic is cheap or expensive relative to the underlying, an arbitrage opportunity might exist. Indeed, there are some options trading firms that specialize in conversions and reversal conversions. These firms typically have advanced tools for identifying opportunities and, most importantly, sufficient pools of capital to buy and sell large blocks of stocks and options.

In addition, there might be other reasons why the puts are expensive relative to calls or vice versa. Maybe the name is due to pay a dividend, or perhaps it is hard to borrow for the purpose of short selling. When rare arbitrage opportunities do arise, the costs of executing the trades in commissions and other fees (like assignment or exercise) need to be factored in as well, as they can be substantial.

In conclusion, there is an important relationship between puts and calls on the same underlying, which is known as put-call parity. It guides us in understanding synthetics and at times can help us determine if certain options strategies might offer an advantage over long or short stock positions. It also helps us to understand how two strategies—like short puts and covered calls—can have similar payoff charts.

Summary

Understanding put-call parity is essential to understanding synthetics and how some options strategies can replicate stock positions. It also helps to explain why two options strategies—like covered calls and short puts—have similar payoff charts.

Meanwhile, there are several components that help determine the prices of both puts and calls. The relationship between the strike price and the underlying asset price is one of them. The changes in the price of the underlying and its volatility are two others. Options are also wasting assets and lose value over time. Finally, dividends and interest rates can affect the price of an options contract as well.

Armed with this knowledge, the reader is now better prepared to understand some of the more advanced strategies like cash-secured puts and calendar spreads that are discussed in later chapters. Before resuming the discussion of strategies, one more thing needs to be addressed. The last chapter in Part II dives into the topic of probabilities to better help you find trading opportunities in the options market that have the best chances of success.

References

www.cboe.com/tradtool/option-calculators.aspx
www.optionseducation.org/getting_started/options_overview/options_
    pricing.html

CHAPTER 9

Probabilities

Option strategies can vary from simple trades that involve just one contract to complex positions with multiple expiration and strike prices. The simple strategies of long calls and long puts were already covered in Chapters 5 through 7. Chapters 10 through 16 will cover more advanced strategies such as vertical spreads, condors, and butterflies.

You will hear a recurring theme throughout the strategy discussions. Namely, all of the strategies in Part III of this book have potential risks and rewards that can be clearly defined beforehand. In addition, every options strategy has a probability of success as well. In fact, the point that I try to drive home when I teach is that options are nothing more than giant probabilities. I determine what the probabilities are, and that helps me determine the optimal prices for buying and selling positions as well as, and perhaps more importantly, the risk I am willing to take.

But what exactly do I mean by *probabilities*? I discuss three distinctly different ones: the probability of expiring in the money (ITM), the probability of profit, and the probability of touching. The probability of expiring ITM is the more widely used measure, as it is the basis for most options pricing models, but you will see that the other two offer unique insights as well. Lastly, this chapter explains how to use delta as a thumbnail for computing probabilities of expiring ITM.

Probabilities are relatively straightforward when dealing with simple strategies like long calls, but the same principles can also be applied to more advanced options plays. You will note that some positions, such as ITM long calls, can have significantly higher probabilities, and others, such as far out-of-the-money (OTM) long puts, have lower ones.

My approach is focused on selling options that are OTM while buying ITM options. My motto is "buy value, sell junk." We will see how probabilities can help support this approach. I also define various probabilities and show how they are used to evaluate strategies. I will answer questions such as: What is the probability of the contract or position expiring ITM? How can delta be used as a thumbnail to calculate this probability? What is the difference between the probability of profit and the probability of touching? So let's get started.

Probabilities 101

Probably, there is a good chance, and *it is likely* are all phrases we hear frequently in everyday conversation when people talk about certain outcomes. There is a good chance it is going to rain this weekend; it is likely that my flight will be delayed tomorrow; or I should probably empty the dishwasher before my spouse gets home.

In a coin toss, the probability of a coin landing on heads is 50 percent, and the probability that same coin will land on tails is 50 percent. Now, just because heads wins over tails twenty consecutive times, the odds don't change. The odds are still 50 percent that it will land on heads, and 50 percent that it will land on tails on the next toss. Over time, the probabilities play out.

Similarly, the probability of an at-the-money (ATM) option being ITM or OTM is equally 50 percent. The current stock price is equal to strike price, and the next move might be higher or lower. This is especially true in the final minutes before the option expires, because the very next move could determine if the contract is ITM or OTM.

Pinning

While there is roughly a fifty-fifty chance that an ATM expires ITM or OTM, it might also expire ATM. In rare instances, the stock is exactly equal to the strike price heading into the final moments of expiration. Traders call this *pinning*. The stock is being pinned to the strike, and the outcome can have important implications for both long and short options holders at that strike price, because there is increased uncertainty about whether exercise/assignment will come into play.

Like with a coin toss, probability analysis assumes that going forward, there is a 50 percent chance a stock moves higher and a 50 percent chance it moves lower. The math is based on basic statistics and concepts like normal distributions, means, and standard deviations that are outside the scope of this particular book. My focus is on option strategies with defined risks and higher probabilities of success.

The probability of an option expiring ITM is also related to its volatility. By ITM, I mean that the option has more than $0.01 of intrinsic value at the expiration. For example, if a stock has been trading in a $35 to $40 range during the past six months, the probability of the stock reaching $45.01 at next month's expiration might be rather low. The 45-strike calls have a low probability of expiring ITM. By way of comparison, a stock that has been trading in a $30 to $50 range in the past six months will have a greater probability of moving to $45.01 in the next month, and therefore, the 45-strike calls will likely have a higher probability of expiring ITM.

If options on higher volatility instruments that are OTM have higher probabilities of expiring ITM (compared to OTM options on lower volatility instruments), it stands to reason that lower volatility securities have lower probabilities. Obviously, these factors also relate to the risk of the underlying security (high volatility versus low volatility) and price (expensive premiums versus low premiums).

Time has an important relationship with the probability of expiring ITM as well. There is a wider dispersion of possible prices for an underlying and a wider spectrum of possible prices over longer stretches of time. For instance, all else being equal, there is a higher probability that an OTM option will expire ITM in six months rather than six days. As you go further out in time, there are more unknowns. In conclusion, there are higher probabilities further out in time, and that, in turn, has important implications for probabilities, options prices, and strategy selection.

Probability of Profit

The probability of profit is the chance that an options position makes at least $0.01 of profit at expiration (transaction costs excluded). For instance, if I buy a 100-strike call on XYZ for $10, what is the chance that XYZ is trading at $110.01 at the expiration? Or, what is the probability that the stock will be $0.01 or more above the breakeven at the expiration? On the other hand, on a short XYZ 100-call sold at $10 per contract, the probability of profit is set at $109.99 per share, or $0.01 below the $110 breakeven.

POP, Not POT

The probability of profit and the probability of touching are discussed here, but the probability of expiring ITM is more widely used throughout the industry. My methodology uses all three, however, and my colleagues and I sometimes refer to the probability of profit as the POP. To avoid confusion, I don't use the acronym POT for the probability of touching.

Probability of Touching

The probability of touching is closely related to the probability of expiring ITM. It reflects the chances that the underlying will move to a certain price at any time prior to the expiration, regardless of how it ends up at the expiration. The probability of touching is computed using a different, but related, model and typically has a value higher than the probability of expiring ITM.

Some traders prefer the probability of touching, particularly for American-style options. European-style options can only be exercised at expiration; therefore, the probability of expiring ITM is the more relevant probability measure. However, American-style options can be exercised any time prior to expiration, so it also makes sense to look at the probabilities of the underlying security reaching certain levels during the entire life of the options contract. The probability of touching can be used for that purpose.

The probability of touching can be used to identify potential extreme prices for the underlying security and to determine if it may be too volatile for an investor's personal risk tolerance. Are you comfortable with the stock if it moves through a certain level? Is the spectrum of possible prices within a range that you can stomach?

The probability of touching is a useful tool, even if you are not yet trading options, because it can help determine possible entry and exit points for stock positions as well. For example, the probability of touching a certain price can be used to identify prices where an investor might want to sell or liquidate stock position. Or, it can be used as a method to exit a position if the stock moves beyond a certain range. In Chapter 17, I will take a closer look at how options can be used instead of stop and limit orders in some situations.

Example

The best way to understand how to use probabilities is with another example. We want to keep our focus on liquid products with sufficient trading activity and where the spreads (difference between bids and offers) are not too wide. This can give us a greater sense of confidence when using probability calculations. Transaction costs are important to consider as well but are not factored into the examples.

Liquid Assets

Liquidity will vary by underlying and can change from one period to the next. Tools for measuring liquidity, such as volume and open interest, were discussed in Chapter 4, "Avoiding Mistakes," and again in Chapter 5, "Options Basics."

Next, we want to find ideas that have probabilities of success of 50 percent or greater. For example, if I am looking at a long call on a stock, my preference is ITM options where the probability of expiring ITM is higher than 50 percent. When I buy options, I tend to focus on shorter-term options, as I am often playing for a quick move and do not want theta (time decay) to affect my premiums as much. However, when I sell options, I typically use options that expire between twenty-one and seventy days, because I find that between roughly three and ten weeks until expiration is optimal for most of the selling strategies I use.

Looking at Figure 9-1, March 115 calls on McDonald's are trading for $9.60 bid and $10.30 ask. With shares of the stock at $124.20, let's say that an investor places an order roughly midmarket and buys one contract for $10, or a $1,000 cash outlay when the multiplier is factored in. At that price, the breakeven of the long call is at $125, which is less than 1 percent above current levels.

The probability of profit is computed based on a move to $125.01 (or better), because at that point, the position is $0.01 above the breakeven and is profitable. (Note that the calls would be subject

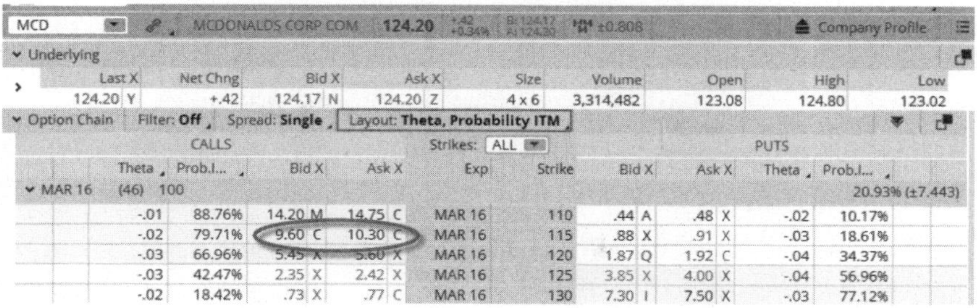

Figure 9-1   McDonald's Options Chain

to auto-exercise if left open through the expiration, and that would have implications for the profit or loss of the position. But for the purposes of POP, the trade is considered to be profitable if the underlying is $0.01 above the breakeven.)

Standard Deviations

I made an effort throughout this book to keep the math simple and avoid digging too deep into statistics. Plenty has already been written in other texts about how options are priced, normal distributions, and bell curves. One statistic worth a few words, however, is the standard deviation (SD), because it is important in assessing probabilities. In this context, SD simply refers to the range of stock prices around the average price or mean. The theory says that a stock will close within one standard deviation roughly 68.2 percent of the time, within two SDs 95.4 percent of the time, and within three SDs 99.7 percent of the time. These numbers are important to keep in mind when looking at probabilities.

Figure 9-2 shows the probability analysis for McDonald's with the stock trading for $124.20 per share. The chart setting is the default at a one standard deviation range (or 68.27 percent), and the level of volatility is 20.6 percent. In this example, the curve is based on probabilities and includes stock price targets of $115.04, $125.01, and $136.91. The stock price is plotted on the vertical *y*-axis and the days until expiration on the horizontal *x*-axis.

The curve on the probability analysis chart represents the probability of the stock trading within a certain range. Notice that the curve

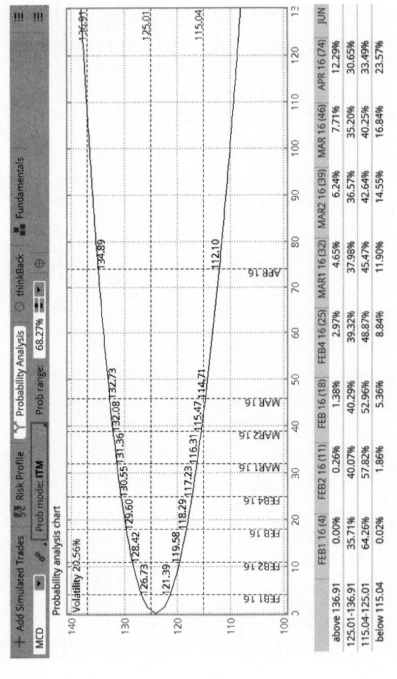

Figure 9-2   Probability of Expiring ITM

116

starts at the left (y-axis) along the stock price line at the current share price of $124.20 and becomes wider as time passes.

For example, at the first February expiration, the stock prices of $121.39 and $126.73 represent the one standard deviation range of stock prices for that time period. Therefore, there is a 31.7 percent probability (or one minus the 0.683 standard deviation) of falling outside that range. Anything inside or in the middle of the curve is within the probability range. Anything outside is outside of one standard deviation. For example, the current price of $124.20 is within the range, but $100 and $140 per share are clearly not.

Looking to the March expiration in forty-six days (Figure 9-2), the expected range for the stock is between $114.71 and $132.73 based on one standard deviation around the current share price. Additional details are provided in the table below the chart. For instance, the probability of expiring between $125.01 and $136.91 is 35.2 percent, and the probability of trading above $136.91 is 7.7 percent. Therefore, the POP is 42.9 percent. If you add up the probabilities within an expiration term, the numbers equal 100 percent, because, together, the numbers capture all of the possible outcomes.

The probabilities of expiring ITM for the short-dated options are higher than for the longer-dated ones. In Figure 9-2, the probabilities of expiring above $136.91 steadily decrease as the curve widens out, because as more time passes, the range of possible outcomes or stock prices become more scattered. Notice that at the first expiration, there was only a 0.02 percent probability of the stock falling to $115.04 or below, but by the March expiration, it is almost 17 percent.

Figure 9-3 shows the probability of touching using the same 68.3 percent, or one standard deviation probability range, and the same $115.04, $125.01, and $136.91 price targets. The y-axis, x-axis, and shape of the curve are all the same as Figure 9-2. However, the models to compute the probability of expiring ITM and the probability of touching are different. As a result, the range of stock prices and the probabilities are very different as well.

Intuitively, the higher stock values and probabilities in Figure 9-3 (compared to Figure 9-2) should make sense because there is a higher probability of a stock touching a certain level rather than closing above or below a certain strike price at expiration.

Using the same March expiration, the one standard deviation range for the stock is $111.53 and $137 for the probability of touching analysis, and that is greater than the $114.71 to $132.73 range for the probability of expiring ITM analysis. Meanwhile, the probability

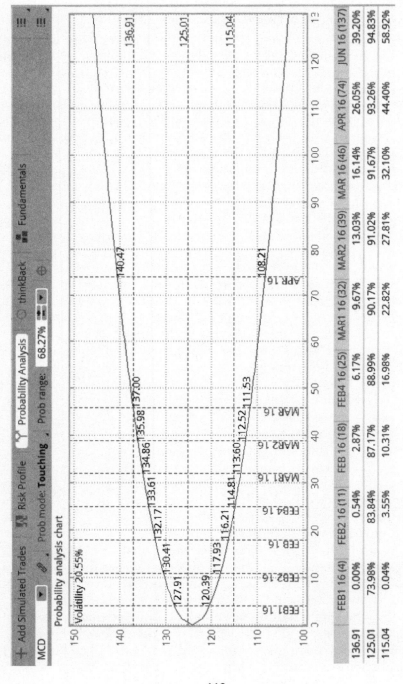

118

Figure 9-3   Probability of Touching

of touching $125.01 per share or better is 90 percent and more than double the POP in Figure 9-2.

As a last note, the probabilities of touching don't add up to 100 percent. That's because while the stock will close at just one price at the expiration, it can touch many different prices along the way. When looking at long stock trades, I prefer ideas with the probabilities of expiring ITM or probabilities of profit greater than 50 percent and probabilities of touching of more than 80 percent.

Additional examples and probability charts will be provided with strategy examples throughout the remainder of this book. While the probability of expiring ITM is widely used in the industry, we also look at the probability of profit and the probability of touching. The goal in all of this is to find potential trading opportunities with clearly defined risks and appealing probabilities of success. Sophisticated trading platforms available in the brokerage marketplace can help make all of this much simpler to do.

Delta to Measure Probabilities

Delta is one of the Greeks that help us make sense of how and why options premiums change in value from one day to the next. (A complete discussion of all the Greeks is provided in Appendix A.) Delta is perhaps the most widely watched, because it measures how much the value of an options contract may change for each one-point move in the underlying.

ATM single stock call options typically have deltas of 0.5, especially as the contract is approaching expiration. If so, the contract is expected to increase in value by $0.50 if the underlying stock moves higher by a point and decrease in value by $0.50 if the stock moves lower by a point. On the other hand, an ATM put will have a delta of roughly -0.50 and will increase in value by $0.50 if the underlying security moves lower by a point and decrease in value for each one-point move higher in the underlying.

Delta Talk

When traders refer to the delta of an option, they often drop the decimal point. A 0.45 delta call is simply 45 delta calls and the -0.65 put is 65 delta puts.

It was noted earlier that when an ATM option is near the expiration, the probability it will expire ITM or OTM is roughly equal. There is a 50 percent probability that it will expire ITM and a 50 percent probability that it will expire OTM. Note that the 50 percent probability is the same as the 0.50 delta.

As a rule of thumb, an option's delta is also a ballpark estimate of this probability of expiring ITM. A call option with a delta of 0.30 has roughly a 30 percent chance of expiring ITM, and a put option with a delta of 0.70 has roughly a 70 percent probability.

In fact, the deltas of a put and a call with the same strike in the same expiration term will approximately equal 1.00 when added together, because one of them will expire ITM (unless both expire exactly ATM). In other words, the sum of the probabilities of expiring ITM of a put and call at the same strike price is 100 percent.

Figure 9-4 offers an example using options on Pfizer (PFE) with the stock trading for $31 per share and five days left until the expiration. First notice that the deltas of the ATM 31-strike puts and calls are −0.50 and 0.50, respectively. Meanwhile, the 30.5-strike calls have deltas of 0.67, and the 30.5 strike puts have deltas of −0.32. It suggests that the 30.5-strike calls have a 67 percent chance of expiring ITM, and the probability of expiring ITM for the 30.5-strike puts is 32 percent. The two deltas sum up to 0.99 and not exactly 1.00, because delta is not a perfect measure of probabilities, especially in further OTM options.

Naturally, options that are far OTM have lower deltas and have a lower probability of expiring ITM. Meanwhile, deep ITM puts and calls have higher deltas, because there is a greater chance of the contracts remaining ITM through the expiration. As we can see from Figure 9-4, the deltas of the calls increase as the strikes decrease, and the put deltas are higher at the higher strikes.

Delta is a useful tool for gauging probabilities, but it is only an indication or an estimate. It assumes, like with a coin flip, that

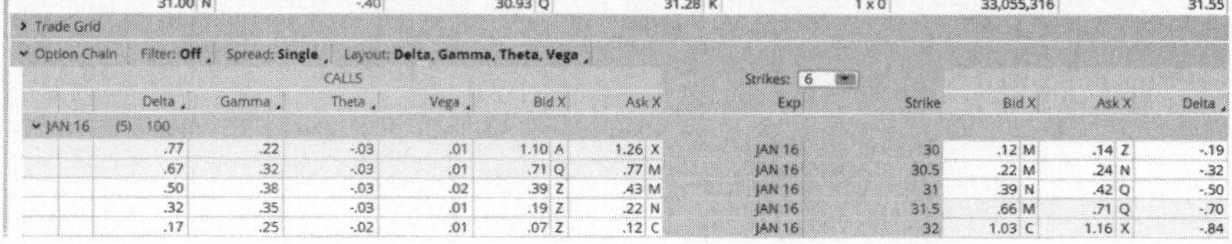

PFE PFIZER INC COM 31.00

Underlying

Last X	Net Chng	Bid X	Ask X	Size	Volume	Open
31.00 N	-.40	30.93 Q	31.28 K	1 x 0	33,055,316	31.55

Trade Grid

Option Chain Filter: **Off** Spread: **Single** Layout: **Delta, Gamma, Theta, Vega**

Strikes: 6

JAN 16 (5) 100

CALLS Delta	Gamma	Theta	Vega	Bid X	Ask X	Exp	Strike	Bid X	Ask X	Delta
.77	.22	-.03	.01	1.10 A	1.26 X	JAN 16	30	.12 M	.14 Z	-.19
.67	.32	-.03	.01	.71 Q	.77 M	JAN 16	30.5	.22 M	.24 N	-.32
.50	.38	-.03	.02	.39 Z	.43 M	JAN 16	31	.39 N	.42 Q	-.50
.32	.35	-.03	.01	.19 Z	.22 N	JAN 16	31.5	.66 M	.71 Q	-.70
.17	.25	-.02	.01	.07 Z	.12 C	JAN 16	32	1.03 C	1.16 X	-.84

Figure 9-4 Pfizer Options Chain with Delta

market movements are random and options are priced rationally —conditions that are not always met in practice. Notice, for example, that combined deltas of the 30-strike puts and calls in Figure 9-4 add up to only 96. Again, this is due to the fact that delta is not as accurate for gauging probabilities for further OTM options.

In addition, it would be a mistake to assume that a put option with a delta of −1.0 has a 100 percent chance of expiring ITM. It has a very high likelihood because it is already deep ITM, but it is not certain to expire ITM. Crazy things can happen, and the underlying could suddenly mover higher instead.

Nevertheless, although not always a precise measure, delta does offer a thumbnail for probabilities in an objective way, and that, in turn, helps to better define risks before placing an options trade. The probability of expiring ITM is a more accurate measure compared to delta. POP and the probability of touching should be considered when looking at potential moves in the underlying as well.

Summary

Probabilities are around us everywhere. There is a chance that it might rain tomorrow, and there is a probability that an airline flight will be on time. In options trading, probabilities can be measured and help you identify optimal trading opportunities. Delta is a quick thumbnail for the probability of expiring ITM.

This chapter also explored the probability of profit and the probability of touching. While delta is available on many options chains and using options-pricing calculators, POP and the probability of touching are best viewed using charting software.

Finally, in order to better understand a strategy's potential using probabilities, you should focus on actively traded and liquid products. Purchases tend to favor ITM contracts, and selling options tend to favor OTM contracts. Time frames are typically twenty-one to seventy days. The probabilities of expiring should be greater than 50 percent and the probability of touching more than 80 percent. A series of examples is provided in Part III of this book, beginning in the next chapter with covered calls.

References

tlc.thinkorswim.com/center/video/videos/Probability-Analysis
www.tastytrade.com/tt/shows/the-skinny-on-options-math/episodes

PART

III

Strategies and Positions

CHAPTER 10

Covered Calls

The basics of investing were covered in Part I, and the reader should now understand where stocks trade, what indicators to watch, and how to place orders. Options basics, including simple strategies of long puts and long calls, were covered in Part II. Part III focuses on a number of other options positions and strategies that I use and that I have taught to investors over the years.

One of the more basic ones—the covered call—is explained in this chapter. Like the protective put, covered in Chapter 7, it is viewed as an entry-level strategy that is a natural extension of stock investing that many investors are already familiar with. There are important differences between long stock and covered calls, however, such as the possibility of being assigned on the call options, the potential profits, and how the breakeven is calculated.

Although it is likely review for many options traders, the covered call is a good starting point for our discussion of various option strategies. Just as an experienced ski instructor doesn't send a student on a black diamond run on day one, an investor with no options trading experience should consider starting with the simplest of strategies first and then moving on to more complex ideas like butterflies, calendar spreads, and others discussed in the last few chapters of this book.

The Covered Call

An investor can learn a lot about options by understanding the covered call, because many important concepts, such as implied volatility (IV), assignment, and dividends, can affect a position during the life of the options. The strategy also builds on buy-and-hold investing in equities, which is already widely understood by most investors. (If not, Chapter 3, "Know the Underlying," offers a primer.) As we will also see, however, the covered call has different risk and reward potential compared to buying stock alone.

> ### Buy-Write
>
> The covered call is also called a buy-write because the investor is buying shares and writing call options against those shares.

The covered call gets its name from the fact that the investor is short calls, which are "covered" by a corresponding long position in the underlying stock. Recall from Chapter 6 that a short call strategy is typically initiated when the investor expects the price of the underlying security to hold below the strike price of the call and is an unlimited risk play because potential losses accumulate as the underlying moves higher, and there's no limit to how high the price of a stock can climb. The short call is considered naked (or uncovered) if the investor has no long position in the underlying (or if the short call is not part of a spread).

The covered call, on the other hand, is short the options but long the underlying security. An example from the equities market is to sell one call option for every one hundred shares of the underlying already held in a portfolio. Or, an investor might buy shares and sell calls at the same time (a buy-write). Indeed, many brokerage platforms today allow the covered call to be initiated as one trade at one price.

In a typical covered call, the investor is neutral or optimistic on the prospects for the underlying security but is not aggressively bullish. After all, writing the call is stating that he is willing to sell the underlying security (or have it "called away") through the life of the options and at the strike price of the contract.

The investor should feel comfortable selling the stock at the strike price of the option through the expiration date. Because the short call obligates the investor to sell the underlying, assignment results in the sale at the strike price. In the equities market, as we get closer to expiration, shares are more likely to be sold if the price of the underlying climbs up beyond the strike price of the option. So before writing the calls, similar to putting in a stock sell order, it's important to ask, "Am I willing to sell the stock at the strike price?" If the answer is not yes, then the covered call is probably not the best strategy for you.

Income is received from the sale of the short calls, and the investor collects any dividends along the way as well. Therefore, the covered call is sometimes used as an income-generating strategy when shares are expected to hold in a range. In addition, selling calls reduces the cost of the stock purchase. In stock market parlance, the call writing reduces the cost of purchasing shares. The net cost is equal to purchase price of the shares minus the premium received for the call options.

Just like with owning stock alone, the breakeven of a covered call is the net cost of the shares. The math is simply the stock price minus the credit received for writing calls. The risk to the strategy is a move below the breakeven (ignoring any dividends paid and transaction costs). If the price of the stock moves above the strike price of the call options, the options are in the money (ITM) and likely to be exercised/assigned. The result is assignment to the holder of the short calls, and the stock is sold at the strike price.

Because equity options are American-style, assignment can happen at any time prior to the expiration. If it is ITM at expiration, the contract will likely be auto-exercised, and assignment is almost guaranteed. At that point, the profit is equal to the strike price of the calls minus the cost of the stock. The shareholder collects any dividends paid as well.

Covered Call Cheat Sheet

Strategy: Buy stock, sell calls

Direction: Bullish or neutral

Debit or Credit: Stock bought, calls sold at credit

Risk: Stock price – Credit

Breakeven: Stock price – Credit

Potential Profits: Strike price – Stock price + Premium received

Figure 10-1 shows a simple risk graph for the covered call. The position generates profits if shares hold above the breakeven and move higher. The gains are limited by the short calls. Losses increase

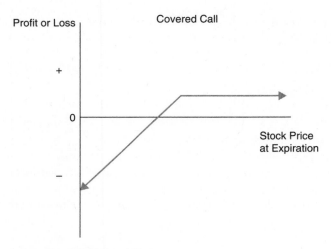

Figure 10-1   Covered Call Risk Graph

as shares move below the breakeven, and like owning shares, the risks are related to the performance of the underlying. If shares fall, significant losses are possible, but the risks are never greater than the stock price minus the credit. In addition, the risks of the covered call are less than owning stock alone, because the investor has collected premium for writing the calls, and that, in turn, helps offset a portion of the purchase price.

The strike price selection of the covered call is important and will depend on the investor's objective. If the goal is to generate income, the ideal situation is for shares to hold just below the strike through the expiration and the options to expire worthless. Then the investor can sell the shares, write additional calls, or simply hold the stock position.

A covered call can also be used as a tool to exit a stock position. For instance, an investor might have accumulated gains in shares and wants to sell (or *liquidate*) his holdings. Rather than selling the shares outright, calls are sold to collect a premium, and the investor is looking for the stock to move above the strike price by expiration. If assigned on the calls, the investor delivers the shares and exits the position. In this way, writing calls against a stock position can also be used instead of a limit order, but the investor is actually getting paid (collecting a premium) when he is ready to get out of the stock at a specific price. Of course, assignment is not guaranteed, because the stock price may never reach or go beyond the strike price while you are holding the short call.

> ## Opportunity Risk
>
> While the risk of a covered call position is similar to owning shares, there is another risk to consider. Namely, if the stock moves substantially higher and the calls are assigned at the strike, the investor will miss out on gains above the strike price if the stock continues to move higher. The *opportunity risk* is certainly an important trade-off to consider when investors collect premiums for writing calls against their stock positions. In general this is a minor risk as most people's biggest problem is not that the stocks they purchase are going up too fast.

After opening the covered call, the ideal situation is for the stock to move toward the strike price of the short call through the expiration but not shoot higher too fast. The goal is to let time decay take a toll on the options. Any decrease in implied volatility before the expiration can help the (short call) position as well.

Writing out-of-the-money (OTM) calls also leaves room to participate on the upside. On the other hand, selling ITM calls certainly limits the upside and will also increase the possibility of early exercise due to dividends paid. That is, if a dividend is expected, a holder of an ITM call is likely to exercise the contract to take delivery of the shares and collect the dividend. Therefore, the possibility of being assigned and taken out of the covered call increases if the options are ITM and an ex-dividend is approaching. There is less early-assignment risk due to exercise when writing OTM calls.

A covered call can typically be closed at any time prior to the expiration. To exit, the investor sells shares and buys-to-close the calls. Or, the investor can close the calls and simply hold the shares. Selling the shares alone, while leaving the short calls open, changes the position to an unlimited risk position known as the naked call. This is not something I would do because it defies the logic of the trade. Finally, if assigned on the short calls, it is too late to close the position. The investor will sell the shares per the terms of the contract. I do not look at assignment as a negative, especially when I am writing OTM calls. I participated for some upside and I can always get back in if I want.

My preference is to continually sell calls against shares. Think of the position as one package of long stock and short calls. When the calls expire, write additional calls against the stock.

Example

Let's say MGM Resorts shares are trading near $20 in mid-January and an investor wants to begin an income strategy using covered calls on the casino company. Keep in mind that the examples, real or hypothetical, are for illustration purposes only. This is not a statement about the company or its outlook, and simply because a strategy worked in the past, that doesn't mean it will work in the future. Market conditions do change. The stock here was selected due to the fact that the stock prices and options prices include some round numbers like $20 per share and $1 per contract. That helps to keep the math simple for the purposes of this example.

Our investor wants to take a position in MGM shares and also write calls. His expectation is that shares might see a modest move higher in the weeks ahead, and while the stock has not been paying a dividend, selling calls against stock can generate a bit of income during this time. Figure 10-2 shows an options chain for various March options on MGM that expire in sixty-five days.

With MGM at $20, the 21-strike calls are $1, or 5 percent OTM. The market was $1.01 to $1.05 at the time. It's reasonable to assume, given the prices, the investor can sell the March 21 calls for $1 against shares at $20. If so, the premium totals 5 percent of the share price ($1/$20). The delta (not shown) is 0.35, and there is an estimated 65 percent probability that the options will expire OTM. (Note: For a refresher on delta and the other Greeks, please turn to Appendix A.)

MGM			MGM RESORTS INTERNATIONAL COM	20.02		B 19.94 A 20.04	ETB	±0.474		Company P
∨ Underlying										
›	Last X	Net Chng	Bid X	Ask X	Size	Volume		Open	High	
	20.02 N	-1.11	19.94 P	20.04 Q	3 x 1	7,811,217		21.35	21.5015	
∨ Option Chain	Filter: **Off**	Spread: **Single**	Layout: **Volume, Open Interest**							
		CALLS			Strikes: ALL				PUTS	
∨ MAR 16	Volume	Open.Int	Bid X	Ask X	Exp	Strike	Bid X	Ask X	Volume	Open.Int
	(65) 100									48.35
	0	3,631	2.02 T	2.08 N	MAR 16	19	1.00 C	1.04 T	2	622
	66	17,657	1.46 X	1.51 X	MAR 16	20	1.43 X	1.53 X	31	3,498
	29	11,074	1.01 C	1.05 X	MAR 16	21	1.95 M	2.02 X	30	1,848
	52	6,449	.68 Z	.70 X	MAR 16	22	2.61 C	2.72 X	0	2,680

Figure 10-2   MGM Options Chain (1/13/2016)

The net cost of the MGM March 21 covered call position is $19 per share, or $20 minus the $1 credit. The investor is not collecting any dividends as MGM does not pay them, but on a dividend-paying name, any dividends collected while the position is open reduces the cost of the covered call as well. In this example, the net cost is $19 (excluding any transaction costs, of course).

Figure 10-3 shows the risk graph of the MGM March 21 covered call for $19. The risk is from a move lower in the shares and is only limited due to the fact that a stock can't fall below zero. So the risk is $19, or $1,900 on one hundred shares (one covered call). While a move below $19 results in losses, the potential profits are to the upside, but the calls will also increase in value as the underlying movers higher. The gains are, therefore, limited.

Moreover, no matter how high the stock climbs, the investor is obligated to sell (or have the shares called) at the strike. With the stock trading $20.02 when you open the covered call, the question to ask yourself is this: Am I comfortable selling the stock at $21 with an effective sale price of $22 in the next sixty-five calendar days?

Upon assignment, the profit is equal to the proceeds from the sale of the shares, which is the strike price of the calls plus the credit minus the purchase price of the stock. In other words, the potential profits equal the strike price minus the net cost. In this example, the investor could potentially make $200 on the MGM March 21 covered call if assigned on the calls, or [$21 − ($20 − $1)] × 100.

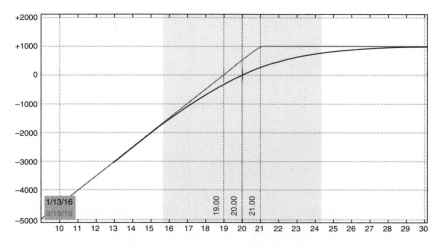

Figure 10-3   MGM March 20 Covered Call Profit/Loss Graph

MGM March 21 Covered Call

Strategy: Buy 100 shares for $20, sell 1 March 21 call at $1

Direction: Bullish or neutral

Debit or Credit: $2,000 for shares – $100 credit

Risk: $20 – $1 = $19

Expiration Breakeven: $19

Potential Profits: $21 – $20 + $1 (premium) or $2

Looking at the probability analysis in Figure 10-4, the one standard deviation range for MGM shares through the March expiration (now in fifty-one days and the stock is at $19.50) is $16.05 to $23.25. There is a 32.6 percent probability that shares will be above $21 and the calls will be ITM. The probability of holding above the $19 per share breakeven and below $21 is 21 percent. Therefore, there is a 53.6 percent probability of success on the trade.

What happens if the stock never reaches $21 through the expiration and the calls are not assigned? There is a 44.7 percent probability that the stock will be below $19 at the March expiration, or 13 percent in the $18 to $19 range and 31.7 percent of closing below $18.

If, for instance, the stock has had a rough go and closes at $18 at expiration, then the calls will expire worthless. The cost of the stock is $19; therefore, the investor is sitting on an unrealized loss of $1, or

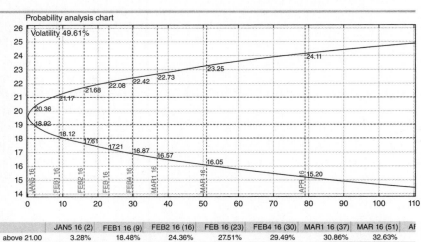

	JAN5 16 (2)	FEB1 16 (9)	FEB2 16 (16)	FEB 16 (23)	FEB4 16 (30)	MAR1 16 (37)	MAR 16 (51)	AI
above 21.00	3.28%	18.48%	24.36%	27.51%	29.49%	30.86%	32.63%	
19.00–21.00	77.91%	46.62%	36.25%	30.67%	27.05%	24.47%	20.95%	
18.00–19.00	17.89%	20.94%	17.91%	15.74%	14.17%	12.98%	11.28%	
below 18.00	0.92%	13.96%	21.48%	26.09%	29.28%	31.69%	35.14%	

Figure 10-4   MGM March 20 Covered Call Probability Analysis

$100 on one covered call with the stock at $18 at the expiration. At that point, the investor can then (1) continue along the same theme by writing additional calls, (2) sell the shares to close the position and book the $100 loss, or (3) do nothing and hold the shares without writing any more calls. Importantly, there is no guarantee that the market will be $18 after trading resumes Monday following the expiration. It might be higher or lower.

On the other hand, if the stock closes at $20.75 and the calls expire without assignment, the investor can sell the shares and monetize the gain, assuming that the stock is still trading for $20.75 on Monday. It might be higher or lower when trading resumes after the expiration. The profit at that level is $1.75, or $175 on one call, as it equals the sale price of the shares minus the net cost, or [$20.75–($20–$1)] × 100. The investor can also write another call option or simply hold the shares.

Collar Me

When looking at the MGM options chain, did you think to yourself, *What if I sell calls to buy puts?* It's not a crazy idea. In fact, the *collar* is another limited-risk options strategy that involves the sale of OTM calls to buy OTM puts. You can think of it as a combination of a protective put and a covered call, and it is sometimes used as a protective strategy to "collar" a position in the underlying. There is more information on this strategy and others in Appendix B.

Lastly, the position can also be closed out prior to the expiration by selling shares and buying back the calls. The profit or loss will depend on the sale prices of the shares, the price paid for the calls, and the transaction costs charged by your broker. That, in turn, will depend on not just the movement in the underlying but also how time decay and implied volatility have affected the options. Time decay is working with the covered call writer. Falling implied volatility can have a beneficial impact as well.

Summary

The covered call is the first options strategy that many new options traders learn because it is simply a combination of being long the underlying and short call options. In the equities market, one call is sold for every one hundred shares. The strategy can be used to generate income beyond any dividends paid. Some investors sell calls on stocks that have rallied and that they are now ready to sell. Therefore, calls are sold as a way to exit a stock position, and whether the stock is sold will depend on where the stock price is relative to the strike at expiration. ITM calls will likely be assigned, per the OCC's auto-exercise rules.

The maximum gains from the covered call are limited due to the strike price and that creates an *opportunity risk* if shares really rally. The investor is collecting a premium, however, and that lowers the cost of simply owning shares. The covered call can also be closed at any time prior to the expiration.

My preference is selling OTM calls with twenty-one to seventy days of life remaining. I want time decay working in my favor. Selling options with high implied volatility can also benefit the covered call writer if volatility moves lower. However, beware of situations when IV is elevated, as there might be some negative headlines surrounding the name that is affecting the price of the shares and the options. Remember the old adage: If something seems too good to be true, it probably is. That's true of covered calls and the remaining options strategies covered in this book as well. Now let's talk about cash-secured puts.

References

www.thinkorswim.com/t/learning.html
www.thinkorswim.com/tos/displayFaq.tos?categoryKey=GENERAL+
    QUESTIONS

11

Cash-Secured Puts

Long puts and protective puts were discussed in Chapter 7. Remember that a put option increases in value as the price of the underlying moves lower. Therefore, being long a put is typically a bearish strategy that is initiated when the investor expects the price of the underlying security to move lower. The protective put is a combination of being long the underlying security and long puts. It is a strategy that is often used to protect (or hedge) an existing position in the underlying, because the long puts will increase in value and offset potential losses if the underlying instrument decreases in value.

This chapter revisits put options but focuses on selling (or writing) rather than buying. If a put buyer is bearish on the underlying, it stands to reason that a put seller might have a bullish view. In fact, the cash-secured put is a strategy that an options trader typically initiates on an underlying security that she already wants to own. Ultimately, the put writer is expressing a willingness to buy (or have put to her) the underlying security at a set strike price through a fixed expiration period.

The term *cash-secured* refers to the fact that the funds to buy the stock stand ready in the investor's brokerage account if the puts are assigned. In the equities market, the investor buys one hundred shares of the stock for every put option that is assigned. The cash needed in the account will therefore depend on the strike price of the option and the number of contracts that are sold.

In some situations, a short put can be used as an alternative to a buy limit order when the investor is a willing buyer at a specific price.

We explore that in more detail in Chapter 17 as well. The advantage is that the investor is getting paid (collecting a credit or premium) for placing the order. If the puts are never assigned and shares stay above the strike, there is nothing to do. The options expire worthless.

If assigned, the strategy is no longer short puts, but long stock. It is a bullish strategy and makes sense if the investor is comfortable buying the underlying at the strike price of the put that was sold. The strategy can also pay off if the investor is writing out-of-the-money (OTM) puts and shares fall, so long as the move lower is not below the strike price of the put.

Short Puts

Selling a put obligates the investor to buy (or have the stock put to him) at the strike price of the option through the option's expiration. In most cases, the investor is selling puts with the intention of taking delivery, such as shares of stock, if required to do so. Having cash in the account to cover the assignment makes the short put a cash-secured put strategy. If not, the put write is considered a short put (or naked put) and will require additional margin.

Naked Put

Have you ever sold puts naked? It has nothing to do with how much clothing you're wearing but refers to selling put options uncovered (with no position in the security) and not as part of a spread. To change a naked put to a cash-secured put, you need to have enough money in the account to cover assignment.

The potential gains from put writing are equal to the credit received. In many cases, the investor is writing OTM puts (where the strike price is below the current market price) and anticipating steady action, or maybe a rally, in the underlying. If the options remain OTM through the expiration and the investor does nothing, the puts will likely expire worthless.

Short Put Cheat Sheet

Strategy: Sell puts

Direction: Bullish or neutral

Debit or Credit: Credit

Risk: Strike price – Credit – 0

Breakeven: Strike price – Credit

Potential Profits: Credit

On the other hand, if the investor wants to take delivery and have the shares put to him, the best-case scenario is for the price of the underlying to be just below the strike price of the options at expiration and for the puts to be assigned at the strike price. At that point, the cost of the shares is the strike price minus the credit. The position then becomes long stock.

Figure 11-1 shows the simple risk graph of the short put. Notice that it is the same shape as Figure 10-1. Like the covered call, the risk to the short put or cash-secured put is from a move lower in the underlying. The worst-case scenario would be getting assigned, buying the stock at the strike price, and then seeing it continue falling to zero. If assigned on the puts, the cost of the stock (which is the strike price) is offset by the premium collected for writing the puts. Therefore, the breakeven equals the strike price minus the credit.

If the puts are in the money (ITM) at expiration, the investor is assigned and will be put the shares. Short puts can also be closed (or covered) prior to the expiration (or before assignment) through an offsetting buy-to-close transaction. Importantly, if ITM,

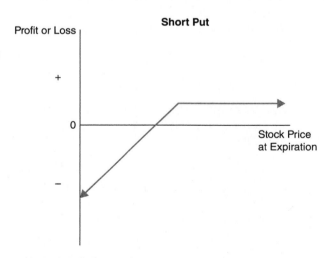

Figure 11-1   Short Put Risk Graph

American-style options might be assigned prior to the expiration as well. If so, it is too late to close the position, and the put writer must take delivery of the underlying. Therefore, it is very important to be comfortable with the idea of taking delivery of the stock at the specified strike before writing the puts.

I like the cash-secured put strategy for stocks that I want to own. The logic is similar to what you have seen earlier in this book, selling puts that are slightly OTM and that have twenty-one to seventy days of life remaining, which can sometimes see a relatively rapid rate of time decay. The puts I write are on names that I feel have strong fundamentals, and by writing the puts, I am stating that I am a willing buyer at that price. Implied volatility (IV) is an important consideration as well, because the short puts not only benefit from time decay, but falling IV during the life of the option can help the position as well.

In most cases, however, I am not looking to cover the puts before expiration, but instead either (1) take delivery of the shares or (2) let the puts expire worthless. The advantage of allowing short OTM puts to expire rather than closing them through an offsetting purchase is that there are no additional transaction costs. Once the puts expire, I can write additional puts in later expirations or simply move on to something else. Lastly, keep one thing in mind: If the goal is to buy the stock due to assignment and you do not achieve your goal because the puts never went ITM, you still make money by getting to keep the premium you received when you sold the put. That is not the case for most strategies.

Example

When the underlying security is a stock, one put write obligates the investor to buy one hundred shares at the strike price through the expiration. For instance, let's say MGM is trading for $20 per share in January, and an investor wants to initiate a short put strategy using March options that expire in sixty-five days. The investor is a willing buyer of one hundred shares of the underlying for $19 per share and, looking at the options chains (Figure 11-2), sees that the March 19 puts are bid at $1 per contract. Let's keep the math simple here and say that with the stock at $20, one contract is sold for a total premium of $100. In other words, the investor will be put the stock at $19 with a breakeven at $18, giving an almost 12 percent downside cushion if shares move lower instead of higher.

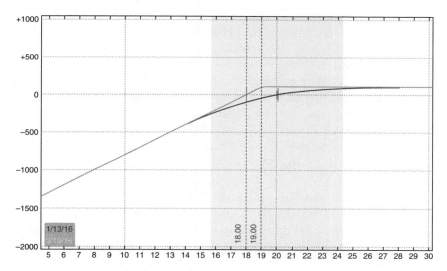

Figure 11-2   MGM Options Chain

Figure 11-3   MGM Short Put

The risk graph of the MGM short put in Figure 11-3 is the same shape as the MGM March 21 covered call from Chapter 10 (Figure 10-3). While the gains are limited, the risks are to the downside. The breakeven is equal to the strike price minus the credit received. In this example, the position shows a loss at expiration if shares are trading below $18 (19 strike minus $1 credit).

Because puts increase in value as shares fall, the risk to a short put is on a move to the downside. If, for instance, the stock loses 25 percent to $15, the puts are $4 ITM at expiration. The loss is $300, or $400 minus the $100 credit collected. Figure 11-3 shows the loss at $13 per share of $500, or $600 minus $100. Potential losses are limited to $18, or $1,800 on one put write, because MGM can't fall below zero.

MGM March 21 Short Put

Strategy: Sell MGM March 19 put at $1

Direction: Bullish or neutral

Debit or Credit: $1 credit

Risk: ($19 − $1) × 100 = $1,800

Breakeven: $19 − $1 = $18 per share

Potential Profits: $100

The potential profits from the short put are limited to the premium collected or, in this case, $100 on one put write. If the options are OTM at expiration, the investor does nothing, and the puts can be left to expire worthless. (*Note:* In rare instances, a slightly OTM or at-the-money [ATM] put might be exercised, and therefore, assignment is a possibility, which is true of any American-style contract that is near-the-money and has little time value heading into expiration.) So if MGM doesn't fall more than 5 percent and holds above $19 through the third Friday in March, the options expire, and the investor gets to keep the $100 collected in his account for writing the puts.

Figure 11-4 shows the probability analysis chart for MGM at the time. While the covered call example in Chapter 10 (Figure 10.4) looked at the probability of expiring ITM, the one in this chapter

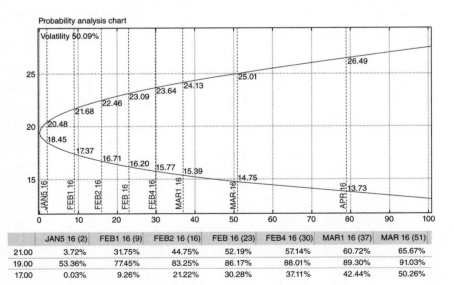

	JAN5 16 (2)	FEB1 16 (9)	FEB2 16 (16)	FEB 16 (23)	FEB4 16 (30)	MAR1 16 (37)	MAR 16 (51)
21.00	3.72%	31.75%	44.75%	52.19%	57.14%	60.72%	65.67%
19.00	53.36%	77.45%	83.25%	86.17%	88.01%	89.30%	91.03%
17.00	0.03%	9.26%	21.22%	30.28%	37.11%	42.44%	50.26%

Figure 11-4   MGM Probability Analysis

is the probability of touching. It assumes a one standard deviation range of stock prices, with MGM at $19.50 and now fifty-one days remaining until the expiration.

The probability of touching $19 is now 90 percent and of falling to $17 is 50 percent. Therefore, there is a 50 percent chance that the stock will fall $1 below the breakeven. However, there is also a 65 percent chance of it touching more than $21 per share. If I am looking to get long the stock, I can live with these probabilities. There is a good chance that I will get assigned at $19 per share, but my real cost of buying the stock is $18. There is also a relatively high probability that the stock will be in the low twenties in the weeks ahead. As most of the assignments happen in the last week of expiration, I prefer to look at probability of expiring ITM when analyzing cash-secured puts.

If the stock drops below the 19-strike but remains above $18, the short put might not profit, depending on the next move in the underlying. If, for instance, the stock is at $18.25 at the expiration, the puts are assigned at $19, and the investor is long stock at $19 minus the $1 credit. The cost is $18, and the stock at $18.25. The next move in shares, higher or lower, will dictate whether the position shows additional profits or if it begins to show losses, but you are starting with a $0.25 edge. Transaction costs (commissions, contract, and assignment fees) need to be factored in as well.

What if the stock really tanks? For instance, the stock closes at $16 at the expiration, the puts are assigned at $19, and the investor buys (has put) one hundred shares for a total of $1,900. He collected $100 on the put write, and therefore, the cost is $1,800, or $18 per share. The stock is closed at $16, and he is long stock at $18 per share. Therefore, the unrealized loss is $2 per share, or $200 on one hundred shares. The investor can then liquidate the shares and book the loss or simply hold the stock in anticipation of a rebound. Remember, an investor would sell the puts anticipating a higher stock move.

Because the investor sold puts with the idea of taking delivery, the more likely strategy is maintaining a long stock position. Importantly, even though the stock may have closed at $16 on expiration Friday, there's no guarantee that the stock will open at $16 on Monday. It could open higher or lower, and there is no guarantee of being able to liquidate at $16.

Selling cash-secured puts rather than naked puts can help avoid the mistake of taking on too much risk or becoming *overleveraged*. Position size is important in this respect. If an investor typically buys and sells five hundred shares of stock at a time, the equivalent number of puts is five contracts. Obviously, the size of the trade will also vary based on whether it is a high- or low-priced stock. Additional tips on risk management and position sizing are covered in Chapter 17, "The Close."

Summary

Like any investment strategy, the short put and cash-secured put strategies are not suitable for every investor. The risks are sometimes hard to define, and if the underlying experiences a dramatic move lower, the losses can be significant, especially for higher-priced stocks or indexes. However, the risk is never greater than the underlying falling to zero.

I personally like the strategy, because it is a tool to enter positions for stocks that I want to own. In the cash-secured put, the investor stands ready to buy the shares at the strike price of the underlying through the expiration. The cash is available in the account to cover assignment. An important point to keep in mind is that there will be margin requirements, and the investor has to be prepared to pay for the stock if assignment occurs.

As we have seen, the risk graph of the cash-secured put is similar to the covered call. Transaction costs can have a significant impact on any potential gains or losses and should be considered when comparing the strategies, as the short put includes only options, and the covered call is a combination of long stock and short calls. In both cases, the investor is optimistic (or bullish) on the outlook for the underlying.

My preference for writing puts is to use shorter-term time frames of between twenty-one and seventy days, because these will typically benefit the most from time decay. Time decay is nonlinear and affects shorter-term options at a faster rate than longer-term contracts. I look for situations when implied volatility is elevated, as the position will benefit from falling IV. Lastly, most of my put writes are options that are between 2 percent and 10 percent OTM.

Lastly, I only sell puts on stocks that I want to own, and the cash is on hand in my account to cover assignment if the options go ITM. In other words, the cash-secured put strategy is a tool to enter stock positions in names that I want to hold for the long-term. Remember that if you don't achieve your goal of purchasing the stock, you still keep the premium received. Chapter 17 will go into more detail about using short puts instead of a buy-limit order to enter a stock position.

12

Long Vertical Spreads

The strategies covered to this point are simple strategies that include just one options contract. The covered call, for example, is the purchase of underlying security along with the sale of call options. Meanwhile, a cash-secured put strategy and the short put strategy involve selling a specific put option. Buying long calls and long puts was covered earlier as well.

The remaining strategies are spread trades that involve more than one contract. One thing to keep in mind with spread trades is that they achieve maximum value if the underlying closes on expiration day at or near the short strike. This chapter explores long vertical spreads. The strategy involves buying one option and selling another option within the same expiration term but with different strike prices. The term *vertical* is due to the fact that the options appear vertically on the options chain. Like a long call or a long put, a long vertical spread is a directional strategy that is typically initiated when an investor is expecting the underlying to make a significant move higher or lower.

First I will consider the long vertical spread with call options. Also known as a bull call spread, the position is simply buying a call at one strike and selling another call at a higher strike. The strategy makes sense when the investor is expecting the underlying to move higher. The bear put spread, on the other hand, is the purchase of a put and the sale of another put at a lower strike. It has a bearish directional bias and is typically initiated when the investor expects the underlying security to fall in price.

Long vertical spreads, whether with puts or calls, have clearly defined risks and also limited rewards. The risks include the loss of principal or the premium paid to enter the spread. The rewards vary based on the strike prices used to create the spread. As we will see, there are times when these long vertical spread strategies offer certain advantages over long calls and long puts alone.

Like when buying long calls or long puts, probabilities help me determine if the price of a vertical spread is worth paying. It is easy to get tempted to purchase out-of-the-money (OTM) spreads that could provide payoffs of two or three times the debit. However, be careful with the leverage. The higher the risk-reward ratio, the lower the probability of success. A couple of examples are provided to illustrate.

Bull Call Spread

Readers were introduced to the long call strategy in Chapter 6. To open the position, an investor pays a premium and enters into a contract that gives him the right, but not the obligation, to buy the underlying security at a fixed (strike) price through an expiration period. The long call is initiated when the investor wants upside exposure to the underlying because he expects the price to move higher.

In addition to the price of the underlying security, changes in implied volatility (IV) and time decay can affect the value of the options contract as well. While the long call loses value over time, an increase in implied volatility will result in an increase in the options premium. Falling IV has a negative impact on the premium.

The long call spread is a long call and the sale of a call at a higher strike price within the same expiration term. The purchase of one call gives the owner the right to buy the underlying security at the strike price, and as has been duly noted in earlier chapters, writing a call obligates the seller to sell the underlying security at the strike price if the call is assigned. The sale of the higher price call offsets some of the premium paid for a long call. Therefore, the investor is paying a smaller debit. The sale of the higher strike call also limits the potential rewards to the upside.

Figure 12-1 shows a simple risk graph of a long call spread. The position generates profits if the price of the underlying security

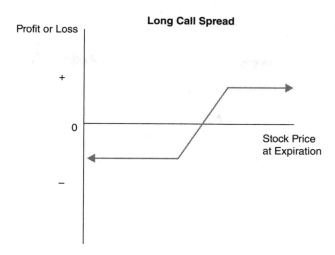

Figure 12-1   Bull Call Spread

moves higher and loses money if it trades lower. The risk of a long vertical spread is the premium paid, and the maximum loss happens if both options expire worthless. Excluding transaction costs, the breakeven equals the lower strike price plus the debit. At that point, the higher strike calls expire worthless, and the intrinsic value of the long call is equal to the debit paid.

The potential gains of a long vertical spread are limited and equal to the difference between the strike prices minus the debit. The maximum profit happens if the price of the underlying is at or above the higher strike of the spread. For instance, say an investor holds a long call spread on XYZ, and the share price closes above the higher strike at expiration. The higher strike calls are assigned, and the lower strike calls are exercised to cover the assignment. The profit is equal to the sale price of shares (higher call strike) minus the purchase price of shares (lower strike) minus the debit paid to enter the position.

A vertical spread can typically be closed at any time prior to the expiration by selling-to-close the same spread. If the credit received for selling the spread is greater than the debit paid, the result is a profit on the trade. If the credit is less than the initial premium, the result is a loss. If both strikes are OTM at expiration and the position is left open, the result is the loss of the premium paid. If only the long call is in-the-money (ITM), the investor will face exercise on the contract if it has not been covered before the expiration and will be buying shares of the underlying stock at the strike price.

Some investors establish long call spreads by selecting a strike to buy and then picking a higher strike that corresponds with their expected price target for the underlying. Like the covered call, selling a higher strike call creates an opportunity risk if shares see a substantial move beyond their target, because the investor is obligated to sell the shares at the higher strike price, regardless of how far the underlying security might rally. The long call, on the other hand, has theoretically unlimited profit potential. Yet, the investor is paying a smaller debit for the call spread, and the sale of a higher strike call also hedges some of the time decay risk, because while the long call is suffering losses due to time decay, the short one is also.

Long Call Spread Cheat Sheet

Strategy: Buy call, sell higher strike call

Direction: Bullish

Debit or Credit: Debit

Risk: Debit

Breakeven: Lower strike + Debit

Potential Profits: High strike – Low strike – Debit

When searching for long call spreads, I always look for underlying stocks that see active trading with significant trading volume (liquidity) and have many listed strike prices to choose from. The thing to focus on with vertical spreads is that they are really all about the option you are buying; the reason you are selling the higher strike call is to lower your net cost.

There are two areas of focus—shorter term or weekly options—where you may be playing for a quick impetus such as earnings. Or the longer-term play that is three to ten weeks in which you believe a more gradual up move will help, but you do not want to commit the capital you would if you purchased the stock itself. I prefer to buy a contract that is ITM and sell a higher strike call that is OTM. That is, the ITM call will have some intrinsic value, while the OTM call is all extrinsic. In other words, like the television character Fred Sanford, I want to buy value and sell junk.

Legging

Many brokerage firms allow investors to initiate spread trades as one order, but an investor can also do the spread one leg at a time. For example, you might buy a long call and then later sell a short call at a higher strike. This is referred to as *legging* into a trade. However, you can often save on transaction costs by executing the trade as one spread rather than legging in one side at a time.

If you are new to spread trading, then consider doing spreads as one trade rather than buying the calls first and then selling the higher strike calls. That is, don't leg into the spread because you know what price you want to pay for the spread. If you leg into it instead and the market moves against you, you won't collect as much on the sale of the upside call. That, in turn, would result in a lower price for the short call and a higher price of the spread. Therefore, after you decided how much you want to pay for the spread (and this holds true of all the strategies outlined in this book), send the order to be executed as one transaction. Also, as I will show later (detailed in Chapter 17), you may want to place the orders between the bids and asks. More on this later.

Example

Let's say an investor has a bullish longer-term view on Apple and wants upside exposure in the name for the weeks ahead, because a move to $100 from $97.34 is expected. Rather than buying shares outright, she is considering opening a limited-risk call spread and, in mid-January, is looking at various strike prices in the March term.

Figure 12-2 shows the nearest strikes with the stock trading for $97.34. The March 90–100 call spread is currently trading for roughly $6, as the market to buy the March 90s is $8.10 and to sell the March 100s is $2.13. She decides to purchase 1 March 90–100 call spread on the stock for $6, or a total debit of $600.

The March 90–100 call spread for $6 has limited risks and rewards. The potential loss is $600 if shares drop back below $90 and the options expire worthless. Excluding transaction costs, the

AAPL ▼	🖉	APPLE INC.COM	**97.34**	+3.25 +3.45%	B: 88.00 A: 97.60	NASDAQ	🔊 +0.925			🔔 Company Profile	

Underlying

	Last X	Net Chng	Bid X	Ask X	Size	Volume	Open	High	Low
>	97.34 Q	+3.25	88.00 Q	97.60 Q	0 x 10	64,416,504	94.79	97.34	94.35

Option Chain   Filter: **Off**,   Spread: **Single**,   Layout: **Volume, Open Interest**,

	CALLS								PUTS		
	Volume,	Open.Int,	Bid X	Ask X	Exp	Strike	Bid X	Ask X	Volume,	Open.Int,	
MAR 16	(48)	100									28.30% (±8.06
	44	2,437	10.00 C	10.15 M	MAR 16	87.5	.85 W	.89 Q	822	3.173	
	861	6,615	7.95 W	8.10 C	MAR 16	90	1.30 C	1.35 W	2,219	31,430	
	280	2,493	6.10 C	6.25 C	MAR 16	92.5	1.94 C	1.99 W	909	5,822	
	1,656	10,171	4.50 C	4.60 M	MAR 16	95	2.85 Q	2.89 W	1,892	15.814	
	1,823	5,049	3.15 C	3.25 Q	MAR 16	97.5	3.95 C	4.05 W	675	7.908	
	5,848	56,525	2.13 C	2.19 M	MAR 16	100	5.40 C	5.55 C	28,193	47.024	
	26,648	30,295	.81 C	.84 Q	MAR 16	105	9.05 C	9.25 W	297	18.309	
	4,015	37,765	.31 Q	.32 Q	MAR 16	110	13.55 C	13.80 W	57	29,937	

Figure 12-2   Apple Options Chain

breakeven is equal to the lower strike plus the debit, or at $96. In this case, the breakeven is below the stock price.

If the stock does nothing, the trade profits, because shares currently trade for $97.34. The intrinsic value at that price is $7.34 and greater than the $6 debit paid for the spread. This is much different than buying the stock outright, because, in that case, the profit depends on the stock moving higher. In this example, the investor makes a profit even though shares did not move as anticipated.

Apple March 90–100 Call Spread Breakdown

Strategy: Buy March 90 call for $8.10 and sell March 100 call at $2.10

Direction: Bullish

Debit or Credit: $600 debit

Risk: $600

Breakeven: $90 + $6

Potential Profits: $100 − $90 − $6

Figure 12-3 shows the risk-reward of the AAPL March 90–100 call spread for $6, and the same information appears in the details above. The potential profits are to the upside and equal the higher strike minus the lower strike (or the spread) minus the debit paid, or $4 per spread.

If both legs of the spread are ITM at expiration, the investor can exit the position by simply letting the exercise and assignment take place, which is likely but never guaranteed. If so, the stock is called at

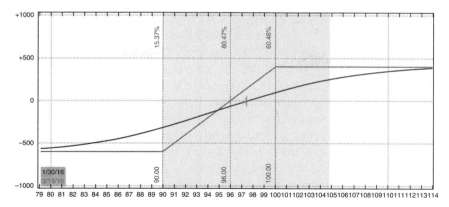

Figure 12-3   Apple March 90–100 Long Call Spread Risk Graph

$90 and sold at $100. In that case, the profit is $100 minus $90 minus the $6 debit, or $400 per spread. (Remember, the multiplier for an equity option is one hundred.)

Using Position Delta

Recall from Chapter 8 that delta expresses the expected change in the value of an option for each one-point price move in the under-lying asset. A position delta can be used to measure the expected change in the value of a spread. In this example, the delta of the March 90 calls is 0.80 and the March 100 calls is 0.20. Because the long calls have positive deltas and short calls have negative deltas, the position delta of the spread is 0.60 and is estimated to see a $0.60 increase for a one-point move higher in Apple shares.

The long call spread could be closed prior to the expiration by selling one March 90 call and buying a March 100 call to close. The profit or loss will depend on the premium collected from selling the spread. If, for example, it's a week before expiration and the stock is trading at $97.50, the March 90s can be sold for $8 and the March 100s can be bought for $1. The investor can exit the position for $7, resulting in a $1 profit on the trade. But if the price of the underlying stock drifts lower and the spread is only worth $3, the position can be covered for a $3 loss.

Or, the investor can close out just one leg of the spread at any time. Closing out only the higher strike through a buy-to-close transaction would leave the investor long the lower strike calls and in a bullish play. On the other hand, selling-to-close only the lower strike leaves the short call naked, which typically has higher margin requirements and exposes the investor to a position with unlimited risk. Personally, I feel it makes more sense to get in as a spread and out of a spread, especially when new to options trading.

The long call can be exercised as well. If, for instance, expiration approaches and the short call is OTM but the long call is ITM, the investor might choose to exercise the contract to buy one hundred shares of Apple for $90 per share. If she holds the short call, then the position becomes a March 100 covered call. However, it typically doesn't make sense to exercise a contract that has time value remaining, because that value is lost upon exercise.

Figure 12-4 offers a look at various probabilities of price ranges for Apple over the life of the March options, or forty-eight days. While the goal is for the stock to move above $100, the $96 breakeven level is also a point of interest. There is a 36.6 percent chance that the stock will rise to $100 (the maximum profit of the spread) and a 16.1 percent chance that it will be between $96 and $100. Therefore, there is a 52.7 percent probability that the stock will be trading above the breakeven at expiration and that the trade will show a profit.

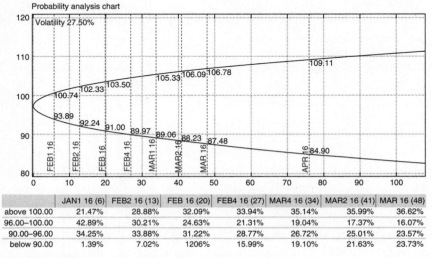

	JAN1 16 (6)	FEB2 16 (13)	FEB 16 (20)	FEB4 16 (27)	MAR4 16 (34)	MAR2 16 (41)	MAR 16 (48)
above 100.00	21.47%	28.88%	32.09%	33.94%	35.14%	35.99%	36.62%
96.00–100.00	42.89%	30.21%	24.63%	21.31%	19.04%	17.37%	16.07%
90.00–96.00	34.25%	33.88%	31.22%	28.77%	26.72%	25.01%	23.57%
below 90.00	1.39%	7.02%	1206%	15.99%	19.10%	21.63%	23.73%

Figure 12-4   Probability Analysis for Apple Inc.

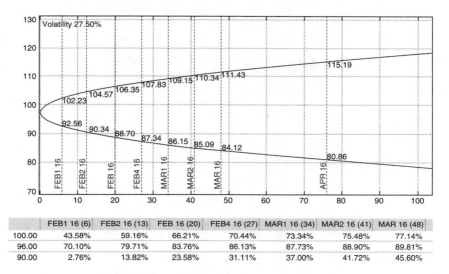

	FEB1 16 (6)	FEB2 16 (13)	FEB 16 (20)	FEB4 16 (27)	MAR1 16 (34)	MAR2 16 (41)	MAR 16 (48)
100.00	43.58%	59.16%	66.21%	70.44%	73.34%	75.48%	77.14%
96.00	70.10%	79.71%	83.76%	86.13%	87.73%	88.90%	89.81%
90.00	2.76%	13.82%	23.58%	31.11%	37.00%	41.72%	45.60%

Figure 12-5   Apple Probability of Touching Analysis

Looking at the probability of touching in Figure 12-5 offers additional insight. There is a 77.1 percent chance that the stock will touch $100 through the life of the options. Because $100 is the short-term target of the spread, the investor might choose to exit the position any time the stock hits that level while the position is open, even if it is not yet near the expiration. In other words, the probability of touching can be useful when looking at potential price targets for the short leg of the long call spread.

As a rule of thumb, the higher the potential profit of the trade, the lower the probability of success. In this case, the investor is risking $6 to make $4. On the other hand, a March 100–110 call spread in Figure 12-2 trades for less than $2. It offers a potential of more than $8 profit. However, the probability of the stock reaching $110 is obviously much less than it reaching $100.

Be extremely careful with the leverage and don't go overboard when buying vertical spreads. The examples presented in this book are for educational and illustrative purposes only and not a recommendation to trade a particular strategy or security. Take some time to find approaches that match your risk tolerance, fit with your trading plan, and also have reasonably high probabilities of success. Practice them on paper or in a virtual trading platform before you go live.

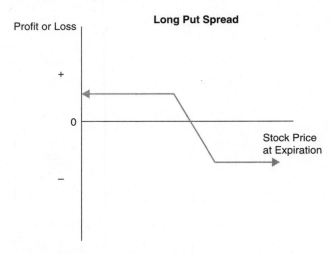

Figure 12-6   Bear Put Spread Risk Graph

Bear Put Spread

The setup for the long put spread is similar to the long call spread, but the directional bias is bearish rather than bullish. The strategy involves buying a put and selling another put at a lower strike price within the same expiration term. The long put gives the investor the right to sell (or put) the underlying stock to someone at a specific strike price, and the short put represents the obligation to buy it at the lower strike price.

Figure 12-6 is the simple risk graph of a long put spread, which is basically the inverse of the risk graph of the long call spread in Figure 12-1. Like the long put, the position loses money as the price of the underlying security moves higher and generates profits if the price falls. The losses associated with buying a put spread are limited to the debit paid, and maximum loss occurs if both legs of the spread expire worthless.

The breakeven of the long put spread equals the higher strike minus the debit. If the stock is at that level at the expiration, the lower strike puts will likely expire worthless, and the intrinsic value of the long put is equal to the debit paid. Excluding transaction costs, there is no loss or gain on the position, and it breaks even.

Long Put Spread Cheat Sheet

Strategy: Buy put, sell lower strike put

Direction: Bearish

Debit or Credit: Debit

Risk: Debit

Breakeven: High strike – Debit

Potential Profits: High strike – Low strike – Debit

Like the long call spread, the maximum potential profit of a long put spread is the difference between the two strikes minus the debit. If, for example, the position is exited through exercise and assignment, the investor is buying (having put) the stock at the lower strike and selling (putting) it to another investor at the higher strike. Also, just like with the long call spread, the position is about the option that you buy. Selling the lower strike put is intended to help lower the net cost.

Like with any options strategy, the long put spread can typically be covered prior to expiration. In this case, the investor sells-to-close the same spread. The gain or loss will depend on how much premium is collected to exit the spread. If the investor collects more of a credit than was paid to open the spread, the result is a profit. On the other hand, the investor suffers a loss if the spread is sold for less than the debit paid to enter the position.

Example

Let's say an investor is concerned about the potential for a substantial market decline in the next few weeks and is looking for downside exposure in the event a sell-off does indeed happen. Looking at an options chain on Goldman Sachs (GS) with shares trading at $161.50, the March 150–170 put spread is trading for roughly $9. That is, the March 170 puts can be bought for $11.65 and March 150 puts sold at $2.65.

Between the Spread

Spreads are often executed as one order rather than buying one side of the position and then selling the other. In addition, just as an investor can place an order to buy a stock between the bid-ask spread, it is also possible to place the order between the bid-ask for the spread. For instance, if the market for a March 150–170 put spread, as in Figure 12-7, is bid at $8.80 and offered at $9.04, an investor might place a limit order to buy the spread for $8.95. There is no guarantee that the trade will be executed at that price, but as the market changes, it is possible that it eventually will. In addition, as we will see in later chapters, there is nothing wrong with trading between the bid and offer. In fact, there may be advantages in doing so.

GS		GOLDMAN SACHS GROUP INC COM		**161.56**	+4.50 +2.97%	B: 150.00 A: 161.75	::: ±1.411			▲ Company Profile	
∨ Underlying											
>	Last X	Net Chng	Bid X	Ask X	Size	Volume		Open	High	Low
	161.56 N	+4.50	150.00 Q	161.75 Q	0 x 1	4,887,892		158.64	161.59	157.78
∨ Option Chain	Filter: **Off**	Spread: **Single**	Layout: **Volume, Open Interest**							
		CALLS				Strikes: ALL			PUTS	
	Volume	Open.Int	Bid X	Ask X	Exp	Strike	Bid X	Ask X	Volume	Open.Int
∨ MAR 16	(48)	100								30.77% (±14.563)
	6	175	13.30 C	13.95 C	MAR 16	150	2.61 M	2.78 A	62	455
	67	288	9.85 X	10.10 T	MAR 16	155	3.85 N	4.10 C	67	262
	75	389	6.65 X	6.90 T	MAR 16	160	5.65 C	5.90 X	64	179
	120	304	4.10 X	4.35 X	MAR 16	165	8.10 M	8.40 Z	15	68
	117	692	2.37 A	2.53 M	MAR 16	170	11.15 M	11.65 Z	0	206
	135	612	1.25 M	1.36 C	MAR 16	175	15.15 C	17.50 X	5	5

Figure 12-7   Goldman Sachs Options Chain

The investor buys one March 150–170 put spread for $9 per spread or a cash outlay of $900 plus transaction costs. (Note: I am using $9 rather than $8.95 in order to work with round numbers in this example.) The risk is the premium paid. If shares rally to more than $170 and the position is left open through the expiration, the options will likely expire worthless, and the premium paid would be lost.

From Figure 12-8, we can also see that the breakeven of the spread is at $161 per share, and that equals the higher-strike 170 put minus the $9 debit. At $161 per share, the 170-strike puts are worth $9, and that equals the debit paid. Profits increase below the breakeven and are limited as shares fall below the lower strike, or $150 per share.

Like with any long vertical spread, the potential gain from the March 150–170 put spread is the difference between the two strikes minus the debit paid. In this case, if the options are ITM at expiration and the position is closed through exercise/assignment, the investor is put the stock at $150 and can sell it in the higher strike of $170. Subtract the $9 debit from the $20 profit from the purchase and sale of the shares. The net profit is $11, or $1,100 on one spread.

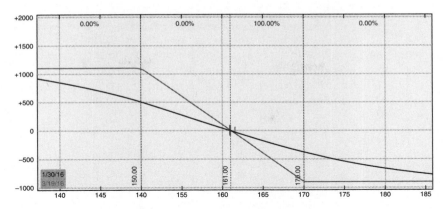

Figure 12-8   Goldman Sachs March 150–170 Put Spread

Goldman Sachs March 150–170 Put Spread Breakdown
Strategy: Buy March 170 put for $11.65 and sell March 150 put
at $2.65

Direction: Bearish

Debit or Credit: $9 debit

Risk: $9

Breakeven: $170 − $9

Potential Profits: $170 − $150 − $9

The gain or loss if the position is sold-to-close prior to the expiration, depends on how the shares performed and the credit received from selling the spread. If, for example, the stock rallies to $170 and the spread is sold at only $2 by mid-February, the position would show a loss of $7 on the spread. Obviously, the investor wants the stock to move lower, not higher.

The probability of expiring ITM analysis in Figure 12-9 shows that the probability of the stock closing between $161 (breakeven) and $150 (maximum profit) at the expiration is 24.1 percent, and the probability of a move below $150 is 27.4 percent. Therefore, the probability of the stock moving below the breakeven is 51.5 percent. The probability of a move above $170 (worst-case scenario) is much less at 30 percent.

In this example, the investor is risking $9 to make $11 over the course of seven weeks. If, for example, the March 150-160 call spread was bought for $3.30 instead, the risk-reward ratio would be much

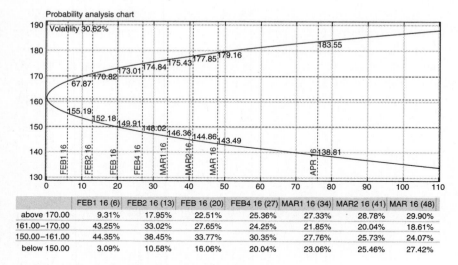

Figure 12-9   Goldman Sachs Probability Analysis

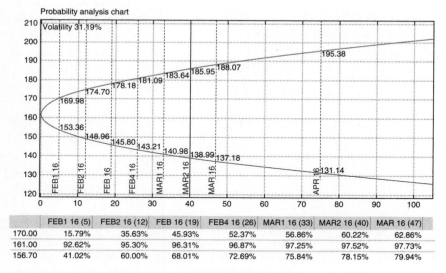

Figure 12-10   Goldman Sachs Probability of Touching

higher on a move to $150. In that scenario, the investor is risking $3.30 to make $6.70. However, the breakeven of the March 150–160 put spread for $3.30 is $156.70 instead of $161. As we can see from the probability of touching analysis in Figure 12-10, there is a substantially higher probability of touching $161 (98 percent) rather than $156.70 (80 percent).

Trading an underlying that has options with many strikes has a number of advantages, and the ability to create a variety of different vertical spreads is one of them. There literally are a lot more options! However, be careful with buying put spreads that are too far OTM. While the risk-reward ratio can be quite high, the probabilities of success are often much lower. As the old adage goes, you get what you pay for. Buy value, not junk.

Summary

Long vertical spreads can be created with puts or calls. The long call spread is sometimes referred to as a bull call spread, because the investor initiates the position when he expects a move higher in the underlying security. The bear put spread makes sense when the investor wants downside exposure in a specific name or market.

When looking for potential trading opportunities, I look at expirations no more than ten weeks out. My focus is call spreads for upside in the short-term, for quick hits with an impetus, or in names that I like for the longer-term. The call spread is merely a vehicle for participating when I am expecting shares to move higher. I only open put spreads on an underlying security that has poor fundamentals or as a short-term hedge against a stock position.

Probability analysis helps me determine whether the price for the spread is worth paying. As a rule of thumb, I am looking for a better than 50 percent probability of the position at least breaking even and an 80 percent or better probability of it touching the higher strike through the expiration.

It might be tempting, for instance, to open a 50–55 strike call spread for $1 with the stock at $45, because the risk–reward ratio seems relatively interesting. The investor is risking $1 to make $4. Odds are, however, that the probability that the stock moves to the higher strike is not extremely high. There are important trade-offs to consider, and you don't want to overdo it with the leverage. It's better to hit singles and doubles rather than swing for the fences every time.

CHAPTER 13

Short Vertical Spreads

Short vertical spreads are the exact opposite of the strategies covered in the previous chapter. I noted in Chapter 12 that a long vertical call spread involves buying a call with one strike and selling another at a higher strike. The investor pays a debit for the long vertical call spread, and the risk is limited to the debit paid. The position offers a maximum payout if the underlying security rises in price and stays above the higher strike of the spread through the expiration. Therefore, the long vertical call spread is typically initiated when the investor has a bullish outlook and expects the price of the underlying security to move higher.

The short vertical call spread is the reverse of the long vertical call spread. The investor is selling a call and buying a call with a higher strike. The trade is initiated at a credit, and the premium collected is the maximum potential profit from the strategy. The risk is also limited, because the call with the higher strike is hedging the risk of the short call with the lower strike. The strategy is typically a bearish play on the underlying security. However, the short vertical call spread, often using out-of-the-money (OTM) calls to take advantage of time decay, can be initiated if the investor expects stock price to hold in a range as well. The ideal scenario is for the underlying to finish below the lower strike of the call spread at expiration and for the options to expire with no intrinsic value.

We will also see that the short vertical put spread is basically the opposite of a long vertical put spread. The strategy is sometimes used instead of a cash-secured or naked put when the investor wants sell puts but also seeks protection from a move lower in the underlying with the purchase of a put at a lower strike. The lower strike put hedges the short put.

So while the long vertical put spread is a bearish play, the short vertical put spread is primarily a bullish or neutral strategy that makes sense when the investor expects the price of the underlying to be above the option's strike price at expiration. It's really all about the option that you are selling. The other option is purchased to hedge or define the risk. In addition, time decay is your friend when initiating the short vertical spread because you start with OTM options. This chapter explores the ins and outs of the short vertical spreads in more detail along with a couple of examples to help illustrate.

Short (Bull) Put Spread

A short vertical put spread is a premium selling strategy that involves selling a put at one strike and buying a put at a lower strike within the same expiration month. Like the cash-secured put from Chapter 10, the idea is to generate income into a portfolio by writing puts on an underlying that an investor is willing to buy (or have put to them) at the strike price. The primary idea is to generate income into a portfolio by writing puts and collecting premium. The primary risk for the investor is having the stock put to them at the higher strike price. The main difference here is that you are trading a spread, so you can manage the spread and avoid being assigned the stock as much as possible. This is a directional play that employs premium selling.

The short vertical put spread includes the purchase of a put with a strike price below the strike of the short put. That limits potential risks if the underlying falls, because the investor has bought the right to sell (or put the underlying) at that strike price. The trade-off is that, compared to simply writing a put, the investor is collecting less of a net credit, because he's also paying a debit to buy the lower strike put. One of the themes that I want to continue is that of limiting reward to limit risk.

Figure 13-1 depicts a simple risk graph for the short vertical put spread. The risks and rewards are limited on both the upside and downside. The maximum potential profit is the credit collected and happens if shares hold above the strike price of the higher strike put through the expiration. At that point, there is nothing to do. The options expire worthless, and the investor keeps any premium

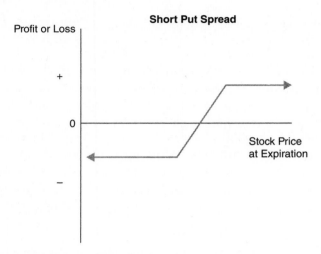

Figure 13-1   Bull Put Spread Risk Graph

from writing the spread, which has the added benefit of no additional transaction costs to exit the position.

The breakeven of the spread is equal to the higher strike minus the credit. If the stock is at that level at expiration, the lower strike puts expire worthless, and the higher strikes have intrinsic value equal to the credit received. Because the investor is short the higher strike puts, the loss there is equal to the credit, and the trade breaks even.

Short Vertical Put Spread Cheat Sheet

Strategy: Sell put, buy lower strike put

Direction: Bullish or neutral

Debit or Credit: Credit

Risk: High strike – Low strike – Credit

Breakeven: High strike – Credit

Potential Profits: Credit received

The amount of risk associated with a short vertical put spread depends on strike price selection. The maximum potential loss is equal to the difference between the two strikes minus the credit collected. If the price of the underlying falls below the lower strike of the spread and assignment at the higher strike occurs, the underlying is bought at the strike price of the short put, and then the long put can be exercised to cover the assignment. In that case, the loss is equal the price paid (higher strike) minus the price received (lower strike) minus the credit.

A short vertical put spread can typically be closed prior to the expiration by buying-to-close, and the profit or loss will depend on the exit price. In most cases, the spread can be, and probably should be, exited as one trade. If the price paid to close the position is more than the initial credit, the trade is a loser. If the spread is bought-to-close for less than the initial credit, then winner, winner, chicken dinner.

What if the underlying closes between the two strikes at expiration? In that case, the short puts are likely to be assigned, but the long put is still OTM and therefore not subject to auto-exercise. In that case, the investor is put the underlying and takes delivery, as with a naked put. From that point forward, the position can be held or closed after the expiration on the following Monday (or Tuesday if Monday is a holiday), and the gain or loss on the position will depend on the price at the time the underlying is sold. This is one of the reasons I like to manage my risk by closing spreads four to ten days before expiration. That is, enter as a spread and exit as a spread.

Closing out only the long put changes the position to a naked put and is still a bullish position on the underlying. On the other hand, if the investor covers the short leg of the spread, the remaining position is a long put and expressing a bearish view on the underlying. This also ruins a bit of the logic of doing a spread to start with, because the nature of the trade has been changed.

In a third, less likely scenario, the investor is assigned on the short put and holds the long put. The new position is long stock and long put (which is the "synthetic" equivalent of a long call position, as discussed in Chapter 7). Reminder: an American-style short put can be assigned at any time prior to the expiration regardless of the in-the-money (ITM) amount. A European-style option can only be assigned at the expiration.

My focus when screening for short vertical put spreads is options that expire in three to ten weeks. Time decay is typically affecting the higher strike puts at a more significant rate compared to the lower strikes. Therefore, even if the underlying moves sideways, the strategy can begin showing profits.

I'm also selling OTM puts that have a relatively low probability of expiring ITM. The underlying might even see a bit of weakness, and the strategy might still pay off, so long as the price of the underlying doesn't fall below the short put strike through the expiration. Unlike the cash-secured put, I am not looking to buy (or have put) the stock, but if I do get assigned, it is not devastating. Because I wrote puts, I'm ready to be assigned and take delivery of the underlying at the strike price through expiration if required to do so.

The key here is time decay. It is a directional play that takes advantage of time working in my favor. I want the options to lose value over time so that I am out of the position at expiration. If so, there are no additional transaction costs to consider, as the options simply expire worthless. Again, this strategy is really focused on the contract that is being sold. The other part of the spread is there to define risk.

Example

A vertical spread is primarily a directional trade that is risk-defined. In the next example, let's say that an investor believes that Apple shares are going higher and wants to put herself, if she is wrong, in a risk-defined situation with a high probability of making money even if nothing happens or she is slightly wrong. To illustrate, let's say Apple is trading for $94.69. Figure 13-2 shows some of the various strikes available for potential vertical spreads in the March options that expire in twenty-four days. (Note that, in this example, the bid-ask for shares is below the last price. The reason for this is that the snapshot was taken afterhours when the bid-asks are still being updated, but the last price is not.)

The March 93 puts, for example, are trading for $1.76 (bid) and $1.79 (ask). The contract is $1.69, or 1.8 percent OTM. The investor

AAPL | APPLE INC COM 94.69 -2.19 -2.26% B: 94.56 A: 94.65 ETB NASDAQ ±0.562 | Company Profile

Underlying

Last X	Net Chng	Bid X	Ask X	Size	Volume	Open	High	Low
94.69 Q	-2.19	94.56 K	94.65 Q	2 x 4	31,839,135	96.40	96.50	94.55

Option Chain Filter: **Off** Spread: **Single** Layout: **Volume, Open Interest**

CALLS				Strikes: ALL		PUTS			
Volume	Open.Int	Bid X	Ask X	Exp	Strike	Bid X	Ask X	Volume	Open.Int
MAR 16 (24) 100									28.17% (±5.54)
72	5	4.90 X	5.00 C	MAR 16	91	1.17 B	1.19 Q	606	215
10	3	4.50 X	4.60 X	MAR 16	91.5	1.29 C	1.32 Q	575	47
44	0	4.15 X	4.25 M	MAR 16	92	1.44 N	1.46 Q	626	169
164	3,804	3.80 X	3.90 M	MAR 16	92.5	1.59 E	1.61 Q	2,244	21,566
126	23	3.50 M	3.55 B	MAR 16	93	1.76 E	1.79 Q	1,313	302
93	1	3.15 C	3.25 X	MAR 16	93.5	1.94 X	1.99 X	866	194
229	103	2.89 A	2.92 Z	MAR 16	94	2.15 Z	2.17 Q	3,117	1,349
433	116	2.61 Q	2.64 Z	MAR 16	94.5	2.36 E	2.40 C	1,795	113
6,168	13,206	2.35 Z	2.37 W	MAR 16	95	2.59 X	2.64 X	8,289	21,876

Figure 13-2 Apple Options Chain

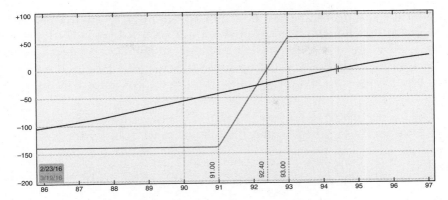

Figure 13-3   Apple March 91–93 Put Spread

is considering selling those puts, because she is expecting the stock
to move higher and wants to define the risk with the purchase of a
lower strike put. The March 91 puts are trading for $1.17 to $1.19.
Therefore, the market to sell the March 91–93 put spread is $0.57,
or $1.76 sell the 93 strike puts and $1.19 to buy the 91 puts. Let's say
that one spread is sold at $0.60 even.

The risk graph of the short vertical put spread in Figure 13-3
confirms that the potential profits are limited to the credit collected, or $60 on one spread. The breakeven is $92.40 per share at
expiration and equal to the higher strike minus the credit. If Apple
closes at $92.40 at expiration, the 91-strike puts are worthless, and
the (short) 93s have $0.60 of intrinsic value, which is equal to the
credit collected.

Here's another way to look at it: If the 91-strike puts are OTM and
the investor is assigned on the puts at $93, the total cost of buying the
stock, excluding transaction costs, is $93 minus the $0.60 credit, or
$92.40 per share. That, in turn, is also the breakeven. Remember, the
investor has to be prepared to buy (or get long) the stock at $93 if the
price falls. Selling the put spread is actually a play on (1) the stock
moving higher and (2) buying the stock for less than current prices,
or, in this example, $92.40.

The potential profit from the short vertical put spread is limited to the credit received. If the stock holds above $93 and both
options expire worthless, the investor does nothing and can move on
to the next trade. Therefore, even if shares fall but hold above $93,
the trade is successful. That's an important point to keep in mind.

Namely, even if the investor is wrong on direction when writing the OTM put spread and the stock heads lower (but not below the higher strike of the spread), the trade can be profitable. There are also no transaction costs to exit if the options are left open through the expiration, which is an advantage to letting the options expire as well.

Probability of Being Profitable for Short Vertical Spreads

A formula that many options traders use to estimate the probability of a short vertical spread being profitable by a penny or more at expiration can be computed by dividing the real risk of the position by the spread itself. That is, it is the real risk (width of the spread minus the premium received) divided by the total risk (width of the spread). In this example, the spread is $2, and the investor is collecting $0.60. The real risk is the difference between the two strikes minus the credit, or $1.40. The probability of the spread being profitable by a penny or more, excluding transaction costs, is therefore $1.40/2, or 70 percent. Note that the probability results from using this formula are theoretical in nature, not guaranteed, and do not reflect any degree of certainty of a particular trade or strategy being successful.

Like with any short vertical spreads, the risks to the position equal the difference between the two strikes minus the credit. In the worst-case scenario, the stock falls sharply and the investor faces assignment on the puts that were sold, requiring him to buy the stock for $93. However, the 91-strike puts represent the right to sell (or put) the stock at $91. The maximum potential loss in that scenario is the price paid ($93) minus the price sold ($91) minus the initial credit received. In this case, the investor is collecting $0.60 and risking $1.40. The theoretical probability of the spread being profitable by a penny or more, as outlined in the formula above, is 70 percent.

Apple March 91–93 Short Put Spread Breakdown

Strategy: Sell March 93 put at $1.79 and buy March 91 put for $1.19

Direction: Bullish or neutral

Debit or Credit: $60 credit

Risk: $93 – $91 – $0.60

Breakeven: $93 – $0.60

Potential Profits: $60

If the price of the stock falls below $93 but stays above $91 and the short puts are assigned prior to the expiration, the investor will be holding a long Apple March 91 put and a long stock position. If the March 91 puts expire worthless (unless also ITM and exercised), the investor is long stock at $92.40.

If the investor has a change of heart and doesn't want to be obligated to buy the stock for $93, the short puts can be bought-to-close. In that case, it typically makes sense to close the spread altogether by also buying-to-close the March 91–93 put spread on Apple. One thing to keep in mind, is that the stock may go slightly below 93, but the exercise risk is usually not great until the last week or so of expiration. The closer to expiration, the greater the risk of exercise/assignment.

My preference is to enter the spread as one trade and close it as one spread. In the event that the options are deep OTM, there is no guarantee that it can be closed out if there is no market to sell the long puts, but in most cases, the spread is sold-to-open and later bought-to-close.

Figure 13-4 shows the probability analysis for Apple through the March expiration and confirms that a drop to $91 or below has a lower (32.4 percent) probability than of it staying above

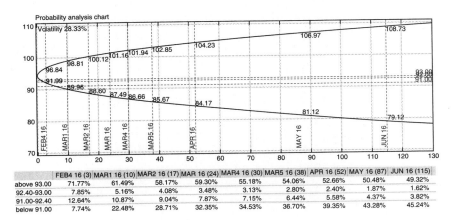

	FEB4 16 (3)	MAR1 16 (10)	MAR2 16 (17)	MAR 16 (24)	MAR4 16 (30)	MAR5 16 (38)	APR 16 (52)	MAY 16 (87)	JUN 16 (115)
above 93.00	71.77%	61.49%	58.17%	59.30%	55.18%	54.06%	52.66%	50.48%	49.32%
92.40-93.00	7.85%	5.16%	4.08%	3.48%	3.13%	2.80%	2.40%	1.87%	1.62%
91.00-92.40	12.64%	10.87%	9.04%	7.87%	7.15%	6.44%	5.58%	4.37%	3.82%
below 91.00	7.74%	22.48%	28.71%	32.35%	34.53%	36.70%	39.35%	43.28%	45.24%

Figure 13-4   Apple Probability Analysis

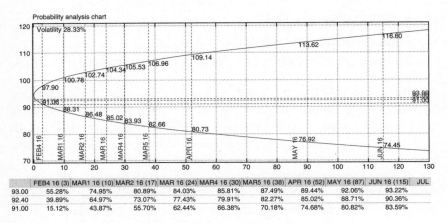

Figure 13-5   Apple Probability of Touching Analysis

$93 (56.3 percent). The probability of it remaining above the $92.40 breakeven equals the probability of staying above $93 and of staying between $92.40 and $93 (3.5 percent). In other words, there is a 59.8 percent probability of shares being above the breakeven through the March expiration.

The probability of touching analysis tells a similar tale. In Figure 13-5, there is an 84 percent probability that Apple will touch $93 through the March expiration in twenty-four days. The probability of it hitting $91 (worst-case scenario) is 62.4 percent. Because there are twenty-four days left until expiration, the probabilities will change as time passes and shares move higher or lower. It doesn't hurt to have an exit strategy in place if the numbers begin to change significantly. Ideally, the stock moves higher, and time decay works in the favor of the position. If not, that's okay too, because the investor is a willing buyer at the 93 strike and keeps the credit for writing the spread as well.

Investors want to be compensated for taking risks. In this example, the risk is $1.40, and the investor is collecting only $0.60. The further you go down in strike prices, the probability of profit typically increases, but the premium collected is less. Again, the focus here is on selling options that are likely to expire worthless, because the investor expects the stock to move higher. The purchase of the long put is a tool to define risk associated with selling puts. In liquid names, there are many strike prices to choose from and numerous ways to create the spreads. Take a look at Appendix B for additional tips when searching for short vertical put spreads.

Short (Bear) Call Spread

Sometimes called a bear call spread, the short vertical call spread is a short call along with the purchase of a higher strike call in the same expiration month. The maximum potential gain from a short vertical spread is limited to the credit received for selling the spread. In this case, the credit equals the premium received for the short call minus the premium paid for the higher strike long call. If the options expire worthless, the position attains its full potential, and as can be seen from Figure 13-6, the risks are to the upside.

The maximum risk to the short vertical call spread is the difference between the two strikes minus the credit. Like with the short vertical put spread, when both legs of the spread are ITM at expiration, the long calls can be exercised to cover the assignment of the short calls. In that case, the investor is selling shares at a lower strike and buying at a higher one. The loss is, therefore, based on the size of the spread minus the credit that was received.

Short Vertical Call Spread Cheat Sheet

Strategy: Sell call, buy higher strike call

Direction: Bearish or neutral

Debit or Credit: Credit

Risk: High strike – Low strike – Credit

Breakeven: Low strike + Credit

Potential Profits: Credit

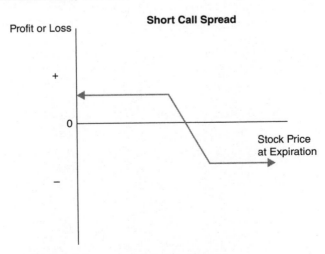

Figure 13-6 Short Vertical Call Spread Risk Graph

The breakeven of the short vertical call spread is equal to the lower strike plus the credit. If the underlying is at that price at expiration, the short calls have intrinsic value equal to the premium collected for writing the spread, and the spread breaks even.

Compared to writing naked calls, short vertical call spreads are less risky, because the purchase of a higher strike call hedges the short option. The trade-off is that buying the higher strike calls also reduces the net credit received from selling the lower strike call. Nevertheless, in both strategies, the ideal situation is for the options to expire worthless. As noted earlier, this also has a nice perk, because there are no additional transaction costs to exit the trade. The short vertical call spread can also typically be closed prior to the expiration by buying-to-close for a debit.

My preference is to sell spreads with twenty-one to seventy days of life remaining. I am selling OTM calls with a relatively high probability of expiring worthless while also buying a higher strike call to define the risk. It's also a play on time decay, because short calls will likely have more time value to lose compared to the deeper OTM calls.

Example

Netflix is trading at $89.56 in early February, and an investor expects shares to see limited upside over the next few weeks and months. The options chain (Figure 13-7) shows that OTM 90-strike calls in the March term, which expires in thirty-seven days, can be sold at $6.40. Because the investor expects the price of the shares to hold below that level over the next few weeks, he decides that those options are worthy of selling.

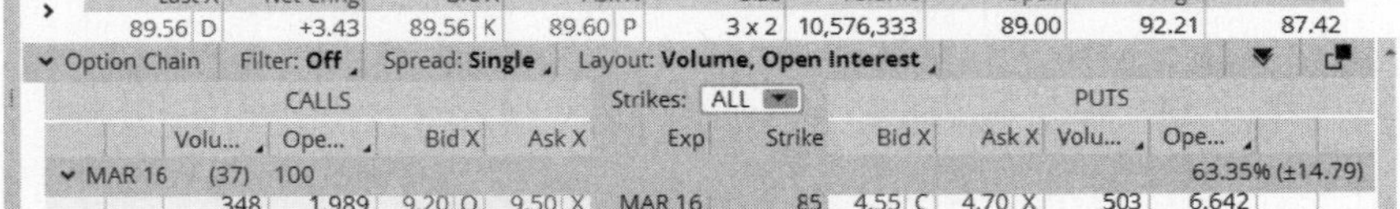
NFLX | NETFLIX.... | 89.56 | +3.43 +3.98% | B: 89.56 A: 89.60 | ETB | NASDAQ | ±1.984 | Company Profile

Underlying

Last X	Net Chng	Bid X	Ask X	Size	Volume	Open	High	Low
89.56 D	+3.43	89.56 K	89.60 P	3 x 2	10,576,333	89.00	92.21	87.42

Option Chain Filter: **Off** Spread: **Single** Layout: **Volume, Open Interest**

CALLS Strikes: ALL PUTS

MAR 16 (37) 100 63.35% (±14.79)

Volu...	Ope...	Bid X	Ask X	Exp	Strike	Bid X	Ask X	Volu...	Ope...
348	1,989	9.20 Q	9.50 X	MAR 16	85	4.55 C	4.70 X	503	6,642
860	6,626	6.40 C	6.60 C	MAR 16	90	6.75 N	6.90 X	452	6,255
795	4,143	4.25 N	4.35 X	MAR 16	95	9.35 X	9.70 X	55	5,377

Figure 13-7 Netflix March Options Chain

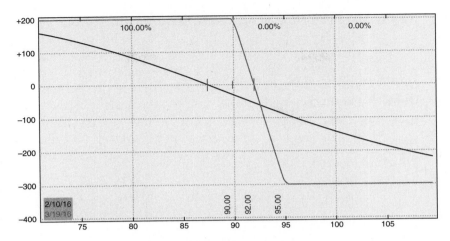

Figure 13-8 Netflix March Call Spread Risk Graph

However, rather than simply selling the March 90 calls naked, a spread is created by purchasing March 95 calls and opening a March 90-95 call spread instead. The March 95s can be bought for $4.35 (Figure 13-7), and for this example, let's say that the investor sells the spread at $2 even.

The risk graph in Figure 13-8 confirms that the potential profits from the short vertical call spread is limited. In this example, the gains max out at $2 per spread, or $200 if the share price holds below $90 and the calls expire worthless. Therefore, as long as share price doesn't move higher and both legs of the spread are OTM through expiration, the investor books the $2 profit.

The breakeven is simply the lower strike plus the credit, or $92. With that price at expiration, the 95 calls expire worthless, but the short 90 calls are worth $2. The loss on the short calls is equal to the premium collected, and the trade breaks even.

If the stock closes anywhere above $92 per share, the spread is losing money. The maximum loss happens if the investor pays the entire spread to cover the position, which would be the case if the position is exited through exercise and assignment. In that case, the loss is $3, or the $5 spread minus the $2 credit. Using the probability of profit formula mentioned in the short put spread example, the theoretical chances of the spread making at least a penny of profit is equal to the real risk divided by the total risk, or $3/5-point spread, or 60 percent.

Netflix March 90–95 Call Spread Breakdown

Strategy: Sell March 90 calls at $6.40 and buy March 95 calls for $4.40

Direction: Bearish or neutral

Debit or Credit: $200 credit

Risk: $95 – $90 – $2

Breakeven: $90 + $2

Potential Profits: $200

The probability of expiring ITM analysis for Netflix in Figure 13-9 shows that chances of a spike to $95 (worst-case scenario) or higher through the March expiration is 35.1 percent. There is a 6.1 percent chance that stock will be between $92 (breakeven) and $95 at expiration. Therefore, there is a 41.2 percent probability that the spread loses money and a 58.8 percent estimated probability of the spread generating a profit.

Lastly, the probability of touching in Figure 13-10 shows that the probability of the stock touching $95 (worst-case scenario) steadily increases over time and reaches 77 percent by the March expiration.

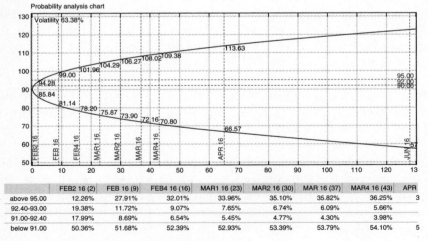

	FEB2 16 (2)	FEB 16 (9)	FEB4 16 (16)	MAR1 16 (23)	MAR2 16 (30)	MAR 16 (37)	MAR4 16 (43)	APR
above 95.00	12.26%	27.91%	32.01%	33.96%	35.10%	35.82%	36.25%	3
92.40-93.00	19.38%	11.72%	9.07%	7.65%	6.74%	6.09%	5.66%	
91.00-92.40	17.99%	8.69%	6.54%	5.45%	4.77%	4.30%	3.98%	
below 91.00	50.36%	51.68%	52.39%	52.93%	53.39%	53.79%	54.10%	5

Figure 13-9   Netflix Probability ITM Analysis

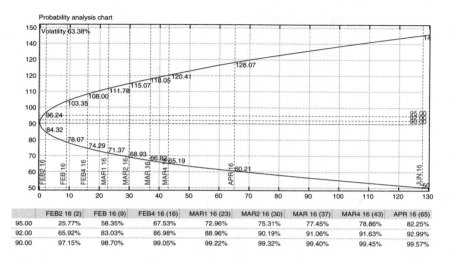

Figure 13-10   Netflix Probability of Touching Analysis

	FEB2 16 (2)	FEB 16 (9)	FEB4 16 (16)	MAR1 16 (23)	MAR2 16 (30)	MAR 16 (37)	MAR4 16 (43)	APR 16 (65)
95.00	25.77%	58.35%	67.53%	72.96%	75.31%	77.45%	78.86%	82.25%
92.00	65.92%	83.03%	86.98%	88.96%	90.19%	91.06%	91.63%	92.99%
90.00	97.15%	98.70%	99.05%	99.22%	99.32%	99.40%	99.45%	99.57%

This confirms that the short vertical call spread makes sense when the investor expects the stock to trade in a range or drift lower in the near term. Rather than selling naked calls, the purchase of the higher strike calls creates a spread that limits the potential profits but also limits the potential risks if there is a major spike in underlying.

In the examples in this chapter, strike prices of the short options are near the underlying and slightly OTM. Selling deeper OTM strikes will increase the probabilities of profit but will obviously reduce the amount of premium collected as well. That's the trade-off. My rule of thumb is to use the probability of profit formula (dividing the real risk by total risk) outlined in this chapter and look for opportunities in the 50 percent to 70 percent range.

Summary

Short vertical spreads can be created with puts or calls. In the bull put spread, the investor is short puts and hedging that position with the purchase of lower strike puts. The bear call spread is a short call with a long call at a higher strike. The potential profit from either spread is limited to the credit collected, and the risks are defined by the difference between the two strikes minus the credit.

Selling OTM options will result in higher probabilities of profitability compared to at-the-money (ATM) or ITM options. The trade-off is that the credit received decreases as you move deeper OTM. The important things to consider are (1) sell premium to take advantage of time decay; (2) remember that it's all about the short option, and the reason to buy the long option is to define the risk associated with selling the premium; and (3) use the probability of profit formula (real risk divided by total risk) and look for opportunities in the 50 percent to 70 percent range. This is a good place to start, as you have a nice combination of premium received and probability of success.

CHAPTER

14

Calendar Spreads

The calendar spread is a strategy that involves buying an option and selling another with the same strike price but in a different expiration month. Also known as a time spread or horizontal spread, the strategy is sometimes initiated when an investor expects the underlying to move in a range around the strike price over the life of short-term contract and then possibly make a directional move thereafter.

The call calendar spread is the sale of a call option and the purchase of another call at the same strike price with a more distant expiration. You can think of it as a combination of a long call and a short call and is a debit transaction because the cost (or premium) of the long option is greater than the premium collected for writing the short call. Calendar spreads are designed to take advantage of time decay as the front month will decay faster than the next month. They also seek to take advantage of increasing levels of volatility.

A put calendar spread is the purchase of a put and the sale of a put at the same strike but a closer expiration month. Both put and call calendar spreads seek to benefit from the nonlinear nature of time decay and the fact that there is a tendency for shorter-term options to lose value due to time decay at a faster rate than longer-term contracts.

If the short option of the put or call calendar spread expires worthless, the strategy has the same risks and rewards as being long a put or long a call option. The investor can choose from several other follow-up actions, such as writing additional short-term options, selling to close their long option position, or exercising it. I will explore the range of possibilities in the examples in this chapter. But keep in mind that, as is the case with all of the strategies covered in this book, I am typically looking to open the spread and then take it off (or cover it as a spread) before the first expiration.

As we will see in this chapter, the risk to the calendar spread is from a sudden move higher or lower in the underlying while both legs of the spread are still open. Therefore, the calendar spread isn't an ideal strategy in very volatile markets that are seeing a lot of vertical movement. Instead, it is more appropriate when the underlying security is expected to move sideways and in a range and can also benefit from an increase in implied volatility. However, as the maximum benefit is at the strike price at expiration, this strategy does have a directional bias.

My focus when looking for opportunities with calendar spreads is typically on long options with fifty to ninety days until expiration, while selling shorter-term contracts with twenty to forty days of life remaining. A couple of examples are provided below to illustrate.

Call Calendar Spread

The call calendar spread is the purchase of a call and the sale of a call at the same strike but a different expiration. The long call has a later expiration date than the short call. The investor pays a debit to enter a call calendar spread, because the premium of the longer-term option is greater than the shorter-term one.

Typically, I will choose a strike price that is just above the current price of the underlying. That is, the calls are slightly out of the money (OTM), and I am expecting the price to stay near that level through the first expiration. The ultimate scenario is for the underlying price to go to the strike price, so the near-term short option likely expires worthless, and the back month, which is now at the money (ATM), has the most time premium.

Figure 14-1 shows the risk graph for a call calendar spread at the first expiration. It isn't as straightforward as other profit–loss lines seen in previous chapters, and that's because the long-term option is still open when the short-term option expires. This makes computing the breakeven a bit problematic. Due to possible changes in implied volatility (IV), it is impossible to predict the value of the long call at the time the short call expires, but the volatilities of the two should be

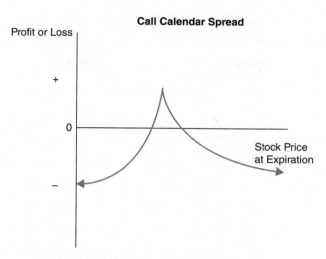

Figure 14-1   Call Calendar Spread Risk Graph

related because they are options on the same underlying instrument. Using software like the tools available on many trading platforms can help you estimate the breakeven.

Long Call Calendar Spread Cheat Sheet

Strategy: Buy a call, sell a short-term call at the same strike price

Direction: Bullish or neutral

Debit or Credit: Debit

Risk: If the short call expires worthless, the risk is limited to the debit paid. There are additional risks to consider due to the possibility of assignment on short calls.

Breakeven: Varies; use trading software to help determine.

Potential Profits: No limit if short call expires worthless. If closed before the expiration, it's the credit received for closing the long call minus the premium paid for closing the short call minus initial debit paid.

Ideally, the underlying is at the strike price of the call calendar near expiration. The investor can cover the position by purchasing the short call to close and selling the long call to close. When closing a calendar spread, the profit or loss is equal to the credit received for the long call minus the premium paid to cover the short call minus the initial debit—in other words, the difference between what you paid for the spread and what you sold it for. After the first expiration, the profit/loss graph is similar to the long call from Chapter 6, with theoretically unlimited upside profit potential and a breakeven equal to the strike price plus the debit paid to enter the position.

> ### Vega
>
> Note that volatility can have an important effect on time spreads. Because implied volatility typically has a greater impact on longer-term options compared to shorter-term ones, increasing IV typically helps the long calendar spread, while falling IV will work against it. Vega is the Greek that is used to estimate how changes in IV might affect an option's premium. It, along with the other Greeks, is covered in more detail in Appendix A.

There is more than one risk associated with a call calendar spread. If the underlying falls in price, the short option likely expires worthless. That's not such a bad thing. However, if the investor holds the remaining long call and the option is OTM at expiration, it too will expire worthless. So one risk is that both options expire worthless, and the entire debit paid to enter the spread is lost.

Another problem can arise if an American-style short call is in the money (ITM) near expiration and is assigned. The investor is hedged with the long call, but there is likely to be time value remaining in the longer-dated option; therefore, exercise may not the optimal way to cover the assignment. The time value is lost if the option is exercised, and the debit paid to enter the spread is also lost.

If the short call is assigned and the underlying is sold (called) per the terms of the contract, the investor can then liquidate the remaining long call, sell additional short-term calls, or exercise the long call. However, investors might prefer to exit the position entirely at this point, because the nature of it has changed. In each case, early assignment of the shorter-term option forces the investor out of the calendar spread, and the position is not playing out as planned.

Therefore, if expiration is at hand and the price of the underlying is above the strike price of the spread (or there is a dividend approaching on an ITM call option), an investor is at risk of being forced out of the call calendar spread due to assignment. This is not a high probability event, but it's something to be aware of because it can occur. Once the short calls are assigned, it is too late to close the short position, and the underlying is called away. Of course, early assignment is not a factor with European-style options, but it's certainly an important consideration when initiating long call calendar spreads with equity options and other instruments that settle American-style. This also is why earlier I discussed closing positions four to ten days before expiration. It can help to keep you out of this situation. If the stock price rises significantly above your strike, it might be time to close the position.

Example

Let's say an investor has an upbeat longer-term view on Facebook (FB) shares, but after a strong run, she expects the stock to see limited upside in the weeks ahead. She is considering a call calendar spread to express this view and, looking at the options chain (Figure 14-2), notices that March 110 calls, which expire in twenty-five days, are trading at $1.79 to $1.81. The stock is trading for $106.21, and these calls are currently 3.6 percent OTM.

Looking further down the options chain (Figure 14-3), the 110 strike calls in the May term, which expire in eighty-eight days, are trading for $5.75 (bid) and $5.80 (offer). Therefore, at current prices, the March-May 110 call spread is trading for approximately $4, or $5.80 to buy the May 110 calls and $1.80 to sell the March 110

FB — FACEBOOK INC COM — ETB — Company Profile

Underlying

Last X	Net Chng	Bid X	Ask X	Size	Volume	Open	High	Low
106.21 D	+1.64	106.21 Z	106.22 Q	1 x 3	5,208,059	105.49	106.54	105.34

Option Chain Filter: **Off** Spread: **Single** Layout: **Volume, Open Interest**

CALLS				Strikes: ALL		PUTS			
Volume	Open.Int	Bid X	Ask X	Exp	Strike	Bid X	Ask X	Volume	Open.Int
MAR 16 (25) 100									33.22% (±7.524)
910	41,683	1.79 Z	1.81 H	MAR 16	110	5.50 M	5.60 X	161	13,968
739	0	1.45 C	1.47 N	MAR 16	111	6.15 M	6.30 X	0	0
54	0	1.16 Z	1.18 Z	MAR 16	112	6.85 X	6.95 C	0	0

Figure 14-2 Facebook March Options Chain

MAY 16 (88) 100									38.91% (±16.485)
38	2,679	8.25 C	8.40 X	MAY 16	105	6.85 M	6.95 M	18	2,209
258	2,075	5.75 C	5.80 H	MAY 16	110	9.30 C	9.40 C	32	583
106	3,717	3.75 C	3.85 X	MAY 16	115	12.30 X	12.45 C	0	2,593

Figure 14-3 Facebook May Options Chain

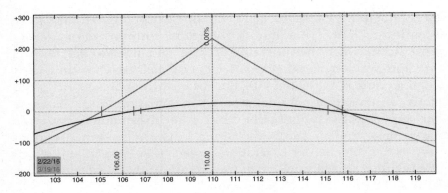

Figure 14-4   Call Calendar Spread Risk Graph

calls. The multiplier on an equity option is one hundred, and an investor takes a position in one spread for a cash outlay of $400.

Figure 14-4 shows the risk graph for one Facebook March-May 110 call calendar spread for $1 through the first expiration. Notice that the max payout happens at exactly $110 per share where the short option is ATM and set to expire worthless.

What about the long call? How much premium is left? It is impossible to know how much it will be worth, but the value can be roughly estimated. In this example, the profit on the spread is expected to be around $225 if the stock is at $110 at the first expiration. Because a $4 debit was paid for the spread, the long call is expected to be worth roughly $6.25 if the stock climbs to $110 into the first expiration. That is, the profit is $2.25 per spread, because the long calls are worth $6.25 and a $4 debit was paid to enter the position. Again, these are only estimates.

Figure 14-4 also shows that the breakevens of the call calendar spread are near $105 and $116. For instance, at $105, the shorter-dated 110 calls are expiring worthless, and the May 110-strike calls have an estimated value of $4, which is equal to the debit paid to open the spread. If the stock continues falling, however, the longer-dated calls will lose additional value, and the spread begins losing money. In the worst-case scenario, the stock falls far enough that there is no market to sell the longer-dated call, and it expires worthless. The debit paid is lost.

On the other hand, on a move toward $106, both contracts have no intrinsic value at the first expiration, but the May calls have sixty-three days of life remaining. That extra time value is expected to be roughly $4 when the first options expire. The trade breaks even at that price. However, as the stock continues climbing, the time value diminishes, because, as you will recall from Chapter 8 on components of options prices, deeper ITM calls have less time value compared to ATM options.

At an unfortunate extreme, both contracts are deep ITM, and the short calls are assigned. The long calls are exercised to cover the assignment. The investor buys and sells one hundred shares of stock for $110. The transaction is a wash, and the $4 debit paid to enter the calendar spread is lost. Therefore, when both contracts are deep ITM, you may want to consider exiting the position.

Facebook March-May 110 Call Calendar Spread Breakdown

Strategy: Buy May 110 calls for $5.80 and sell March 110 calls at $1.80

Direction: Bullish or neutral

Debit or Credit: $400 debit

Risk: If the short call expires worthless, the risk is limited to the debit paid. There are additional risks to consider due to the possibility of assignment on American-style short calls.

Breakeven: Varies; use trading software to help determine.

Potential Profits: No limit if short call expires worthless. If closed before the expiration, it's the credit received for closing the long call minus the premium paid for closing the short call minus initial debit paid.

Probability of expiring ITM analysis (Figure 14-5) shows that through the life of the near-term option in twenty-five days, the odds of a move to between $110 and $115.80 is 19.1 percent and a move beyond $115.80 is 16 percent. Therefore, the probability of the short option expiring ITM is just 35.1 percent, and the probability of it remaining below $110 (OTM) is almost 65 percent.

Meanwhile, the May 110 call has a 40 percent probability of expiring ITM. If the March option expires, the investor may want to revisit the curve based on the current stock values, because the only position now is the long call. At that point, it might make sense to write another short-term call against the long call, exit the position entirely, or simply hold the long call. Exercising the call is not likely the best strategy at this juncture, because any time value remaining

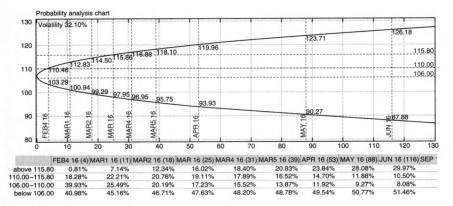

Figure 14-5   Probability of Expiring ITM Analysis

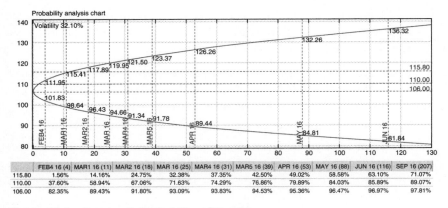

Figure 14-6   Facebook Probability of Touching

in the long call would be lost once it is exercised. (If you are not sure what to do, you can always contact your broker and ask for help.)

While probability of expiring ITM indicates that there is a 65 percent chance that the short option will expire OTM, probability of touching (Figure 14-6) confirms that there is a greater chance that stock will move higher through the May expiration compared to the shorter-term March expiration. For example, the probability of touching $115.8 through the March expiration is 32.4 percent, compared to 58.6 percent through the May term.

In the end, buying a slightly OTM call calendar spread, as in the Facebook example, is a directional play. The ideal situation is for the stock to edge toward the strike price of the spread in the near term but not rise above it. Time decay will do a lot of the work to help the position, but certainly favorable action in the underlying is desired as well. The higher the strike prices selected, the more aggressive the trade, as the risk to losing the debit paid to enter the spread is higher.

I prefer to sell short-dated, slightly OTM options with twenty to forty days of life remaining that have a high probability of expiring worthless while buying longer-term call options that have fifty to ninety days until expiration. I buy calendar spreads on stocks where I expect a volatility increase and, in this case, an upside impetus. As I mentioned earlier, since this is a spread, I will enter it and exit the trade as such. One mistake I see new investors make is just sitting with the long call after the first expiration. This ruins some of the logic of the trade. They are using the time decay in the front month to finance the longer term option. So if they keep the long call after the first month expires, they go from a positive theta (time decay) position to a negative theta. Therefore, defeating the purpose of this trade.

Put Calendar Spread

The put calendar spread is the same strategy as a call calendar spread, with an obvious difference. To create the spread, the investor sells a put and also buys a longer-dated put at the same strike but with a different expiration month. A typical example is to sell a put option that expires in one or two weeks and buy one with an expiration that is two or three months out. Ideally, the underlying stays in a range around the strike, but not falling below it, and time decay eats away at the short-term option at a faster rate compared to the longer-term contract. Remember that these positions also benefit from volatility increase.

Figure 14-7 shows that the risk graph of the put calendar spread is the same as the call calendar (Figure 14-1). The investor pays a debit to enter the spread, and that debit is at risk if the position is left open and both options expire OTM. At that point, the entire debit is lost.

The debit can also be lost if the short put is assigned and the long put is exercised to cover assignment. In that scenario, the investor is buying (having put) the underlying and selling (putting) it at the same price. Excluding transaction costs, there is no gain or loss on the purchase and sale of the underlying, but the initial debit

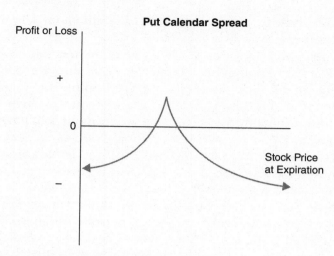

Figure 14-7   Put Calendar Risk Graph

paid is lost. Therefore, the worst-case scenario for the put (or call) calendar spread can arise from a substantial move higher or lower in the underlying.

Long Put Calendar Spread Cheat Sheet

Strategy: Buy a put, sell a short-term put at the same strike price

Direction: Bearish or neutral

Debit or Credit: Debit

Risk: Debit

Breakeven: Varies; use trading software to help determine.

Potential Profits: If closed before the expiration, the credit received for closing the long put minus the premium paid for closing the short put minus the initial debit paid. After the expiration, the risk is only limited to the price of the underlying falling to zero.

Ideally, the underlying instrument stays in a range around the strike price, and the investor can cover the position near the expiration of the short option by selling-to-close one leg of the spread and buying-to-close the other. At that point, any profit is equal to the credit received for one put minus the debit paid for the other minus the initial debit. If, on the other hand, the short-term put expires worthless, the investor is now holding a long put and to stay with the logic, should close that put also.

The maximum potential profit through the first expiration happens if the stock price is equal to the strike price of the spread and the short-term option expires worthless. At that point, the longer-term contract has remaining time value, and the potential profit is equal to the value of the long put at that time minus the debit paid to enter the spread. The amount of value will vary based on changes in implied volatility and can only be estimated using special software. Similarly, because there are two expirations in the spread, breakeven levels can only be estimated as well.

My same rules of thumb apply to put calendar spreads, but my outlook on the underlying is typically cautious or bearish rather than bullish. I want to sell short-term options that are slightly OTM and likely to see time decay at a faster rate compared to the longer-term contract.

The put options will increase in value as the underlying moves lower, but a move below the strike price close to the first expiration (ten days or less) is likely to force me out the spread. Instead, I want range-bound action in the underlying or a gradual move through the first expiration. At that point, I revisit the profit–loss potential to decide the best follow-up course of action.

Example

Another example can help illustrate how the put calendar spread can potentially generate profits through a combination of time decay and a favorable directional move in the underlying. Let's say it's mid-February and an investor is anticipating weakness in The Home Depot shares, but only after the company reports earnings in early April. Steady trading in the stock is expected between now and then. A put calendar spread seems like an interesting idea to express this view.

The March 115-strike puts on the stock are 7 percent below the current stock price of $123.71. The investor notices on the options chain (Figure 14-8) that the recent quote for the puts is $1.29 to $1.34. Scrolling through the later expiration months (Figure 14-9), the May 115 puts on the home improvement retailer are trading for $3.30 to $3.45. Therefore, at current prices, it is possible to buy the March-May 115 put spread on the stock for roughly $2 or buy the May 115 puts for $3.30 and sell March 115s at $1.30.

| HD ▼ | ⌖ | HOME DEPOT INC COM | 123.71 | +2.02 +1.66% | | ETB | ⚙ ±4,079 | | | ⬧ Company Profile | ⋮⋮ |

▾ Underlying									
>	Last X	Net Chng	Bid X	Ask X	Size	Volume	Open	High	Low
	123.71 D	+2.02	123.69 N	123.73 N	4 x 3	1,864,088	123.00	124.47	122.84

▾ Option Chain Filter: Off ⌄ Spread: Single ⌄ Layout: Volume, Open Interest ⌄   ▾ ⌷

		CALLS			Strikes: ALL ▾				PUTS		
	Volume ⌄	Open.Int ⌄	Bid X	Ask X	Exp	Strike	Bid X	Ask X	Volume ⌄	Open.Int ⌄
▾ MAR 16 (25) 100										32.21% (±8.49)
	32	891	9.60 C	9.80 X	MAR 16	115	1.29 N	1.34 C	331	2,435
	0	0	8.70 C	8.95 X	MAR 16	116	1.47 Q	1.51 Z	11	0
	0	0	7.80 X	8.10 E	MAR 16	117	1.65 Q	1.73 C	10	0

Figure 14-8   The Home Depot March Options Chain

	Volume ⌄	Open.Int ⌄	Bid X	Ask X	Exp	Strike	Bid X	Ask X	Volume ⌄	Open.Int ⌄
▾ MAY 16 (88) 100										29.98% (±14.712)
	0	83	19.40 C	20.85 C	MAY 16	105	1.59 X	1.67 I	31	345
	41	486	15.50 C	15.90 C	MAY 16	110	2.39 C	2.40 C	6	1,940
	7	1,335	11.55 X	11.75 X	MAY 16	115	3.30 X	3.45 X	17	3,434
	58	1,296	8.05 X	8.25 X	MAY 16	120	4.80 X	5.00 X	94	1,340
	75	2,182	5.20 X	5.35 X	MAY 16	125	6.90 C	7.10 X	28	498

Figure 14-9   The Home Depot May Options Chain

The profit/loss line on the risk graph in Figure 14-10 of The Home Depot 115 put calendar spread for $2 shows that the maximum gain happens if the stock closes at $115 per share at its expiration. At that point, the short-term put expires worthless, and the long put has remaining time value. Looking at the line (the upside-down, V-shaped one) shows that the profit is expected to be roughly $350 for one spread if the stock is at the 115-strike at the expiration. Because $2 was paid for the spread, it is estimated that the May 115 put will be worth $1.50 if shares drift down to $115 over the next twenty-five days, because $1.50 plus the debit paid equals $3.50. Again, these are estimates and not precise calculations.

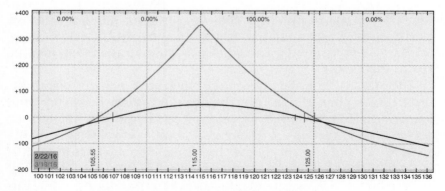

Figure 14-10   The Home Depot March-May Put Calendar

The breakevens are expected to be around \$105.55 and \$125.50. If the stock price sees a move higher above the upper breakeven through the first expiration, the value of the long put should decrease and is estimated to be worth less than the \$2 paid for the spread. The position is losing money, and the maximum risk is that the long put is left open, it expires worthless, and the entire debit paid for the spread is lost. In addition, depending on the magnitude of the move in shares, if the long put becomes deep OTM, there is no guarantee that there will be a market (bid), and it may not be possible to sell the contract to close.

On the other hand, a dramatic move lower can create problems, because as both contracts become deeper ITM, time value is no longer helping the position. The contracts are trading more at intrinsic rather than extrinsic value so this is a time to consider closing the spread, taking the loss and moving on. Remember, the calendar spread trader wants time to work in his favor, and this works best if the contracts are near the money and not deep ITM. The risk of assignment also increases, because this is an American-style option and can be exercised any time prior to the expiration.

The Home Depot March-May 115 Put Spread Breakdown

Strategy: Buy May 115 put for \$3.30 and sell March 115 put at \$1.30

Direction: Bearish or neutral

Debit or Credit: \$200 debit

Risk: \$200 debit

Breakeven: Varies; use trading software to help determine.

Potential Profits: If closed before the expiration, it's the credit received for closing the long put minus the premium paid for the long put minus the initial debit paid. After the expiration, the risk is only limited to the price of the underlying falling to zero.

If assigned on the short put, it's too late to close the position. The investor is obligated to purchase the shares per the terms of the contract. At that point, he can sell the shares and the long put on the open market or exercise the put to sell the shares. Again, your goal is to close the spread before it comes to this point.

The probability of expiring ITM analysis in Figure 14-11 confirms that it is statistically more likely that the stock falls below

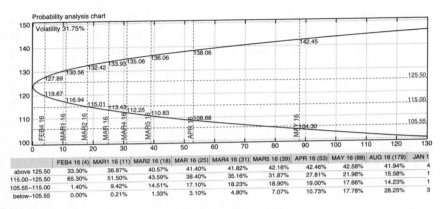

	FEB4 16 (4)	MAR1 16 (11)	MAR2 16 (18)	MAR 16 (25)	MAR4 16 (31)	MAR5 16 (39)	APR 16 (53)	MAY 16 (88)	AUG 16 (179)	JAN 1
above 125.50	33.30%	38.87%	40.57%	41.40%	41.82%	42.16%	42.46%	42.58%	41.94%	4
115.00–125.50	65.30%	51.50%	43.59%	38.40%	35.16%	31.87%	27.81%	21.98%	15.58%	1
105.55–115.00	1.40%	9.42%	14.51%	17.10%	18.23%	18.90%	19.00%	17.66%	14.23%	1
below–105.55	0.00%	0.21%	1.33%	3.10%	4.80%	7.07%	10.73%	17.78%	28.25%	3

Figure 14-11   The Home Depot Probability Analysis

$115 through the May expiration rather than at the March weekly expiration. Specifically, there is 20.2 percent probability that it drops below $115 over the next twenty-five days and a 35.5 percent chance through the May expiration. Again, once the short-term contract expires, it makes sense to exit the position entirely.

Probability of touching also indicates that a move to $115 or below over the life of the longer-term option is more likely than in the short-term option. Figure 14-12 shows that through the short-term expiration, the probability of touching $115 is less than 40 percent, and by the May expiration, it is 66.7 percent.

It should not come as a surprise that, in this example, it is more likely that The Home Depot will fall below $115 during the next

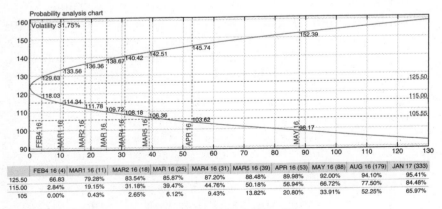

	FEB4 16 (4)	MAR1 16 (11)	MAR2 16 (18)	MAR 16 (25)	MAR4 16 (31)	MAR5 16 (39)	APR 16 (53)	MAY 16 (88)	AUG 16 (179)	JAN 17 (333)
125.50	66.83	79.28%	83.54%	85.87%	87.20%	88.48%	89.98%	92.00%	94.10%	95.41%
115.00	2.84%	19.15%	31.18%	39.47%	44.76%	50.18%	56.94%	66.72%	77.50%	84.48%
105	0.00%	0.43%	2.65%	6.12%	9.43%	13.82%	20.80%	33.91%	52.25%	65.97%

Figure 14-12   The Home Depot Probability of Touching

eighty-eight days rather than the next twenty-five days. There is a wider spectrum of possible stock prices over longer periods of time. The calendar spread is not just a play relative to the probabilities of movement in the underlying, but also attempts to benefit from the fact that time decay will affect the short option more than the long one. All else being equal, time is your friend when you buy a put or call calendar spread so long as the underlying doesn't see a dramatic move higher or lower.

Summary

Calendar spreads can be created in different ways. For example, if the investor is mildly bullish on the underlying, he might sell calls that are slightly OTM and buy longer term calls at the same position. Remember when you are starting out that staying disciplined and entering and exiting these as spreads can help you in the long term.

Ultimately, the success of a calendar spread hinges on the underlying moving to the strike price selected, although keep in mind that theta (time decay) and increasing volatility (vega) can help. Because the strategy includes buying and selling two expiration months, the strategy is sometimes called a time spread or horizontal spread. That's in contrast to the vertical spreads covered in the previous two chapters. Next, my focus turns to strategies with three and four legs—butterfly spreads (Chapter 15) and condor spreads (Chapter 16).

Butterfly Spreads

The term *butterfly* might sound a bit unusual to describe an options play, but the strategies are relatively straightforward and are basically combinations of the vertical spread trades that were discussed in Chapters 12 and 13. For example, a butterfly, sometimes just called a fly, can be viewed as a short call spread and a long call spread. Or, a spread can be created by combining a short call spread and a short put spread. That's the case with an *iron butterfly*.

The long call butterfly and long put butterfly are debit transactions with limited risks and rewards. Iron butterflies are credit spreads that also have defined risks and profit potential. Still, these are more advanced plays that are best suited for sophisticated investors with previous options trading experience.

While many options strategists use the butterflies when they expect the underlying to trade in a range around current levels, the spreads can also be structured to profit from a move higher or lower in the underlying. These spreads are designed to benefit primarily from a move of the underlying to the middle strike.

A few examples are provided to illustrate but are for educational purposes and not a recommendation to trade a specific name or strategy. Market conditions can and do change. Also, please keep in mind that these strategies, which include three and four legs within the spreads, can entail significant transaction costs, including multiple commissions, which will impact any potential returns. The actual amount charged will vary by brokerage firm.

Butterfly Spread

The long call butterfly spread is a strategy that includes the purchase of a call, the sale of two calls at a higher strike, and the purchase of another call at yet a higher strike. All of the options are within the same expiration term, and the strategy is combination of a long call spread and a short call spread, where the higher strike of the long spread is the same as the strike of the short spread. All three strike prices are equidistant apart. (Note that there are other variations of this strategy with strikes that are not equidistant apart, but that is for a later time.) Keep in mind that although these often trade at a low price, they also have low probability of profit.

Figure 15-1 shows a simple risk graph for a butterfly spread. It is a debit transaction. This should make sense because the investor is buying a long call spread and selling a short call spread at a higher strike. The best-case scenario is that the price of the underlying is at the middle strike (or the body) of the fly at the expiration. At that point, the middle strikes and the higher strike expire worthless. The remaining lower strike call is in the money (ITM), and the profit is equal to the middle strike (which is the same as current underlying price) minus the lower strike minus the debit paid. Or stated another way, the profit is the full value of the difference between those strikes or the full value of that vertical spread. As I mentioned earlier, going to the short strike is the best case scenario.

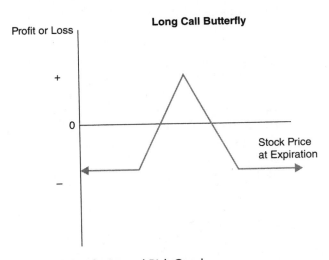

Figure 15-1   Long Butterfly Spread Risk Graph

The risk to the long call fly is the debit paid and can be lost in two ways. On the one hand, if the price of the underlying is below the lower strike and the position is left open through the expiration, the options are out-of-the-money (OTM) and the calls have no remaining value. The options expire worthless and the entire debit paid to enter the spread is lost.

Long Call Butterfly Spread Cheat Sheet

Strategy: Buy call, sell two higher strike calls, buy an even higher strike call

Direction: Depends on strike price selection

Debit or Credit: Debit

Risk: Debit

Breakeven: (1) Low strike + Debit; (2) High strike – Debit

Potential Profits: Middle strike – Low strike – Debit

If the position is closed prior to the expiration, the gain or loss will depend on whether the credit received from selling the butterfly is greater or less than the debit paid for the position. Time decay is generally working in favor of the position, because the investor wants all but the lower strike calls to expire worthless. If the middle strikes (body) are losing value faster than the other two legs (wings), that's a good thing.

On the other hand, if the price of the underlying is above the higher strike of the spread and the position is open at expiration, the middle strike (short) options will be assigned. If so, the investor can exercise the higher and lower strikes to fulfill the assignment. The stock is bought (called) at the higher and lower strike prices and sold at the middle strike. Because the strikes are equidistant apart and the average of the higher and lower strikes equals the middle strike, the purchase and sale of the stock yields no profit or loss (except transaction costs), and the debit paid for the spread is lost. Therefore, as the goal was not to have a stock position to start, it makes sense to just close out of the whole position.

Early-Assignment Risk on American-Style Options

When trading butterfly spreads using single stock options or other products with American-style settlement, assignment on the short options is possible before the expiration. If the calls are ITM and have little or no time value remaining, the possibility of being assigned on short options increases. In addition, if an ex-dividend date is approaching, an investor might exercise a call option to buy the stock and collect the dividends and the potential for early-assignment increases as well. If assigned, it is too late to close the position, and in a butterfly, the investor would be forced out of the position.

There are two breakevens to consider with any butterfly spread. In a long call fly, the breakevens are: (1) the lower strike plus the debit and (2) the higher strike minus the debit. At the first breakeven, the underlying is trading above the lower leg of the spread but below the other two strikes at expiration. The middle and higher strikes are OTM and expire worthless. Meanwhile, the lower strike has (intrinsic) value that is equal to the debit, and the spread breaks even.

If the price of the underlying is equal to the higher strike minus the debit at expiration, the position breaks even as well. At that point, the lower and middle strikes are ITM. There is a profit on the long call spread portion of the butterfly that can be monetized through exercise and assignment. That leaves the short call spread where the higher wing is expiring worthless, but the other leg is ITM. The loss on the short call is equal to the debit paid for the spread, and the trade breaks even. If this is confusing, don't worry; the following example should help make it clear.

Example

Let's say Facebook is trading for $107.20 in late February, and the investor expects the stock to trend higher in the weeks ahead. A long call butterfly spread seems like an interesting idea to express this view. Looking at the March options that expire in twenty-four days (Figure 15-2), there are many strikes to choose from, and all are actively traded with significant open interest.

One play being considered is a March 106-110-114 call butterfly on Facebook. The spread can be initiated at the time by purchasing one March 106 call for $4.25, selling two March 110 calls at $2.13, and buying one March 114 call for $0.91. The net debit is equal to $4.25 minus $2.13 minus $2.13 plus $0.91, or $0.90 for the spread.

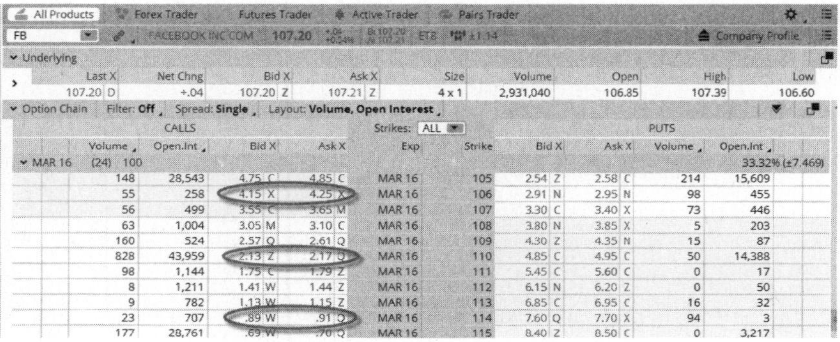
All Products | Forex Trader | Futures Trader | Active Trader | Pairs Trader

FB | FACEBOOK INC COM 107.20 | Company Profile

Underlying

Last X	Net Chng	Bid X	Ask X	Size	Volume	Open	High	Low
107.20 D	+.04	107.20 Z	107.21 Z	4 x 1	2,931,040	106.85	107.39	106.60

Option Chain Filter: Off Spread: Single Layout: Volume, Open Interest

CALLS				Strikes: ALL		PUTS			
Volume	Open.Int	Bid X	Ask X	Exp	Strike	Bid X	Ask X	Volume	Open.Int
MAR 16 (24) 100									33.32% (±7.469)
148	28,543	4.75 C	4.85 C	MAR 16	105	2.54 Z	2.58 C	214	15,609
55	258	4.15 X	4.25 X	MAR 16	106	2.91 N	2.95 N	98	455
56	499	3.55 C	3.65 M	MAR 16	107	3.30 C	3.40 X	73	446
63	1,004	3.05 M	3.10 C	MAR 16	108	3.80 N	3.85 X	5	203
160	524	2.57 Q	2.61 Q	MAR 16	109	4.30 Z	4.35 N	15	87
828	43,959	2.13 Z	2.17 Q	MAR 16	110	4.85 C	4.95 C	50	14,388
98	1,144	1.75 C	1.79 Z	MAR 16	111	5.45 C	5.60 C	0	17
8	1,211	1.41 W	1.44 Z	MAR 16	112	6.15 N	6.20 Z	0	50
9	782	1.13 W	1.15 Z	MAR 16	113	6.85 C	6.95 C	16	32
23	707	.89 W	.91 Q	MAR 16	114	7.60 Q	7.70 X	94	3
177	28,761	.69 W	.70 Q	MAR 16	115	8.40 Z	8.50 C	0	3,217

Figure 15-2 Facebook March Options Chain

For the sake of keeping the math relatively simple, we will say that one butterfly spread is bought for $1 even. (Remember, however, it often makes sense to place the order below the current asking price or midmarket.)

> **How many options to buy?**
>
> The examples here use just one contract, but the same ratios apply when trading more than one contract. For example, if the investor buys three contracts for each of the wings, then six contracts would be sold for the body. The ratio of wings to body on the fly is always 1:2:1.

The risk graph of the Facebook March (Figure 15-3) 106-110-114 call butterfly shows the potential profits and losses. The risk is the $1 debit paid (or $100 on one spread, because the multiplier is one hundred). If the options are left open through the expiration and the stock is trading for less than $106, all legs of the butterfly spread should expire worthless, and the debit paid is lost.

On the other hand, if the stock is trading north of $114 and the long calls are exercised to cover assignment of the short calls, the investor buys (calls) two hundred shares for an average of $110 and sells two hundred shares at the middle $110 strike (due to assignment). The stock transactions are a wash, excluding transaction costs, and the debit paid to enter the spread is lost. Therefore, the risk is

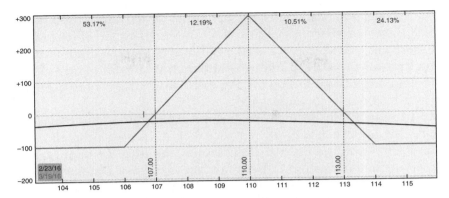

Figure 15-3   Facebook March 106-110-114 Call Butterfly Risk Graph

the debit if shares make a move below $106 or above $114 through the expiration in two weeks.

The first breakeven of the Facebook March 106-110-114 call butterfly is computed the same as a long call or long vertical call spread. It simply equals the lower strike plus the debit, or $107 per share. At that point, the middle and higher strikes are expiring OTM, and the lower strike has $1 of intrinsic value, which is equal to the debit paid for the spread.

The second breakeven equals the higher strike minus the debit. If the stock is trading for $113 at the expiration, the March 106-110 call spread is worth $4. That leaves one short March 110 call and one long March 114 call. The 114 strike call is OTM and has no value. However, the 110 call is $3 ITM if shares are at $113. Because the 110-strike calls were sold, the investor has a $3 loss on those calls. Subtract that amount from the $4 profit on the 106-110 long call spread, and the spread is worth $1 at expiration, which is equal to the debit paid. The position breaks even.

Facebook March 106-110-114 Call Butterfly Breakdown

Strategy: Buy one March 106 call, sell two March 110 calls, buy one March 114 call

Direction: Bullish

Debit or Credit: $100 debit

Risk: $100

Breakeven: $107 and $113 per share

Potential Profits: $300

Now the good part: The potential profit of the March 106-110-114 call butterfly on Facebook for $1 is $3 and happens if the price of the underlying is at the middle strike of the spread at expiration. If the stock is trading for $110 at the expiration, the 110 strike and 114 calls have no intrinsic value, and the 106 calls are worth $4. Therefore, the profit is $4 minus the debit paid.

You can also exit the position prior to expiration and that is typically my preference. If, for instance, the stock suddenly fell below the $106 lower strike price after a week, the investor might opt to sell-to-close the position rather than run the risk of the stock falling further and losing the debit if the options expire OTM. If the spread is sold at $0.50, for example, the loss is $50, because the debit paid was $1 and the multiplier on a single stock option is one hundred.

Similarly, if the stock is trading for $110 or $114 after a week, the investor might choose to close the position as well. The gain or loss will depend on whether the spread is sold at a price (credit) greater than the premium paid (debit) to enter the position.

Probability of expiring ITM analysis helps to see the potential ranges for the stock through the expiration. Figure 15-4 shows that the probability of the stock holding between $107 (breakeven) and $113 (breakeven) through the expiration in twenty-four days is relatively low at less than 25 percent. This is not unusual for a butterfly spread where the middle strikes (or body) are OTM.

In other words, selling OTM strikes for the body creates a strategy with a directional bias. In this case, the success depends

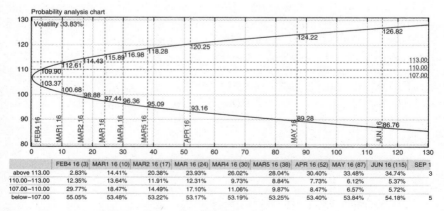

	FEB4 16 (3)	MAR1 16 (10)	MAR2 16 (17)	MAR 16 (24)	MAR4 16 (30)	MAR5 16 (38)	APR 16 (52)	MAY 16 (87)	JUN 16 (115)	SEP 1
above 113.00	2.83%	14.41%	20.38%	23.93%	26.02%	28.04%	30.40%	33.48%	34.74%	3
110.00–113.00	12.35%	13.64%	11.91%	12.31%	9.73%	8.84%	7.73%	6.12%	5.37%	
107.00–110.00	29.77%	18.47%	14.49%	17.10%	11.06%	9.87%	8.47%	6.57%	5.72%	
below–107.00	55.05%	53.48%	53.22%	53.17%	53.19%	53.25%	53.40%	53.84%	54.18%	5

Figure 15-4   Probability of Expiring ITM Analysis

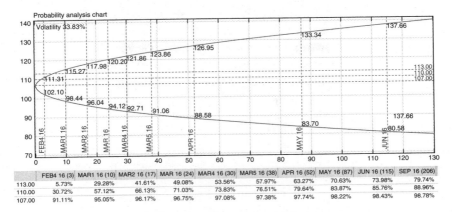

Figure 15-5   Facebook Probability of Touching Analysis

on the underlying moving higher and reaching $110. The trade-off is the large potential gains if the shares move as anticipated. Recall that the investor is paying $1 for the potential to make $3, or a 200 percent gain in just twenty-four days. There, again, is the leverage.

Figure 15-5 shows the stock's probability of touching various prices over several expirations. Notice that the probability of touching the $110 sweet spot of the spread through the March expiration in twenty-four days is relatively high, at more than 70 percent. Because the 110 is the price target for the spread, some strategists might choose to exit the butterfly as one spread once this price is reached, even if it is well before the expiration.

A long butterfly can be created with puts as well. For instance, if an investor is expecting the price of Apple shares to fall to $95 from $100 through the February expiration, he might sell two February 95 puts, buy one February 100 put, and buy one February 90 put. The payoff is equal to the difference between strikes minus the debit, and the risk is the debit paid. When the underlying has American-style options, the advantage of using puts rather than calls is there isn't the same type of early-assignment risk due to dividends if the short options are ITM on the ex-dividend date. But American-style short options can still be assigned at any time prior to expiration, regardless of the ITM amount. (Take a look at Appendix B for additional suggestions for put butterfly spreads.)

While the examples so far are butterfly spreads with a directional bias, the strategy is sometimes used if an investor expects the stock to hold in a range through the expiration as well. In the Facebook example, with shares trading near $107, a March 105-107-109 call (or put) fly could be created to express the view that shares will hold around $107. The cost of the spread at the time was $0.35 with the potential to make $1.65 (or the difference between the highest and middle strike minus $0.35 debit). The risk-ratio in that case is nearly 5:1 if shares simply hold at current levels.

While the percentage gains can be substantial, be careful with the leverage when opening butterfly (or condor) spreads. The debits might seem quite small relative to the potential profits, but the probabilities of reaching the breakevens or the sweet spots of the position can be low as well. Set reasonable targets and use the middle strike of the spread as a guide for entering and exiting the position. In many cases, it makes sense to close the position before the expiration.

Lastly, don't overlook the impact of volatility on the butterfly spread. In a typical spread, the higher the implied volatility (IV) of the options, the lower the butterfly price (because the body of the fly will be richer) and vice versa. Therefore, all else being equal, the lower the IV, the more the spread will cost. Higher IV in the options will typically result in a smaller net debit. Therefore, once the position is entered, it will benefit from a decrease in volatility, as the body loses value at a faster rate compared to the wings.

Vega Revisited

While falling volatility can work in the favor of the long butterfly, this can change if the underlying is approaching the high or lower strikes of the spread. Then, the investor might want the wings (the ones you own) to see an increase in volatility, especially as expiration approaches, because higher IV will affect the near-the-money strikes more than the body or middle strikes. If you are not sure how volatility will affect the position, look at the vega of the options, which is covered in more detail in Appendix A.

Iron Butterfly Spread

This is a much more advanced strategy, but one you should be aware of, which can be used to take advantage of high volatility. The call butterfly spread can be thought of as a long call spread and a short call spread. Similarly, a put butterfly spread is a short put spread and a long put spread. The iron butterfly is a combination of a short call spread and a short put spread. All of the options are within the same expiration month.

To create the iron butterfly, the investor is selling puts and calls at the same strike and the same expiration (a position that is also known as a short straddle). The purchase of a lower strike put and a higher strike call (or a long strangle) serves to hedge the short options. The short options are the body of the fly, and the two long options are the wings. The overall position is designed to be a credit transaction.

Ideally, the underlying trades at or very near the middle strike (or the body of the fly) through the expiration. If the middle strike options are at the money (ATM) at expiration, all of the options expire worthless, and the maximum profit potential is attained, which is equal to the credit minus any transaction costs. Therefore, the middle strike of the spread is the target price for the underlying through the expiration.

As the profit-loss line in Figure 15-6 shows, the risk to the iron butterfly is from a substantial move higher or lower in the underlying. In one worst-case scenario, the calls are in the money, and the position is exited through assignment/exercise at expiration. At that point, the loss is equal to the spread (higher strike minus middle strike) minus the credit received. The opposite is true if the price of the underlying falls and the put spread is ITM. The loss is also equal to the difference between the two strikes minus the credit.

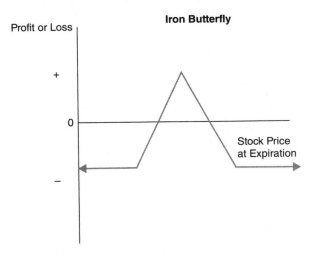

Figure 15-6   Apple Iron Butterfly

The first breakeven of the iron butterfly is equal to the middle strike plus the credit. If, at expiration, the underlying is trading at that level, the puts and the higher strike call expire worthless. Meanwhile, the loss on the remaining (short) call is equal to the credit received for the iron butterfly spread. For the same reasons, the second breakeven is equal to the middle strike minus the initial credit.

Iron Call Butterfly Spread Cheat Sheet

Strategy: Buy put, sell higher strike put, sell call at same strike as higher strike put, buy higher strike call

Direction: Depends on strike price selection

Debit or Credit: Credit

Risk: High strike – Middle strike – Credit

Breakeven: (1) Middle strike + Credit; (2) Middle strike – Credit

Potential Profits: Credit

The iron fly is designed to benefit from time decay, especially when the middle strikes are ATM and the middle strike of the fly is near the underlying price. After all, the investor wants all of the options to expire worthless and therefore wants the position to lose value over time. The spread can also be closed at any time through the expiration (unless assigned first) with a closing purchase. (However, note again that if the underlying has made a substantial move and the options are deep OTM, there is no guarantee that there will be a market to close the position.) If the debit paid to cover the spread is less than the credit received, the result is a profit on the position. However, if the debit is more the credit, then the result is a loss plus transaction costs.

Example

An investor notices that shares of Goldman Sachs (GS) have been trading around the $150 level for several days and expects the trend to continue in the days ahead. Looking at the options chain of short-term puts and calls that expire in two days (Figure 15-7), the February 145-150-155 iron butterfly seems like a reasonable strategy in anticipation of quiet trading in the short term.

In this example, the investor can sell the February 150 puts and calls (or the straddle) for a combined $4.30. Meanwhile, the February 145 puts and 155 calls (strangle) can be bought for $1.25. At those

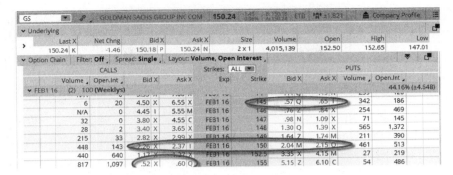

Figure 15-7   Goldman Sachs February Options Chain

prices, the spread fetches a $3.05 credit. The decision is made to sell the February 145-150-155 iron fly of Goldman Sachs at $3 even, or $300 for one spread when one factors in the multiplier.

Goldman Sachs Iron Butterfly Breakdown

Strategy: Buy February 145 put, sell February 150 put, sell February 150 call, buy February 155 call

Direction: Neutral

Debit or Credit: $300 credit

Risk: $200

Breakeven: $147 and $153

Potential Profits: $300

The profit/loss line in Figure 15-8 is the shape of the butterfly spread. The maximum profit potential is the $3 credit and happens if shares are trading at $150 at the expiration. The breakevens equal $150 plus or minus $3, or $147 and $153. The potential loss is equal to the difference between strikes minus the credit. In this case, the risk is $2, or $200 on one spread, if the stock moves substantially higher or lower and the position is covered. The spread can likely be closed at any time prior to the expiration, and as we get close (four to ten days from expiration), probably should be to avoid assignment/exercise risk.

Probability of expiring ITM analysis (Figure 15-9) shows that there is a greater than 50 percent probability that the stock will be between the two breakevens at the expiration (26.3 percent that it will be between $150 and $153 and 25.3 percent that it falls between

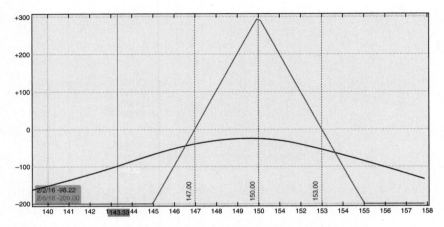

Figure 15-8   Goldman Sachs February 145-150-155 Iron Butterfly

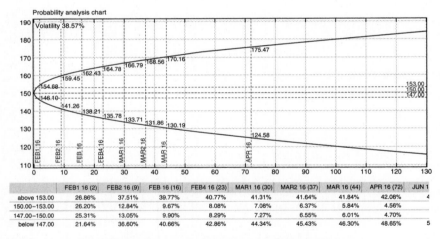

Figure 15-9   Goldman Sachs Probability Expiring ITM Analysis

$147 and $150). The probabilities of staying in that range diminish rapidly as time passes. For example, the probability of the stock being between $147 and $153 at the last expiration in March is less than 12 percent. This is another way of stating the obvious—in other words, the probabilities of staying within the breakevens of the fly are greater in the short term rather than the long term.

Probability of touching analysis (Figure 15-10) also shows that the probabilities of the stock touching the upper and lower breakevens

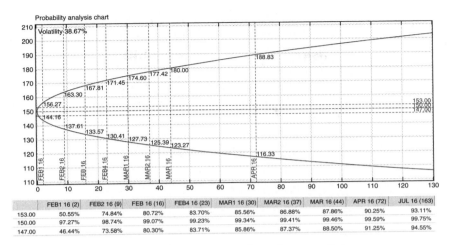

Figure 15-10   Goldman Sachs Probability of Touching Analysis

are much less than the probability of touching \$150, which is the sweet spot of the spread. Those probabilities change considerably as time passes as well. By April, there is a greater than 90 percent probability of the stock touching \$147 and \$153.

Because the iron butterfly is intended to target a certain price around the current price of the underlying, shorter-term time frames are typically preferable over longer-term ones. However, the amount of premium collected on the spread might be less when dealing with shorter-term options as well. There is another trade-off. My preference is on shorter-term time frames of three weeks or less for this play. That's when the options will experience the fastest rate of time decay.

Summary

Butterfly spreads are advanced strategies best suited for seasoned options traders. The positions can be viewed as combinations of other strategies covered in this book. The iron butterfly, for instance, is a credit strategy that combines a short call spread and a short put spread. It makes sense when the investor expects the underlying to move toward the middle strikes of the spread.

Meanwhile, long butterflies can be created with either puts or calls. A call fly for example, is simply a long call spread and a short call spread. The strategies are debit transaction with limited risks and rewards. The debit is at risk if the underlying moves outside of the higher and lower strikes (the wings). The best-case scenario is that the underlying is trading at the middle strike (the body of the fly) at the expiration. The further the middle strike is from the current price of the underlying, the more aggressive the directional bias.

Practice these strategies using virtual trading platforms before implementing them (and risking real money) so you can better understand how to enter the trades and manage them. Set a price target for the underlying and sell the body that corresponds with that target. Consider entering the spread as one transaction and exiting as one spread once the price target is reached, even if that happens to be before the expiration.

CHAPTER

16

Condor Spreads

If the butterfly spread from Chapter 15 made sense to you, the strategies in this chapter will, build upon those. Indeed, condor spreads are similar to butterflies with one important difference. In a typical fly, the investor is purchasing an option, selling two options at a different strike, and buying yet another option at a third strike, all within the same expiration term. The middle two options are the body of the butterfly, and the other two strikes are the wings.

By contrast, the condor is a four-legged options spread that involves the purchase of an option, the sale of another option at a different strike, the sale of a third option at a further strike, and finally, the purchase of another option at yet a different strike, all in the same expiration month. The middle two strikes are the body of the condor. The highest and lowest strikes are the wings.

Like the butterfly, the condor is an advanced play that can be considered a combination of vertical spreads covered in Chapters 12 and 13. For instance, a long call condor is a long call spread along with a short call spread at a higher strike. The last strategy in this text, the iron condor, is the combination of a short put spread and a short call spread. If this seems murky, don't fret. A couple of examples follow to illustrate.

Because four option legs are employed to implement these strategies, they can entail significant transaction costs, including multiple commissions, which will impact any potential returns. Of course, the actual amount charged will vary by brokerage firm.

Condor Spread

The long call condor is a four-legged spread that is designed for use in anticipation of a horizontal or vertical move in the underlying. The investor pays a debit to enter the position because he is buying a long call spread and simultaneously selling a short call spread at a higher strike. For example, a condor can be created by purchasing a 50-strike call, selling a 55-strike call, selling a 60-strike call, and buying a 65-strike call, all within the same expiration month. The outer 50s and 65s are the wings. The middle 50 and 55 strikes are the body.

Figure 16-1 shows the simple risk graph of a condor spread. The best-case scenario is that the price of the underlying is between the two middle strikes (or the body) of the spread at the expiration. At that point, the long call spread has reached its maximum profit potential, and the short call spread expires worthless. Therefore, the best potential profit is equal to the difference between two strikes (the long call spread) minus debit paid.

The potential risk of the long call condor strategy is the debit paid and that debit can be lost if the price of the underlying is above or below the wings of the spread at expiration. On the one hand, if the underlying is below the lower strike and the position is left open through the expiration, the options all expire out-of-the-money (OTM). They have no remaining value, and the entire debit paid is lost.

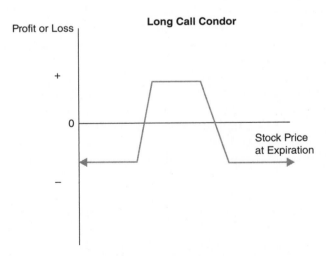

Figure 16-1   Long Condor Spread Profit-Loss Line

Long Call Condor Spread Cheat Sheet

Strategy: Buy call, sell higher strike call, sell even higher strike call, buy even higher strike call

Direction: Depends on strike price selection

Debit or Credit: Debit

Risk: Debit

Breakeven: (1) Low strike + Debit; (2) High strike – Debit

Potential Profits: Middle strike – Low strike – Debit

On the other hand, if the price of the underlying is above the higher strike of the spread and the position is open at expiration, all the options are in-the-money (ITM). As we saw with the long call butterfly, the gains from the long call spread are offset by losses in the short spread. If the position is closed through exercise and assignment, it's a wash, and the debit paid to enter the spread is lost.

The position can be closed prior to the expiration as well, and the gain or loss will depend on whether the credit received from selling the spread is greater or less than the initial debit. (As noted in previous chapters, there is no guarantee that the position can be closed if the underlying makes a dramatic move, because there might not be a bid for deep OTM options.)

The two breakevens of the long call condor are computed in the same fashion as the butterfly. The trade breaks even at expiration if the underlying price is equal to the lower strike plus the debit. At that point, the long calls (with the lower strike) have intrinsic value that is equal to the debit paid. The second breakeven is the higher strike minus the debit. If the underlying is at that price at expiration, the long call spread has attained its full potential. The highest strike call is expiring worthless, but the losses on the remaining (ITM) short call plus the debit offset any gains from the long call spread. The trade breaks even.

Example

Let's say Facebook (FB) is trading near $106 per share in late February, and an investor expects the stock to make a climb to the $106 or $108 range through the next few weeks. A long call condor spread is being considered as a relatively inexpensive way to play the move, and looking at the March options chains (Figure 16-2),

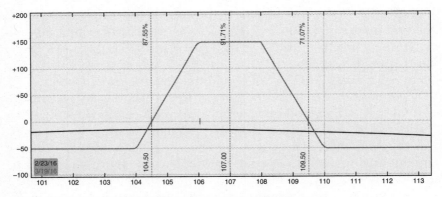

Figure 16-2   Facebook March Options Chain

Figure 16-3   Facebook March 104-106-108-110 Call Condor

the 104-106-108-110 call condor is trading for $0.47, or $4.80 minus $3.55 minus $2.58 plus $1.80. For this example, let's say that one spread is bought for $0.50 (or $50 because the multiplier for an equity option is one hundred).

The profit/loss line for the March 104-106-108-110 call condor appears in Figure 16-3. The risk is the $0.50 debit paid and happens if the position is open at the expiration and the underlying is above or below the wings of the spread. If, for instance, it falls below the lower strike through the expiration and the position is left open, all of the options expire, and the debit paid is lost.

On the other hand, if all of the legs are ITM and the position is closed through exercise and assignment, the debit is also lost because the resulting purchase and sale of stock result in no gains or losses. In other words, the long call spread loses the same amount as the short call spread if all the contracts are ITM at the expiration.

Excluding transaction costs, the breakevens of the Facebook March 104-106-108-110 call condor for $0.50 are equal to $104.50 and $109.50. At the lower breakeven, the 104-strike call is the only contract that is ITM. It has $0.50 of intrinsic value, which equals the debit paid. The trade breaks even.

If shares are trading for $109.50, the 104-106 call spread is ITM and worth $2. The 110 calls are expiring worthless. The short 108 call is $1.50 ITM. Therefore, the profit is $2 on the 104-106 call spread minus the $1.50 of intrinsic value in the 108 calls. The net gain is $0.50 on the spread, which equals the debit paid to open the position. It breaks even.

Facebook March 104-106-108-110 Call Condor Breakdown
Strategy: Buy March 104 call, sell March 106 call, sell March 108 call, buy March 110 call

Direction: Neutral

Debit or Credit: Debit

Risk: $50 Debit

Breakeven: $104.50 and $109.50

Potential Profits: $150

Meanwhile, the best potential profits from the spread happen if shares settle between $106 and $108 at the expiration. At that point, the 104-106 call spread that was bought is worth $2, and the 108-110 call spread, which is short, expires worthless. The profit is $2 minus the $0.50 debit, or $150 on one spread.

Probability of expiring ITM analysis in Figure 16-4 shows that the likelihood of the stock closing between the $104.50 and $109.50 breakevens through the first expiration is relatively high at 52.8 percent and steadily decreases over later expiration terms. This is basic statistics because there is a greater likelihood that the stock will move outside of a trading range over time.

However, probability of touching (Figure 16-5) shows that there is a strong likelihood of touching $107 at the middle of the condor through the March expiration. The probability is more than 91 percent. Like with the butterfly spread in the previous chapter, the spread can be covered prior to the expiration once the sweet spot of the condor has been touched.

The long call condor is a strategy that is typically used when the investor wants to target a range of strike prices for the underlying in

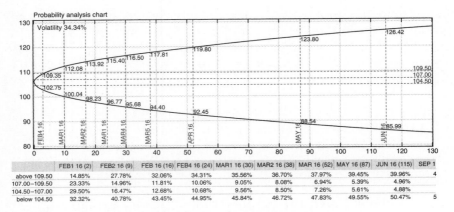

Figure 16-4   Facebook Probability Expiring ITM Analysis

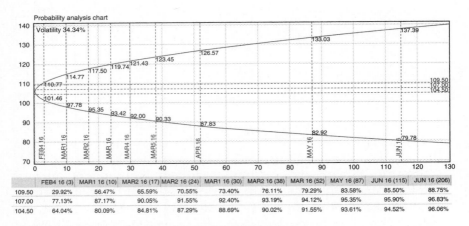

Figure 16-5   Facebook Probability of Touching Analysis

the short term. It is not as well-suited for volatile markets where the underlying is moving higher and lower in dramatic fashion. While time is working in favor of the spread, vertical movements can result in losses if the underlying moves too far in one direction or the other.

The probabilities of moving outside of the higher or lower strikes (wings) will increase as time passes. That's why I focus on options that expire in a few weeks or less when initiating this play. The same is true of long put condor spreads, which have the same payoff charts as when using calls. Appendix B has further details on put condors. For now, our attention turns to the iron condor.

Iron Condor Spread

If you understand the iron butterfly described earlier, and particularly how vertical spreads work, the next and final strategy of this book will be straightforward. The difference between the iron butterfly and the iron condor is that the condor is a higher probability trade which, similar to short vertical spreads, takes advantage of time decay. To initiate the play, the investor buys one put, sells a higher strike put, sells an even higher strike call, and buys an even higher strike call. A good starting point is to have all of the strikes equidistant from the stock, and use options that are within the same expiration cycle. This so-called iron condor is simply a combination of a short put spread and a short call spread. Therefore, it is a credit strategy.

> **Iron Call Condor Spread Cheat Sheet**
>
> **Strategy:** Buy put, sell higher strike put, sell even higher strike call, buy even higher strike call
>
> **Direction:** Depends on strike price selection
>
> **Debit or Credit:** Credit
>
> **Risk:** High strike – Middle strike – Credit
>
> **Breakeven:** (1) Middle strike put – Credit; (2) Low strike call – Credit
>
> **Potential Profits:** Credit

Figure 16-6 shows the basic profit and loss line for an iron condor. The best profits from the spread happen if the underlying is between the two middle strikes at expiration. At that point, the options expire worthless, and the profit is equal to the credit minus transaction costs.

Just as with the iron fly, the risks with the iron condor are from a significant move higher or lower. Because the investor is short put and short call spreads, if the underlying moves above or below the highest and lowest strikes through the expiration, one of the spreads will be ITM. The result is a loss equal to the difference between the two strikes minus the credit.

The breakevens of the iron condor equal the strike price of the short put minus the credit and the strike price of the short call plus the credit. At that point, the intrinsic value on one of the short options (either the put or the call) is equal to the credit received to open the spread, and the position breaks even. If an iron condor is

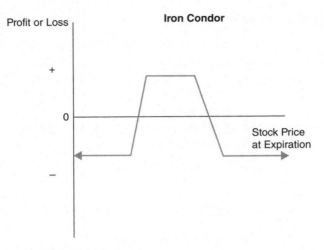

Figure 16-6   Iron Condor Risk Graph

closed before the expiration, the profit or loss will depend on the prices at the time of exit. If the debit paid to close the position is more than the credit received, the result is a loss. If the debit is less than the initial credit, the spread has generated a profit.

Fly or Condor

The payoff charts for butterflies and condors are similar, but the spreads are different, and one is not necessarily better than the other. The butterfly probably makes more sense when the investor wants to target a very specific price for the underlying at expiration. The condor can be used to target a range of prices between the two middle strikes. Another factor to consider is transaction costs, as condors (and iron butterflies) have four legs, and long butterflies have only three. Depending on the broker, one strategy might have lower commissions than the other. Lastly, while the put and call butterflies and condors are typically lower probability trades with larger payoffs, the iron butterflies and condors are higher probability with lower payoff potential.

Example

An investor expects shares of Coach (COH) to trade in a range in the coming months and is seeking to bag some profits based on those

COH	▼	🔗	COACH INC COM	36.95	+.77 +2.13%	B: 36.83 A: 36.95	ETB				

✓ Underlying

	Last X	Net Chng	Bid X	Ask X	Size	Volume	Open	High	Low
>	36.95 N	+.77	36.83 P	36.95 P	1 x 3	4,919,152	36.23	38.40	36.18

✓ Option Chain   Filter: **Off**,   Spread: **Single**,   Layout: **Theo Price**,   Theo Price: **02/23/2016** Stock: **+0.00$** Vol: **+0.00%** ,

	CALLS					Strikes: ALL ▼		PUTS		

	Theo Price ,	Bid X	Ask X	Exp	Strike	Bid X	Ask X	Theo Price ,
✓ APR 16 (52) 100								31.95% (±3.592)
	N/A	5.10 A	6.50 M	APR 16	31	.25 T	.35 C	.30
	N/A	4.30 A	5.40 C	APR 16	32	.35 X	.45 X	.40
	3.95	3.40 C	4.50 X	APR 16	33	.50 A	.60 X	.55
	3.50	3.30 M	3.70 X	APR 16	34	.70 M	.80 X	.75
	2.68	2.60 C	2.75 C	APR 16	35	.95 C	1.10 C	1.03
	2.05	2.00 A	2.10 A	APR 16	36	1.35 T	1.45 C	1.40
	1.50	1.45 C	1.55 C	APR 16	37	1.80 T	1.90 X	1.85
	1.05	1.00 C	1.10 C	APR 16	38	2.35 T	2.45 C	2.40
	.70	.65 C	.75 C	APR 16	39	3.00 M	3.10 M	3.05
	.45	.40 X	.50 X	APR 16	40	3.70 X	3.90 M	3.80
	.25	.20 X	.30 M	APR 16	41	4.30 C	4.80 C	4.55
	.15	.10 C	.20 C	APR 16	42	5.20 M	5.70 M	5.45

Figure 16-7   Coach Options Chain

expectations using an iron condor. Shares of the fashion products company are trading for $36.95, and Figure 16-7 shows the numerous strikes listed on the stock in the April monthly options that expire in fifty-two days.

One idea is to initiate an iron condor by selling the April 32-34 put spread and selling the April 40-42 call spread. The latest prices indicate that, using midmarket prices, the put spread is trading at $0.35 and the call spread at $0.30. The investor sells one Coach April 32-34-40-42 iron condor at $0.65. That equals a net credit of $65 on one condor, because the multiplier for a standard equity option is one hundred.

The potential profit from the COH April 32-34-40-42 iron condor is limited to the $0.65 credit, or $65 on one spread. As we can see from Figure 16-8, the best profits happen if shares are trading between $34 and $40 (or the body of the condor). At that point, all of the options expire worthless, and there is nothing left to do except to move on to another trade.

Because the strikes of the call spreads and the put spreads are two points apart, the risk (excluding any potential risk due to early assignment mentioned earlier) to one spread is $1.35, because the maximum loss is the difference between the two strikes minus the credit. The max loss can be suffered if either the put spread or the call spread is ITM at expiration, but obviously not both.

For instance, if Coach is trading above $42 at expiration, the short call spread is ITM and is worth $2. On the other hand, the short put spread has widened to $2 if shares fall below $32. Because $0.65 was collected, the risk is $1.35 (or $135). Figure 16-8 shows it graphically:

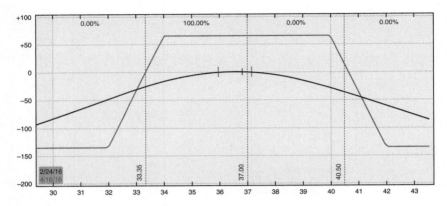

Figure 16-8   COH April 32-34-40-42 Iron Condor

The investor is collecting $65 and risking $135. Table 16-4 shows the same data.

Coach April 32-34-40-42 iron condor breakdown

Strategy: Sell April 34 puts, buy April 32 puts, sell April 40 calls, buy April 42 calls

Direction: Neutral

Debit or Credit: $65 credit

Risk: $135

Breakeven: $33.35 and $40.65

Potential Profits: $65

The breakevens of the COH April 32-34-40-42 iron condor at $0.65 each are equal to $33.35 and $40.65. This is the same math as the breakevens for short vertical spreads covered in Chapter 13. If the stock is at $33.35 at expiration, the short 34-strike puts are $0.65 ITM (all other options expire worthless), and that is equal to the initial credit. On the other hand, the short 40 calls are $0.65 ITM if the stock is trading for $40.65 at the expiration. Therefore, the position breaks even at that level as well.

Short Vertical Spread Probabilities Revisited

Recall from Chapter 13 that a useful tool for computing the probability of a short spread making at least a penny profit is to divide the real risk of the spread by the total risk. For instance, in the Coach spread, the strikes are two points apart (short call and short put spreads, that is), and the investor is collecting $0.65. The spread is two points wide; therefore, the total risk is $2. The real risk is the total risk minus the credit, or $1.35. Therefore, the probability of making money on the spread is 1.35/2, or a 65 percent probability of making money.

Probability of expiring ITM analysis in Figure 16-9 shows that there is 58.7 percent probability of the stock staying within the breakevens of the iron condor through the expiration in fifty-two days (27 percent chance that it will be between $37 and $40.65 and 31.7 percent between $33.35 and $37). Notice that the probabilities of a move outside the breakevens increase in later expiration terms.

Lastly, the probability of touching in Figure 16-10 shows that there is a high probability of the stock touching the $37 and being within the sweet spot of the iron condor in the next fifty-two days, and that's because the stock is currently near that level. The probability of touching the breakevens steadily increases over time, and therefore, at the risk of stating the obvious, the longer the stock stays in a range within the body of the condor, the better the probabilities of success.

Iron condors are a lot like iron butterflies, and the selection of the right expiration month is important. That's because the probabilities of a move outside of the wings of the spread steadily increase

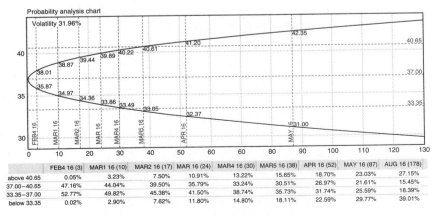

	FEB4 16 (3)	MAR1 16 (10)	MAR2 16 (17)	MAR 16 (24)	MAR4 16 (30)	MAR5 16 (38)	APR 16 (52)	MAY 16 (87)	AUG 16 (178)
above 40.65	0.05%	3.23%	7.50%	10.91%	13.22%	15.65%	18.70%	23.03%	27.15%
37.00–40.65	47.16%	44.04%	39.50%	35.79%	33.24%	30.51%	26.97%	21.61%	15.45%
33.35–37.00	52.77%	49.82%	45.38%	41.50%	38.74%	35.73%	31.74%	25.59%	18.39%
below 33.35	0.02%	2.90%	7.62%	11.80%	14.80%	18.11%	22.59%	29.77%	39.01%

Figure 16-9   Coach Probability of Expiring ITM Analysis

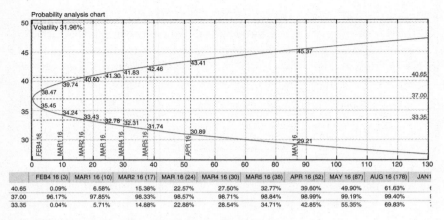

	FEB4 16 (3)	MAR1 16 (10)	MAR2 16 (17)	MAR 16 (24)	MAR4 16 (30)	MAR5 16 (38)	APR 16 (52)	MAY 16 (87)	AUG 16 (178)	JAN1
40.65	0.09%	6.58%	15.38%	22.57%	27.50%	32.77%	39.60%	49.90%	61.63%	
37.00	96.17%	97.85%	98.33%	98.57%	98.71%	98.84%	98.99%	99.19%	99.40%	
33.35	0.04%	5.71%	14.88%	22.88%	28.54%	34.71%	42.85%	55.35%	69.83%	

Figure 16-10   Coach Probability of Touching Analysis

over longer time frames. Therefore, the risks must be balanced with the premium paid (or collected for iron flies and condors) to open the position. Strike price selection is a key element to consider as well, because, ultimately, we want the underlying staying in (or moving to) the body of the spread through the expiration. It's important to note that I used an example with fairly equidistant strikes to start, but you can skew this bearish or bullish if you like.

Summary

Butterfly and condors spreads are the most complex strategies covered in this book, but the reader should now understand that they are merely combinations of the vertical spreads covered in Chapters 12 and 13. The iron butterfly, for instance, is a credit strategy that combines a short call spread and a short put spread. It makes sense when the investor expects the underlying to move toward the middle strikes of the spread. The same is true of iron condors.

Long butterflies or condors can be created with either puts or calls. A call fly, for example, is simply a long call spread and a short call spread. The strategies are debit transactions with limited risks and rewards. The debit is at risk if the underlying moves outside of the higher and lower strikes (or the wings). The best-case scenario is that the underlying is trading at the middle strike (or the body) of the fly at the expiration. The further the middle strike is from the current price of the underlying, the more aggressive the trade.

As I mentioned earlier, these are complex strategies, so entering and exiting as one spread, particularly when new to trading is a good idea. You may want to also consider practicing in a virtual trading account to get used to the logistics of the trade before using real money.

In addition, using European-style index options eliminates the risk of being assigned on the short legs of the spread, so don't overlook the S&P 500 Index for opportunities to implement the strategy. Lastly, as noted in the previous chapter, condor and butterfly spreads are advanced options plays that are best suited for sophisticated investors with previous options trading experience. Practice them using virtual trading platforms before implementing them (and risking real money), so you can better understand how to enter and manage the trades.

17

The Close

You have learned a lot about options! You know the basics of puts and calls; what variables affect options prices; and how different strategies can be used to express bullish, bearish, and even neutral outlooks relative to underlying securities.

Some strategies, such as protective puts and covered calls, are extensions of the buy-and-hold investing that you were probably already familiar with. Advanced strategies, such as butterflies and calendar spreads, are more complex and best suited for more sophisticated investors with previous options trading experience.

Regardless of the experience level, the strategies used, or whether an investor is bullish or bearish, one concept is relevant to all options traders: risk management. After all, it's easy to be enticed by the leverage offered with certain options plays. The potential for large gains on relatively small amounts of capital is a double-edged sword, however. The potential for large losses is high as well.

This final chapter explores some of the basics of risk management, such as position sizes and not putting all your eggs in one basket. We also consider order entry techniques and position adjustments. The book concludes with a brief discussion about social media, including what information is worthwhile and what is likely to be fleeting.

Risk Management

Leverage—You have heard the term and have seen examples many times throughout this book. That's because options give you leverage to control relatively large amounts of the underlying security with relatively small amounts of capital. The options represent the right to buy or sell an underlying, and that gives you exposure to price movements of the underlying. As an example, Facebook (FB) has been an actively traded name in 2016 and has been trading at around $100 per share. Buying one hundred shares outright is a $10,000 investment.

Buying one long call (Chapter 6) on Facebook represents the right to buy one hundred shares. If one contract is trading for $5, the investor is controlling $10,000 worth of stock for only $500 (the multiplier for one single stock option is one hundred). The ability to control a substantial amount of an underlying security with relatively small amounts of money increases the potential for large percentage profits but also for big percentage losses.

It's important not to overdo it with this leverage. I use this analogy: Leverage is like fire. When used properly, it can have enormous positive benefits. Of course, we all know what can happen when fire gets out of control.

The first tip is to trade options positions that are similar to your stock trades. If, on average, the investor is buying five hundred shares at a time on stocks that trade for between $20 and $30, the equivalent is to buy or sell five contracts on these stocks, because five contracts control five hundred shares. The rule of thumb applies to simple strategies like cash-secured puts (Chapter 11) or more advanced ones like butterflies (Chapter 15).

Consider the notional value of the position as well. For instance, if a stock is trading for $5 per share, the notional value of one call with a $5 strike is $500 (or 100 × the 5-strike price). However, if an index is trading at 5,000, one 5,000-strike call has a notional value of $500,000. Because options are agreements to buy or sell the underlying, understanding the notional value of the trade can help the investor to decide if she is really comfortable buying or selling the underlying if exercise or assignment come into play.

Most of us have probably heard the saying, "Don't put all your eggs in one basket." That's certainly true in investing. Some seasoned traders focus on percentage amounts for each position. For instance, one position shouldn't equal more than 5 percent of his portfolio. Or maybe an investor might not allocate more than 10 percent of the portfolio to aggressive trading strategies like long call spreads (Chapter 12) and condors (Chapter 16).

Diversification should not be overlooked. A portfolio can be diversified by owning securities in different market sectors, such as energy, sector, and financials. Investing in different asset classes—such as commodities, fixed income (bonds), and stocks—is also a way to diversify a portfolio. The last way to do so is to invest in different types of option positions diversifying over volatility levels. As noted in Chapter 1, decisions about strategic investments should be considered as part of an investor's financial goals and trading plan. If you are not sure what opportunities exist outside of stocks and options, I strongly urge you to consult with an experienced financial adviser or use the tools in your trading platform to educate yourself.

I hope that this book has helped you realize another area of diversification, and in my opinion the most overlooked—using a combination of different strategies. I like to think of diversifying my approach to the market, even if it is only in a few products. That way, I am trading things I know but with a different approach to them.

Options Orders

The ability for individual investors to open complex options strategies online is a relatively new development. When I started my career, very few individuals were using options strategies beyond covered calls. Options quotes were not as readily available, transaction costs were high, and trade executions were slow. The infrastructure was not yet in place to allow self-directed investors to easily participate in the options market.

All that has changed. Sophisticated trading platforms now available to retail investors have helped level the playing field. Investors now have access to real-time price quotes and advanced order-entry tools, as well as the ability to analyze trades. This applies to combination stock and options plays like protective puts or covered calls in addition to more advanced spreads such as condors (Chapter 16) and calendars (Chapter 14).

For example, Figure 17-1 shows a snapshot of an order to buy a butterfly spread (Chapter 15) on Facebook with the stock trading near $100. The order includes one price for the entire spread. In this case, the order is for five butterfly spreads (ten contracts for the body) for a limit order of a $1 debit per spread. Total cash outlay in this example would be $500 (5 contracts × $1 debit × 100 multiplier, plus transaction costs).

Trading instruments that see a significant amount of daily trading volume and placing the order between bid-ask spread is also preferred. Recall from Chapter 4 that *slippage* refers to the costs of trading that an investor incurs due to the difference between bid prices

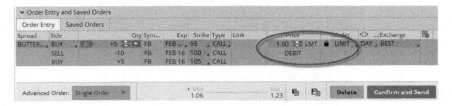

Figure 17-1   Example of an Advanced Order Entry Screen

and ask prices. We can minimize the impact of slippage by focusing on options that have active markets because the bid-ask spreads are typically smaller. Placing limit orders between the bid and asking prices can reduce the impact of slippage as well.

Computing Bids and Asks on Spreads

The quote for an option contract is easy to find, and computing the bid-ask prices for a spread is straightforward as well. For example, if Facebook January 100 calls are trading for $4.90 bid and $5 ask and the January 110 calls are $1 bid and $1.10 ask, the ask price for the long January 100-110 call spread is computed using the asking price for the January 100 calls and the bid price for the January 110s, because the investor is buying the 100s and selling the 110s. Therefore, the market price to buy is $4, or $5 ask on the 100s minus $1 bid for the 110s. The opposite is true if selling the spread, because the January 100s are sold and the January 110s are bought. The bid-ask for the Jan 100-110 call spread is therefore $3.80 to $4, in which case, whether buying or selling, I would try to do so at $3.90.

Returning to the previous example, the market on the February 95-100-105 call butterfly on Facebook at the time was $0.90 to $1.23. That is, the bid was $0.90 (not shown in Figure 17-1), and the asking price was $1.23. At the bottom of Figure 17-1, we can see that the natural market (or asking price) for the spread was $1.23, which is the price an investor might be expected to pay if the order is sent as a market order (discussed in Chapter 4). Midmarket (or simply mid) in Figure 17-1 is $1.06. That means that midway between the bid-ask (or the average) is $1.06. In this example, the limit price of $1 is not only below the asking price but below midmarket as well.

When placing limit orders to buy below the current market (or sell orders above the current market), it might take some time for the order to be executed (or to fill) at that price. It might not be executed at all. In the Facebook example, the stock would probably need to move lower for the butterfly spread to trade for $1 even, because the current price to buy the spread is $1.23 and midmarket is $1.06, so I prefer midmarket for my orders.

There is no assurance that a limit order will be executed, however. Using a market order increases the possibility of rapid execution, but the investor has no control over the price that is paid. By trading smaller, more manageable positions, it decreases the needed urgency to be filled immediately for the order. You can focus on doing the options play or spread at a price you are comfortable with. In short, a market order increases the possibility of an execution but also increases the risk of not getting filled at the price you want. Whereas a limit order keeps you in control of the price, but your order may never get filled, which should be okay, as knowing this will help keep your positions at manageable sizes.

Using Options to Reduce Capital Commitment

Options are tools that allow investors to control underlying securities. One single stock call option, for instance, gives the owner the right to buy one hundred shares of stock. The investor is under no obligation to do so, but he can call the stock and take ownership of shares if he chooses to.

When looking for bullish exposure in a stock, an investor might sometimes want to buy the call instead of buying one hundred shares outright at current prices. The investor is stating that she doesn't want to buy it right now but might want to call it at a later date. The contract lasts only through the expiration and can only be exercised at one price, known as the strike price.

In this context, the investor is comparing the benefits of buying the stock now versus a call option that gives the right to buy at a fixed price through a fixed period of time. Similarly, an investor might also consider selling an existing position in stock now and replace it with a call option instead. This is known as *stock replacement* and is a strategy used when an investor wants to maintain upside exposure in a name but reduce the dollar amount of risk associated with holding shares.

For instance, returning to the Facebook example, the investor has a position in shares with the stock trading for $100 and is concerned about a possible decline in the share price but is longer-term bullish. Rather than liquidating the position entirely and moving to the sidelines, the investor sells one hundred shares of stock at $100 and buys one 100-strike call for $5. He collects $10,000 on the stock sale and pays $500 for the call, excluding transaction costs.

If the stock continues moving higher, the investor has the right to call it for $100 regardless of how far it climbs. The breakeven of a 100-strike call bought for $5 is at $105 per share (or the strike price plus the debit), and any move beyond that level results in profits.

On the other hand, if the stock falls, the investor is under no obligation to buy (or call) it. If, for example, Facebook falls to $90 from $100 and the options expire worthless, the investor loses the $500 premium paid for the calls. However, that is less than the $10 per share (or $1,000) loss suffered if the shares had been held instead.

Transaction costs, the potential for missing out on dividends, and tax consequences should be considered carefully before swapping out stock for calls or other options plays, but in some situations, an options strategy (long call, short put, call spread, etc.) can offer bullish or bearish exposure with less risk (in dollar, not percentage, terms) than investing in the underlying itself.

In addition, knowing when to sell (or exit) a position is often just as important as deciding when to enter one. In other words, buying a stock at a low price and seeing it move higher is great, but how do you decide when to sell and book the profit? Options can also help in that respect.

For example, let's say an investor initially bought one hundred shares of IBM for $90 per share, and the stock is now trading at $99. The investor has an unrealized gain of $9 per share (or $900). If that investor is a willing seller at $100 per share, she could sell a 100-strike call at $5 to reflect that view. If price of the shares rises above $100 prior to or at expiration and the calls are assigned, one hundred shares are sold per the call option at $100 per share, which can be added to the $5 that was collected for selling the calls. In this case, a covered call is similar to placing a stop order to sell the stock (Chapter 4), but writing calls generates a premium—which the investor keeps regardless of whether the calls are assigned.

> ## Stop versus Stop Limit
>
> A stop limit order to sell shares can be used to specify a price to sell the stock if that price is reached. The order is triggered at a specific price and then becomes a limit order. The limit price or better is "guaranteed" with a limit order, but actual execution of the order is not guaranteed. On the other hand, an investor can place a stop order to sell, which becomes a market order once a certain price is touched and seeks immediate execution without regard to price.

A short put or a short put spread, on the other hand, can be used as a tool to set an entry price for the purchase of a stock position. If an investor is a willing buyer of IBM at $85, selling a put with an 85-strike will express that view, because if the shares fall below that level prior to or at expiration, the put is assigned and the investor buys one hundred shares at the strike price.

Rolling with Spread Trades

In the options market, a *roll* is not something you find on your dinner plate but rather, a position adjustment when an investor wants to close one contract and open another. The roll might move a block of options from one strike price to another. An investor might also roll an options position from one expiration term to the next. Or, the action might adjust both the strike price and expiration month.

To illustrate, let's say an investor has purchased January 100-strike calls on Netflix for $5 per contract, and the stock has increased in value during the past few months. It is trading for $110. The 100-strike calls are now worth $10, and the investor wants to monetize the profit but also position for additional gains by purchasing 110-strike calls for $5. The position in January 100 calls can be rolled to the January 110 strikes by selling the January 100-110 call spread at $5 (or selling-to-close the January 100 calls at $10 and buying-to-open the January 110s for $5). Most electronic order entry tools will recognize that the spread is closing one leg or another. Therefore, the short call spread (Chapter 13) is a way to roll a block of long calls (Chapter 6) up in strike price.

While vertical spreads (Chapters 12 and 13) can be used to roll positions from one strike to a higher or lower one, calendar spreads or diagonal spreads (Chapter 14) are used to adjust positions from one expiration to the next. For instance, rather than selling the January 100-110 call spread, an investor might initiate a January 100-February 110 (diagonal) call spread to roll the position up ten strikes and out one month.

Knowing when to close or adjust positions is an important part of the investing process. There is no secret formula or precise set of rules when exiting or rolling a position. Instead, I suggest setting price targets and stop-losses at the time the options play is opened. Map out the game plan before the position is initiated using payoff charts (Chapter 8) and probabilities (Chapter 9) and take profits or cut losses according to the game plan. One thing to keep in mind in rolling: only do so if you want the new position. Too often it is done to "save" a losing position, which often just makes the hole deeper.

Investing and Social Media

It's easy to fall victim to information overload. In today's electronic world, financial news and data flow freely and abundantly. Social media also drives increased interaction among investors and encourages the sharing of experiences and ideas. Without a doubt, all of this is a positive development that has provided self-directed investors with more information than ever before.

The challenge is filtering out the noise and recognizing the info that is likely to be fleeting versus research that can help in the longer-term investment decision-making process. Economic news and headlines related to individual companies, industries, and commodities can obviously have immediate impact on market share prices. For that reason, many brokerage firms today offer their customers real-time news feeds like the one in Figure 17-2, which screen for news by options ticker or for the entire market.

Many of us are on social media as well. My colleagues and I often use Twitter to share information about company events or direct our followers to interesting stories. I like to follow people who highlight interesting news or market activity that I might have overlooked. LinkedIn, Facebook, and YouTube have been useful to me as well.

While it is somewhat overwhelming at times, social media can be a source of useful market information if you filter the list down and narrow it to a handful of trusted and knowledgeable groups of people and companies. You may even want to separate your social

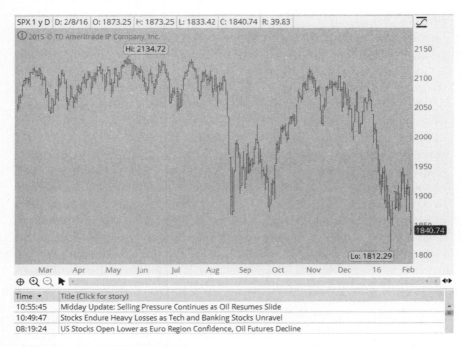

Figure 17-2   Charting and News

media accounts into two categories: one for your personal life and a second for the purpose of trading and investing.

Lastly, there is no substitute for self-education, be that through research on positions or on options strategies. After several decades trading options, I can assure you that there are no free lunches. The best way to invest with confidence and for the longer term is to have strong conviction in the investments and strategies that are part of your trading plan. The only way to develop that conviction is by making decisions based on reliable information, facts, and thorough research. I can't emphasize enough the importance of education and knowing the products you are trading. Lastly, never take on positions you do not understand. Take some time to learn the ins and outs of each strategy before initiating them with real money.

Final Thoughts

Congratulations. Your thirst for knowledge has brought you to the conclusion of this book. Hopefully, you now understand the basics of puts and calls, including how to find current prices, what are the determinants of the premiums, and how to place orders for both simple and complex strategies.

My rules of thumb are provided to illustrate my approach, and my approach will not be suitable for every investor. These methods are the ones I learned after more than twenty years trading on the Chicago Board Options Exchange (CBOE) and that I now use for my own personal account. Trading options involves significant risk, including potential loss of principal.

However, no two investors are alike, and the suitability of any investment strategy must be considered within the larger context of an individual's long-term investment goals, risk tolerance, and trading plan. Options trading is certainly not suitable for everyone, and as a self-directed investor, you must decide if an approach or methodology is right for you. Market conditions can and do change. Simply because a strategy has worked in the past or in a virtual trading environment, does not guarantee it will work in the future, which is why I talk about diversifying strategies even more than stocks.

Hopefully, the strategies outlined in this book provide you with enough information to fully understand what options are available today (yes, that is an intentional pun) and give you tools to help make better, more-informed investment decisions. If you have never traded options before, take some time to learn the strategies through a virtual paper trading platform. Practice, practice, practice.

And always ask yourself, "How much can I lose on this position?" Knowing your risk beforehand is one of the keys to success. Once you have defined the risk and you are comfortable with that, it will make your decision-making process so much clearer. Lastly, don't be afraid to start with small trades until you have achieved some success.

Thank you for taking time to read this book, and I truly hope that it helped build a better understanding of options and options trading. Good luck in your pursuits, and remember—investing is not a sprint but a marathon.

APPENDIX A

The Greeks

Understanding the Greeks makes us smarter options traders. By Greeks, I don't mean Zeus, Plato, or Aristotle, but rather delta, gamma, theta, vega, and rho. While these concepts are somewhat complex in the beginning, you don't need a degree in quantum physics to understand the concepts or to use them in real-world trading.

Indeed, while computing the Greeks requires the use of options pricing models, many websites and brokerage platforms offer the information for free, but a few traders actually compute the numbers themselves. It is much easier to pull up an options chain with the numbers already computed.

If you have already traded puts and calls, you know that options prices change as the price of the underlying moves higher or lower. But have you ever purchased a call option only to see it lose value despite a move higher in the underlying? That might happen when other factors, such as time decay (theta) or volatility (vega), chip away at the options premiums. The Greeks can help us understand why this happens and what factors are having the greatest influence on options premiums.

In fact, it's a common mistake to assume that the change in the price of the stock, index, or other underlying instrument is the only factor that determines the value of the options contract. Although it is the one that changes most often, there are other important determinants of options prices as well. The Greeks are variables that isolate how factors such as time and volatility impact the value of the contract. Let's start with a discussion of delta.

Delta Defined

If Zeus was the king of the gods in Greek mythology, delta is the Zeus of the Greeks in the world of options trading. Understanding how it works helps make sense of why options prices are changing as the stock, index, or underlying instrument moves higher or lower. Knowing the position delta is valuable when trading more advanced strategies with more than one options contract.

But let's not put the cart before the horse. While the underlying instrument, like a stock, has a fixed delta of 1.0, each individual options contract has a unique delta that is always changing. It tells us, approximately, how much the value of the options contract can be expected to change for each one-point change in the underlying asset.

Call options have positive deltas ranging from 0 to 1, because they increase in value when the underlying asset moves higher. Put options have negative deltas of between −1 and 0, because the value of the contract will typically increase as the price of the underlying instrument heads lower. Very low delta options see relatively little reaction to the underlying's move. High delta options approaching 1 or −1 move almost point-for-point with the underlying.

An equity call option with a delta of 0.25 can be expected to increase in value by $0.25 for a $1 move higher in the underlying stock. Because the multiplier for a standard options contract is one hundred, an increase of 0.25 equals $25. On the other hand, a put with a delta of −0.25 can be expected to increase in value by $25 for each $1 decline in the underlying stock price.

As we saw in Chapter 9, delta is sometimes described as the thumbnail probability that an option will expire in-the-money (ITM) by at least a penny. It's not an actual calculation; it's simply a thumbnail and a useful way of thinking about delta.

For example, an at-the-money (ATM) call option, which has a strike price equal to the stock price, should have a delta of roughly 0.50 because there is a 50 percent chance that it will expire ITM. This should make sense given that an ATM call has an equal probability of being ITM or out-of-the-money (OTM) at expiration because there is a fifty-fifty chance that the stock will move higher or lower from current levels.

As expiration approaches, the delta of an OTM option will approach zero and see little reaction to the underlying. After all, the contract is about to expire worthless. On the other hand, the delta of an ITM call option will approach 1, and an ITM put will move toward −1 heading into the expiration.

Changes in the value of the underlying can lead to very fast changes in delta as expiration approaches because of the rapidly decreasing or increasing probabilities of the option expiring ITM or OTM. This fast change in delta is measured by another Greek called gamma, which we cover after I explain the concept of delta neutral.

Delta Neutral

Each options contract has a unique delta. When combined into strategies with multiple contracts or shares, the total delta of the trade is called the position delta. A stock has a delta of 1. Therefore, a position in one hundred shares of stock and one ATM put with a −0.5 delta has a position delta of 0.5. The position is expected to increase in value by $0.50 if the underlying gains $1 or lose $0.50 if shares drop $1. Again, because the multiplier is one hundred, a 0.5 delta would equal $50 for every one hundred shares held (and one put).

The term *delta neutral* refers to a position that theoretically doesn't react at all to price changes of the underlying instrument. To create a position that is neutral with respect to delta with call options with a 0.5 delta, the investor might sell short one hundred shares and buy two call options. The result is a position delta of 0, or 0.5 plus 0.5 minus 1. Or, an investor could buy two −0.5 delta puts against a stock and create a protective put, or a short-term hedge. Of course, the delta will change as the price moves higher or lower, and a true delta neutral strategy will continually buy or sell shares or options as needed. Position deltas can also be greater than one hundred. For instance, buying ten 0.5 delta options will yield a position delta of 500 (10 × 0.50).

While a market maker or some other institutional investor, rather than an individual investor, is more likely to initiate a strictly delta neutral strategy, the concept of position delta is relevant to all options strategists. It can help make sense of why positions, whether simple or complex, change in value as the underlying instrument moves higher or lower. As you start out, this is not as important a concern. However, make sure that you understand how many deltas you are long or short, as that is theoretically how many dollars you are risking with a one dollar move in the underlying.

Of the Greeks, delta seems to make the most sense intuitively. As the price of the underlying asset moves higher, calls will increase in value and puts will decrease in value. On the other hand, if the price falls, calls decrease in value and puts increase in value. The same is true for more complex strategies, and the position delta is the way of quantifying the expected changes in premiums.

Importantly, delta and the other Greeks are computed using options pricing models, and the calculations are theoretical. The option might or might not behave exactly as the models suggest. Therefore, delta is really a guide and not a precise measure of potential changes in options premiums as the price of the under-lying moves higher or lower. The same is true of the other Greeks. In addition, delta is dynamic and constantly changing. A call option with a delta of 0.25 might have a delta of 0.33 after a $1 move higher in the underlying stock and a 0.5 delta if the stock moves $2 higher.

Gamma

If deltas are constantly changing as the price of the underlying moves higher and lower, gamma measures the change in delta for every point change in underlying. If delta is speed, gamma is the accel-erator, and the options with the highest gammas see the greatest reactions to changes in the underlying.

Gamma is a positive number (or sometimes zero) for both puts and calls. Unlike delta, it is not a measure of the changes in premi-ums. It only reflects changes in delta. In addition, gamma will be the greatest near the ATM strikes, while steadily decreasing moving out to the further ITM and OTM strikes.

An option that is near the money heading into the expiration will have high gamma because the delta can change quickly from a low number to a high value if shares go through the strike price. For instance, an OTM call might have a delta of 0.25 the day before expiration, but if shares rally through the strike price of the con-tract on expiration day, the call might suddenly see its delta increase to 1. It has very high gamma. Note that if you are having trouble getting your arms around this, do not fret; it takes a while, and clos-ing your positions out before expiration week will limit your exposure to gamma.

Theta

Options are wasting assets. Have you heard that before? The adage refers to the fact that options lose value over time and suffer from time decay. Theta measures the amount of time value that is expected to be lost with each passing day. It is always expressed as a negative number, because both puts and calls lose value over time.

You can think of time loss like a snowman melting after the winter. It slowly melts away when temperatures are still cold, but the speed will increase as the weather gets warmer. Similarly, time decay is nonlinear and affects short-term options at a faster rate than longer-term ones. Time decay is the greatest in the days and hours immediately before expiration.

Meanwhile, ATM options will have higher thetas (relative to ITM or OTM options), because there are greater losses in premiums (as measured in dollars and cents) at those strike prices. In other words, there is more to lose in the bigger time value of ATM or near-the-money strikes, and that's where time decay occurs the most. That's because these are the options with the highest amount of premium as well.

Theta only relates to the extrinsic (or time) value of the option and has no impact on intrinsic value. Meanwhile, OTM strikes will have lower thetas than ITM, because there is less time value. However, the percentage losses associated might be greater for OTM strikes because of the smaller absolute levels of time value. After all, losing $0.02 per day on a contract trading for $0.50 is a much larger percentage loss than losing $0.03 on a contract trading for $5.

Vega

Vega is not actually a Greek letter, but in the world of options trading, it is considered one of the Greeks. It offers estimates about the potential changes in options prices for each one-point move in the volatility of the price of the underlying. As volatility increases, the value of the option increases. Falling volatility results in lower premiums. Like theta, changes in vega only affect the extrinsic (or time) value of the option.

Each options contract has a measure of volatility known as implied volatility (IV). Computed using an options pricing model and always in a state of flux, IV is a percentage and will vary from one option to the next. Even two options on the same underlying stock can have very different levels of implied volatility. Vega measures how much the premium might change as IV moves 1 percent higher or lower.

Vega is always a positive number regardless of whether the option is a put or call. It is typically higher for ATM or near-the-money options and declining in the further ITM or OTM strikes. Lastly, longer-dated options can often have substantially higher levels compared to short-term ones as well. The higher vega option premiums are more responsive to changes in implied volatility. In addition, longer-dated options are slower to respond to volatility changes, but when they respond, it is in a much bigger way.

An options pricing model is a useful tool to see how changes in implied volatility (and other factors) affect premiums for puts and calls. Figure A-1 shows an example from The Options Industry Council website (www.optioneducation.net/calculator/main_advanced.asp). In this example, we are looking at a stock option expiring in March with a $105 share price and a 105 strike price. We assume a 0.50 percent interest rate, no dividend payments, and implied volatility of 25 percent.

With shares at $105, both the 105-strike puts and calls are ATM with deltas of −0.47 and 0.53, respectively. The prices are $4.92 and $4.81 per contract, respectively. Now, suppose the implied volatility of the options increases to 35 percent from 25 percent, or ten points. Because vega was 0.194 and implied volatility moved ten points higher, both options should increase by roughly $1.94.

As we can see from Figure A-2, if implied volatility is changed to 35 percent from 25 percent, the premiums increased to $6.86 for

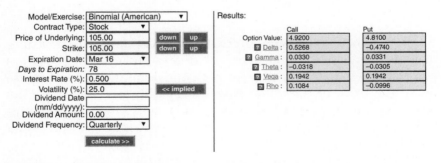

Figure A-1   Options Calculator
Source: Options Industry Council

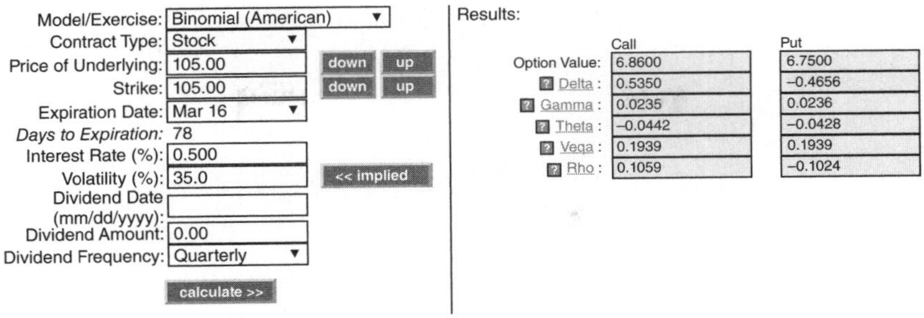

Figure A-2   Options Calculator
Source: Options Industry Council

calls and $6.75 puts, respectively. On the other hand, a ten-point drop would see the premiums drop by roughly $1.94 per contract. The fact that changes in implied volatility can have an important impact on premiums helps explain why a call option might lose value, even if shares move higher. In that case, the impact of vega was larger than the impact of delta.

Using an options calculator, we can also substitute out IV with other measures of volatility to see theoretical options prices. One measure often used with pricing models is historical volatility (HV, also called statistical volatility, actual volatility, or realized volatility). While IV is computed using options pricing models, HV is computed using the past prices of the underlying asset over a number of previous trading sessions. Mathematically, it is the annualized standardized deviation of stock returns and is also expressed as a percentage. (See Appendix C for more on HV in the section about volatility studies.)

Indeed, volatility is always changing and will vary for each underlying asset. Even individual contracts listed on the same underlying can have very different levels of implied volatility. Vega helps us understand how the next changes in IV might affect the premiums.

Lastly, it's also possible to see vega and some of the other Greeks using an options chain in a trading platform. Figure A-3 provides an example of one using Microsoft (MSFT) March options. In addition to the bid-ask prices, the columns include delta, gamma, theta, and vega.

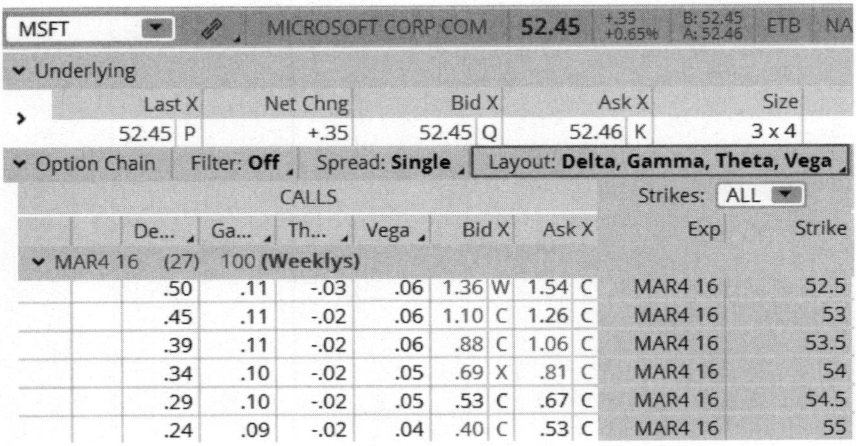

| MSFT ▼ | 🔗 | MICROSOFT CORP COM | **52.45** | +.35 +0.65% | B: 52.45 A: 52.46 | ETB | NA |

∨ Underlying

>	Last X	Net Chng	Bid X	Ask X	Size
	52.45 P	+.35	52.45 Q	52.46 K	3 x 4

∨ Option Chain   Filter: **Off**   Spread: **Single**   Layout: **Delta, Gamma, Theta, Vega**

| | CALLS | | | | | | Strikes: | ALL ▼ |

		De...	Ga...	Th...	Vega	Bid X	Ask X	Exp	Strike
∨ MAR4 16 (27) 100 (Weeklys)									
		.50	.11	-.03	.06	1.36 W	1.54 C	MAR4 16	52.5
		.45	.11	-.02	.06	1.10 C	1.26 C	MAR4 16	53
		.39	.11	-.02	.06	.88 C	1.06 C	MAR4 16	53.5
		.34	.10	-.02	.05	.69 X	.81 C	MAR4 16	54
		.29	.10	-.02	.05	.53 C	.67 C	MAR4 16	54.5
		.24	.09	-.02	.04	.40 C	.53 C	MAR4 16	55

Figure A-3   Options Chain with the Greeks

Rho

Rho is the Greek that measures how the options value may change due to a 1 percent change in interest rates. Rho for a call is positive, because the contract will increase as rates rise. The rho for a puts has a negative value. If overall rates are at low levels, the impact from rates on options premiums are not a major factor. However, in periods of higher interest rates, the changes to options premiums are sometimes more meaningful. Rho is the measure for gauging the potential impact. Again, try using an options calculator to see how changes in rates and other variables can affect the prices of puts and calls.

Reference

www.optioneducation.net/calculator/main_advanced.asp

B

Strategy Recap

Every options strategy has risks and rewards that can be plotted on a profit/loss line, payoff chart, or risk graph. While many trading software packages can do this in real time with live market prices, what follows is a summary of the simple risk graphs for the strategies outlined in this book. For the sake of simplicity, transaction costs (commissions, contract fees, exercise, and assignment fees) are not accounted for in the examples that follow. But keep in mind that many of the spread strategies discussed utilize two, three, and even four options legs, and the resulting transaction costs should be considered carefully, especially if the strategy might involve the exercise and assignment of more than one contract. In that case, transaction costs can be significant.

Recall that a payoff chart includes a vertical *y*-axis that shows the profit and loss and a horizontal *x*-axis that represents changes in the price of the underlying security. The simple risk graph of being long stock (Figure B-1) makes sense, because as share prices move higher, the position increases in value and profits accumulate. As share prices move lower, shares lose value and losses increase. Where the risk line crosses the *x*-axis, there is no gain or loss. This is the breakeven level. While the breakeven of a long stock is the price paid, the breakeven level for an option or options strategy is the price of the underlying at expiration.

Long Call

The long call strategy is covered in more detail in Chapter 6. An investor typically buys calls when he expects the price of the underlying to move higher. Therefore, the directional bias of the

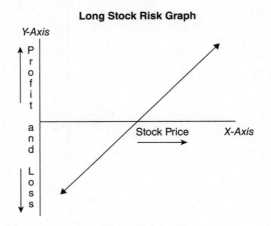

Figure B-1   Long Stock Payoff Chart

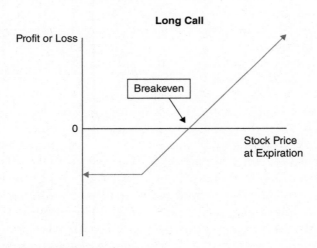

Figure B-2   Long Call Payoff Chart

long call is bullish, which is reflected on the risk graph (Figure B-2). It is a debit transaction, and the expiration breakeven is computed as the strike price plus debit paid. The risk is limited to the debit, and theoretically, there is no limit to potential profits.

Strategy: Buy call
Outlook: Bullish
Debit or Credit: Debit

Risk: Debit

Breakeven: Strike price + Debit

Potential Profits: No limit

JJ's Tips for Long Calls

- Be careful with the leverage, as losing on long calls can result in 100 percent loss of capital committed to the trade, including transaction costs.
- While out-of-the-money (OTM) options often seem "cheap," the probability of profit is typically higher with in-the-money (ITM) calls. But the amount of capital at risk will likely be higher also.
- Use delta as a thumbnail for probability of expiring ITM; 50 deltas or higher is preferred.
- Buy when implied volatility (IV) is low, as expensive calls can lose value due to falling IV, even if shares tick higher.
- Time decay is not your friend. Focus on short-term options.
- Only trade products with open interest at least fifty times larger than the number of contracts you trade (applies to all strategies).

Short Call

The short call is a credit strategy that was explained in more detail in Chapter 6. When selling calls without a covering position in the underlying or as part of a spread trade, the play is also called an uncovered (or naked) call write. The profit is limited to the credit received, and as we can see from Figure B-3, the risks to the upside are theoretically unlimited because there is no cap on how high the price of a stock can climb. The breakeven is equal to the strike price plus the credit received.

Strategy: Sell calls

Outlook: Bearish or neutral

Debit or Credit: Credit

Risk: No limit

Breakeven: Strike price + Credit

Potential Profits: Credit

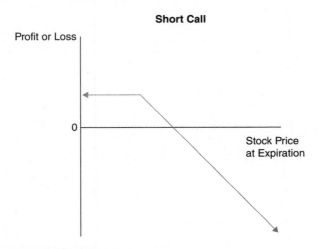

Figure B-3   Naked Call Risk Graph

JJ's Tips for Short Calls
- Consider short vertical call spreads rather than naked calls, as risks are better defined.
- Be careful with naked calls as risks are *not* defined. They are best suited for sophisticated options traders with the highest risk tolerance.
- The higher the strike, the less premium received and the higher probability of profit.
- When selling calls, focus on OTM options with a high probability of expiring OTM.
- Look for high implied volatility, as the position benefits from falling IV.
- Time is on your side, because short calls benefit from time decay.

Long Put

The long put was covered in detail in Chapter 7. Because puts typically increase in value as the price of the underlying falls, options traders go long puts when prices are expected to fall or as a hedge (also see the protective put). As shown in the profit/loss line in Figure B-4, the risk to buying puts is the debit paid, and the breakeven is the strike price minus the debit. The potential profits are only limited due to the fact that an underlying security can't fall below zero.

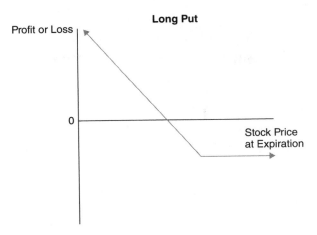

Figure B-4   Long Put Risk Curve

Strategy: Buy puts

Outlook: Bearish

Debit or Credit: Debit

Risk: Debit

Breakeven: Strike price – Debit

Potential Profits: Strike price – Debit – Current price of the underlying

JJ's Tips for Long Puts
- Buying puts can be an alternative to shorting stock, but with defined risks.
- Look for low implied volatility situations, as puts increase in value as IV moves higher.
- When buying puts, ITM contracts have greater probabilities of success but higher capital outlay versus OTM puts.
- Time decay works against the put buyer.
- Consider buying puts only as a short-term play with expirations less than seven weeks out.
- If held through the expiration, long puts can expire worthless, and if this happens, the entire investment is lost.

Protective Put

Examples of the protective put were provided in Chapter 7. The position is long stock and long puts. As we can see from Figure B-5,

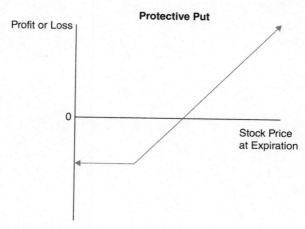

Figure B-5   Protective Put Risk Graph

the strategy has a bullish bias because the investor wants the stock to move higher, but the risk is defined by the strike price of the put. The breakeven equals the stock price plus the debit paid.

Strategy: Long stock and long puts

Outlook: Bullish

Debit or Credit: Debit

Risk: Stock purchase price − Strike − Debit paid

Breakeven: Stock price + Debit

Potential Profits: Unlimited above the breakeven

JJ's Tips for Protective Puts

- Consider a protective put to hedge an existing stock position during periods of increased volatility, but this can be expensive due to the premium paid for the put.
- It can be used as a type of stop order to exit a position.
- If the stock price continues to fall, you might still lose money, but the losses will likely be less than if no puts had been purchased.
- Compare to buying a long call instead, as the payoffs are similar.
- After the position is established, an increase in implied volatility helps the puts, but time decay works against it.
- You want the stock to move higher, higher, higher...and for the puts to expire worthless.

Covered Call

The ins and outs of the covered call or buy-write strategy are covered in Chapter 10. The position is created by selling calls against a new or existing stock position. If it's a standard equity option, the investor sells one call option for every one hundred shares. The risk is a move lower in the stock. The breakeven equals the net cost (stock price minus credit received). The upside is capped by the strike price of the short call, and the maximum profit equals the strike price minus the net cost of the stock (the original purchase price minus credit received from selling the call) plus any dividends collected. Maximum loss happens if the stock falls to zero and equals the stock purchase price minus the credit received.

It bears repeating that this strategy can limit the upside potential of the underlying stock position, as the stock would likely be called away in the event of substantial stock price increase. That's why Figure B-6 shows limited upside along the profit/loss line. Also, the risk of the stock being called away increases the closer you get to the ex-dividend day. If you are assigned prior to the ex-dividend date, eligibility for receiving the dividend is lost.

Strategy: Buy stock, sell calls

Outlook: Bullish or neutral

Debit or Credit: Debit (Cost of stock − Credit)

Risk: Stock purchase price − Credit

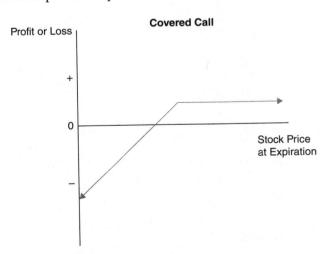

Figure B-6   Buy-Write Risk Graph

Breakeven: Stock price − Credit

Potential Profits: Strike price − Breakeven

JJ's Tips for Covered Calls
- The covered call is not aggressively bullish, as upside potential to holding shares is capped by the strike price of the calls.
- This is a position that helps you lower the net cost of your stock purchase.
- You can continue to collect dividends but may lose that benefit if assigned.
- When selling calls, OTM options are preferred.
- The position benefits from falling implied volatility and time decay.
- Compare to a cash-secured put strategy, as it has a similar payoff chart.
- Consider using covered calls as a way to exit a position by selling a strike price that equals the price at which you're willing to sell the stock.

Collar

Chapter 10 explores the ins and outs of the covered call or buy-write strategy, and Chapter 7 explains the protective put. The collar is a combination of the two strategies and, as we can see from Figure B-7, is a limited risk-reward play. To initiate this play, the investor sells calls and buys puts against a new or existing stock position. One call is sold and one put is bought per one hundred shares of the underlying. The strategy has limited risks and limited rewards. While the put hedges the downside risk to the stock, the short calls limit the upside potential. The trade can typically be initiated for a small credit or debit, depending on the value of the puts versus the calls. A zero-cost collar is one where the sale of the call equals the premium for the put.

Strategy: Buy stock, sell call, buy put

Direction: Bullish or neutral

Debit or Credit: Depends on strikes

Risk: Breakeven − Put strike

Breakeven: If opened for a credit, the BE is stock price minus credit. On debit trades, it's the stock price plus the debit.

Potential Profits: Call strike − Breakeven

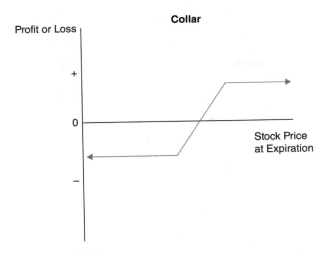

Figure B-7   Collar Payoff Chart

JJ's Tips for Collars

- If you're mildly bullish but worried about the potential for a drop in the stock, consider putting a collar around it.
- Sell OTM calls to leave upside for shares.
- Look to finance the puts with the calls and initiate for zero-cost or better.
- Time decay will work against the puts but will help the calls. Similarly, changes in implied volatility in calls are being offset by the puts, and therefore, it is typically a volatility neutral strategy.
- The strategy involves the risks of both covered calls and protective puts.

Cash-Secured Put

The cash-secured put is duly covered in Chapter 11. The strategy gets its name from the fact that the put writer has sufficient cash in the account to cover assignment. Premium is collected for writing the puts, and the potential profits are limited to the credit received. As we can see from Figure B-8, losses accrue as the price of the underlying moves lower, and therefore, the put sale is typically viewed as a bullish strategy, although it can also yield profits (the credit received) if shares see little upward movement (staying above the strike price) and the options expire worthless. The breakeven equals the strike price minus the credit.

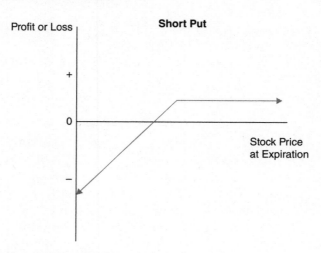

Figure B-8   Short Put Risk Graph

Strategy: Sell puts

Outlook: Bullish or neutral

Debit or Credit: Credit

Risk: Strike price − Credit

Breakeven: Strike price − Credit

Potential Profits: Credit

JJ's Tips for Short Puts

- Be careful with writing puts, because the risk is defined, but only because the stock price cannot fall below zero.
- Keep enough cash in the account to cover assignment and be sure you really want to buy the underlying at the strike price sold.
- Only sell puts on stocks you want to own and keep in mind that one put represents the obligation to buy one hundred shares for equity options.
- Higher implied volatility will result in higher premium received, but typically greater volatility in the price of the underlying security.
- Short puts will benefit from time decay.
- There is a risk of purchasing the stock at the strike price at a time when the price of the stock will likely be lower and could continue to fall.

- The nice thing about letting the puts expire worthless is that there are no additional commissions to pay.
- This strategy is good to lower the net cost of stock already owned (due to credit received).

Long Call Spread

Sometimes called the bull call spread, the long call spread is covered in Chapter 12. The play involves buying a call and selling a call with a higher strike price. Figure B-9 shows that the strategy has a bullish bias and offers a maximum payout if the underlying security moves to the higher strike or better through the expiration. At that point, the profit is equal to the difference between the two strikes minus the debit. The debit is at risk if the options expire worthless, and the breakeven is equal to the lower strike plus the debit.

Strategy: Buy call, sell higher strike call

Outlook: Bullish

Debit or Credit: Debit

Risk: Debit

Breakeven: Lower strike + Debit

Potential Profits: High strike − Low strike − Debit

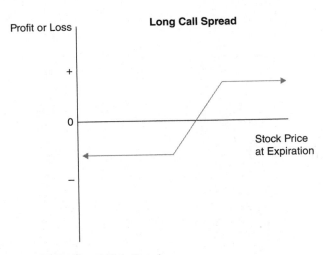

Figure B-9   Bull Call Spread Risk Graph

JJ's Tips for Long Call Spreads
- Buy ITM and sell OTM.
- Focus on shorter-term time frames between three and seven weeks.
- Don't overdo it with the leverage, as "cheap" long vertical spreads have lower probabilities of profit.
- The impact from time decay and implied volatility on the long call are somewhat offset by the short call.
- The maximum value of the spread is usually realized at or very near the expiration.
- It's best to execute the spread as one trade rather than legging into one option at a time, because you want to enter the spread at a set price and exit at one price as well (applies to all spreads).

Long Put Spread

The long put spread, covered in Chapter 12, is also called a bear put spread and is typically initiated when the investor expects the underlying security to decline in value. The strategy involves purchasing a put and selling a put with a lower strike price. It has limited risks and rewards, as depicted in Figure B-10, and offers a maximum payout if the underlying security moves to the lower strike or below through

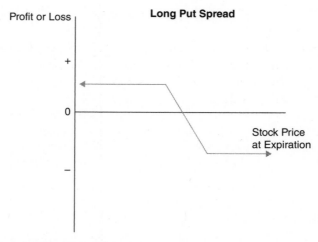

Figure B-10   Bear Put Spread Risk Graph

the expiration. At that point, the profit is the difference between the two strikes minus the debit. The debit is at risk if the options expire worthless. The breakeven equals higher strike minus the debit.

Strategy: Buy put, sell lower strike put

Outlook: Bearish

Debit or Credit: Debit

Risk: Debit

Breakeven: Higher strike − Debit

Potential Profits: High strike − Low strike − Debit

JJ's Tips for Long Put Spreads
- Buy ITM and sell OTM.
- Changes in time decay and implied volatility of the long put will be offset somewhat by the short put.
- When implied volatility is high, buying put spreads is an attractive alternative to long puts, because you are buying and selling puts. The impact of falling implied volatility on the long put is somewhat offset by the short puts.
- Long put spreads are sometimes used to partially hedge against a price decline in the underlying.
- Focus on options that expire in the next three to seven weeks.

Short Call Spread

Short vertical spreads are covered in Chapter 13. When selling call spreads, the strategy involves writing a call and buying a call with a higher strike within the same expiration. In the typical scenario, the investor wants the stock to stay below the lower strike price and the options to expire worthless. The potential reward is limited, as we can see from Figure B-11, and equals the credit received for selling the spread. The breakeven is at the lower strike plus the credit. The risk is equal to the difference between two strikes minus the credit, and maximum losses happen if the underlying is trading above the higher strike of the spread at expiration.

Strategy: Sell call, buy higher strike call

Outlook: Bearish or neutral

Debit or Credit: Credit

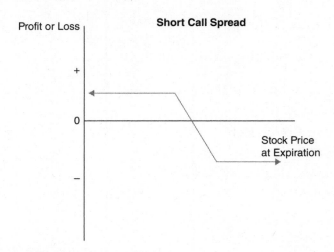

Figure B-11   Short Call Risk Graph

Risk: High strike − Low strike − Credit

Breakeven: Low strike price + Credit

Potential Profits: Credit
JJ's Tips for Short Call Spreads
- Consider a short call spread as a defined risk alternative to naked calls.
- Sell calls that are OTM.
- Use probability of expiring ITM to select the best spreads.
- If both options expire worthless, the strategy has reached its full potential, and there are no additional commissions to pay.
- Time is on your side as the position loses value due to time decay.
- Short-term options see faster rates of time decay, and short call spreads with less than seven weeks until expiration are preferred.
- Don't overdo it with the leverage, as even one loss can wipe out the profits from several successful short vertical spreads.

Short Put Spread

Like selling puts, a short put spread is sold when the investor expects the stock to hold above a certain level and is also willing to buy (have assigned) shares at the strike of the short put. The strategy involves writing a put and buying a put with a lower strike. Figure B-12 shows

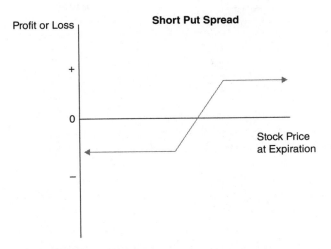

Figure B-12   Short Put Spread Risk Graph

that the risks and rewards are limited, with the best payout happening if shares are above the higher strike at expiration. In the spread, the losses are limited by the lower strike put, and the maximum loss is the difference between the two strikes minus the credit received. The potential profit is the credit, and the breakeven is equal to the higher strike minus the credit.

Strategy: Sell puts, buy lower strike puts

Outlook: Bullish or neutral

Debit or Credit: Credit

Risk: High strike − Low strike − Credit

Breakeven: High strike − Credit

Potential Profits: Credit

JJ's Tips for Short Put Spreads
- Consider this a directional play when you expect the stock to move higher and want to enter a defined-risk strategy.
- The play is similar to a short call vertical spread but in the opposite direction.
- Time decay is helping the position.
- You want both legs of the spread to expire worthless, and there are no additional transaction costs if they do.
- Use probability of expiring ITM to find optimal spreads.

Call Calendar Spread

Chapter 14 is all about the calendar (or time) spread. The call calendar is a debit spread strategy that involves buying calls and selling calls at the same strike but of shorter duration. Ideally, the stock goes to the strike price through the first expiration and then moves higher, at which time you can take off the spread for maximum profit. The breakeven can be estimated, but there is no exact formula because there are two expirations and a number of variables to consider, such as changes in implied volatility and time decay. As Figure B-13 shows, the maximum gain of the position during the life of the first option is limited due to the fact that the investor is both short and long the same strike. But if the short option expires worthless, the risk graph becomes the same as the long call. As mentioned earlier, entering and exiting as a spread is the preferred mode of trading.

> **Strategy:** Buy call, sell short-term call
>
> **Outlook:** Bullish or neutral
>
> **Debit or Credit:** Debit
>
> **Risk:** Debit (but can be greater if assigned early on short calls)
>
> **Breakeven:** Use software to estimate
>
> **Potential Profits:** Limited through the first expiration (short call); then the position becomes a long call, which is why you would consider closing at that point

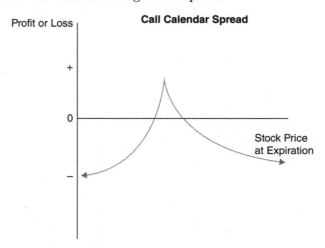

Figure B-13   Call Calendar Time Spread

JJ's Tips for Long Call Calendar Spreads
- Computing breakevens with calendar spreads is tricky and can only be estimated because there are two expirations.
- The strategy is designed to take advantage of the nonlinear nature of time decay.
- Sell options that expire in twenty to forty days and buy options that expire in fifty to ninety days.
- Place the calendar spread with strike above the current stock price.

Put Calendar Spread

The put calendar is covered in Chapter 14 as well. The strategy involves buying puts and selling shorter-term puts at the same strike. As we can see from Figure B-14, the risks and rewards are similar to the call calendar. Best-case scenario: The stock holds above the strike price through the expiration of the short-term option and then moves lower during the remainder of the life of the longer-term contract. The risks, rewards, and breakevens can be estimated, but there is no exact formula because there are two expirations and a number of variables to consider, such as implied volatility and time decay.

Strategy: Buy puts, sell shorter-term puts

Outlook: Bearish or neutral

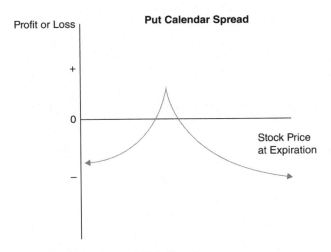

Figure B-14   Put Calendar Spread Risk Graph

Debit or Credit: Debit

Risk: Debit

Breakeven: Use software to compute

Potential Profits: Limited through the first expiration (short put); position becomes long put after first option expires

JJ's Tips for Put Calendars
- Consider this play if the stock is expected to trade in a range in the near term and then go to the short strike.
- After the short put expires, the risk graph turns into a long put, which generally ruins the initial logic of the initial position.
- Know how to handle assignment if assigned on the short puts.
- Use software to see the risk graphs for calendar spreads.
- Sell options that expire in twenty to forty days and buy options that expire in fifty to ninety days.
- If you exit at or before expiration, the profit or loss equals the credit for the long put minus the debit for the short put minus the initial debit.

Call Butterfly Spread (Long)

Butterflies and condors are covered in Chapter 15. The long call fly is run by purchasing one call, selling twice as many higher strike calls, and buying an even-higher strike call all within the same expiration month. All strikes are also equidistant apart. The middle strikes are the body, and the other two are wings. The sweet spot of the spread at expiration, which is the highest point on the profit/loss line in Figure B-15, happens if the underlying is trading at the middle strike. At that point, the maximum profit is achieved and equals the difference between the strikes, minus the debit. The risk is the debit paid. There are two breakevens: the lower strike plus the debit and the higher strike minus the debit.

Strategy: Buy call, sell two higher strike calls, buy one even-higher strike call

Outlook: Depends on strike prices

Debit or Credit: Debit

Risk: Debit

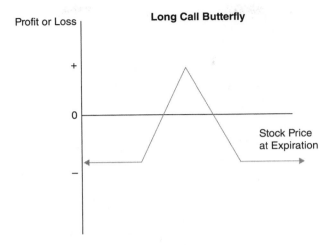

Figure B-15   Long Call Butterfly Risk Graph

Breakeven: (1) Higher strike − Debit; (2) Lower strike + Debit
Potential Profits: Middle strike − Lower strike − Debit

JJ's Tips for Long Call Butterflies
- The long butterfly has defined risks and rewards that vary based on strike prices selected.
- A call fly with strikes above the stock price will have a bullish directional bias.
- The further OTM the options, the cheaper the fly and also the lower probability of success.
- Consider call butterflies on stocks with bullish fundamentals and sell middle strikes (body) that correspond with your expected price target.
- Create spreads with options that expire in less than seven weeks.

Put Butterfly Spread (Long)

The long put butterfly spread involves buying a put, selling two lower strike puts, and buying an even-lower strike put. The spread (or difference) between the low and middle strikes (middle strike minus low strike) and the high and middle strikes (high strike minus middle strike) are the same distance apart. There are two breakevens to the trade: the higher strike minus the debit and the lower strike plus the debit. The maximum payout happens if shares

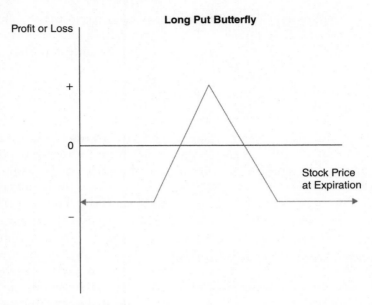

Figure B-16   Long Put Butterfly

settle at the middle strike (body) at the expiration and equals the difference between the high and middle strike (or middle and low strike) minus the debit. Figure B-16 shows that the risks and rewards of the strategy are similar to the long call fly.

Strategy: Buy put, buy two lower strike puts, buy one even-lower strike put

Outlook: Depends on strike prices

Debit or Credit: Debit

Risk: Debit

Breakeven: (1) Higher strike − Debit; (2) Lower strike + Debit

Potential Profits: Higher strike − Middle strike − Debit

JJ's Tips for Long Put Butterflies
- Focus on shorter-term options for ATM butterflies.
- The middle strike is the "sweet spot" for the spread.
- Put flys with strikes below the stock price will have a bearish directional bias.
- Experienced traders might consider using index options for butterfly spreads because they are typically less volatile than

individual stocks, and there is no early assignment risk with
European-style options.
- Time decay is your friend, as you want all but the higher strike
puts to expire worthless.

Iron Butterfly

An iron butterfly uses both puts and calls. In contrast to long call or
long put flys, the strategy is initiated for a credit rather than a debit.
The investor is selling puts and calls at the same strike while buying a higher strike call and a lower strike put. All options strikes are
equidistant apart and in the same expiration term. The best payout
happens if the underlying is at the middle strike at the expiration,
and we can see on Figure B-17 that the profit/loss line is a lot like
the put and call butterfly spreads. At that point, the options expire
worthless, and the profit is the credit. The two breakevens are equal
to the middle strike plus and minus the credit. The maximum loss
is the difference between the low and middle strikes (or middle and
high strike) minus the credit.

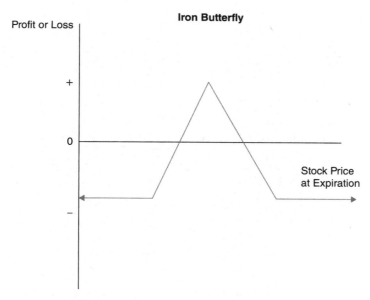

Figure B-17   Iron Butterfly

Strategy: Buy put, sell higher strike put, sell call at same strike as higher strike put, buy higher strike call

Outlook: Depends on strike

Debit or Credit: Credit

Risk: High strike (or low strike) − Middle strike − Credit

Breakeven: (1) Middle strike + Credit; (2) Middle strike − Credit

Potential Profits: Credit

JJ's Tips for Iron Butterflies
- Think of an iron fly as being short a put spread and short a call spread.
- A significant move higher or lower will result in losses.
- Time is on your side, as the best-case scenario is that all options expire worthless.
- Consider running this play with short-term options that have a few weeks of life remaining, or even less.
- Know what to do when one of the short options is ITM into the expiration and you get assigned.

Call Condor Spread (Long)

Condors are covered in detail, along with butterflies, in Chapter 15. A long call condor involves buying a call, selling a higher strike call, selling an evenhigher strike call, and buying an even-higher strike call. The distances (or spreads) between all of the strikes are the same, as are the expirations. The position is initiated for a debit, which is the maximum risk of the long condor. The best potential profits happen if the share price settles between the middle two strikes at expiration, and maximum gain is equal the difference between the lowest strike and second lowest strike minus the debit. The two breakevens are the lower strike plus the debit and the highest strike minus the debit. As we can see from Figure B-18, the worst-case scenario is if the underlying moves higher or lower beyond the breakevens.

Strategy: Buy call, sell higher strike call, sell even-higher strike call, buy even-higher strike call

Outlook: Depends on strike prices selected

Debit or Credit: Debit

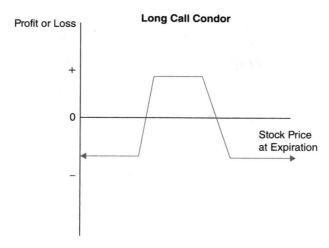

Figure B-18   Call Condor Risk Graph

Risk: Debit

Breakeven: (1) Lowest strike + Debit; (2) Highest strike − Debit

Potential Profits: Difference between the first two strikes − Debit

JJ's Tips for Long Call Condors

- Consider starting with basic options plays before moving on to condors, as these are the most complex of the strategies covered here.
- Choose two middle strikes that capture a targeted range for the underlying.
- The further the middle strikes are from the underlying price, the lower the probability of success.
- Shorter time frames, like two to three weeks, are preferred over longer-term condors.
- Experienced traders might consider using index options for condors and butterflies, as there is no early-assignment risk on European-style options. (Note: Most, but not all, index options are European-style.)

Put Condor Spread (Long)

The long put condor involves buying a put, selling a lower strike put, selling an even-lower strike put, and buying an even lower strike put. The strikes are equidistant apart, and all the options are in the

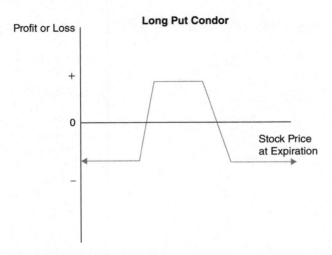

Figure B-19   Long Put Condor Risk Graph

same expiration month. The maximum potential loss is the debit paid for the spread. The best potential profits happen if share price settles between the middle two strikes at expiration and is equal the difference between the highest strike and second highest strike, minus the debit. The two breakevens are equal to the highest strike minus the debit and the lower strike plus the debit. The profit/loss line for the long put condor, as seen in Figure B-19, is the same as the long call condor.

> **Strategy:** Buy put, sell lower strike put, sell even-lower strike put, buy even-lower strike put
>
> **Outlook:** Depends on strike prices selected
>
> **Debit or Credit:** Debit
>
> **Risk:** Debit
>
> **Breakeven:** (1) Lowest strike + Debit; (2) Highest strike − Debit
>
> **Potential Profits:** Difference between the highest two strikes and the debit

JJ's Tips for Long Put Condors
- Think of the strategy as a long put spread and a short put spread.
- At expiration, you want the maximum profit from the long put spread, and you want the short put spread to expire worthless.

- Focus on shorter-term time frames, such as two to three weeks when time decay is the greatest.
- Consider using middle strikes near the underlying stock price to increase probability of success.
- Run this strategy in low volatility markets. A move outside the wings results in losses.

Iron Condor

The iron condor involves buying a put, selling a higher strike put, selling a higher strike call, and buying an even-higher strike call. It is simply selling two vertical spreads—an OTM call vertical spread and an OTM put vertical spread. The maximum payout from the position happens if the share price settles between the two strikes at expiration and is equal to the credit received. The maximum risk is the difference between the first two strikes minus the credit, and as you can see in Figure B-20, this occurs if the underlying makes a move higher or lower. The breakevens are computed as the higher strike put minus the credit and lower strike call plus the credit.

Strategy: Buy puts, sell higher strike put, sell even-higher strike call, buy even-higher strike call

Outlook: Depends on strike prices selected

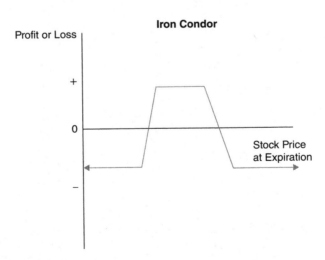

Figure B-20   Long Iron Condor

Debit or Credit: Credit

Risk: Credit

Breakeven: (1) High strike put − Credit; (2) Low strike call + Credit

Potential Profits: Credit

JJ's Tips for Iron Condors
- Think of the iron condor as being short call spread and short put spread.
- Consider picking middle strikes that are equidistant from the underlying stock price.
- Using strikes far away from the current underlying stock price decreases the probability of success.
- As they are just two short vertical spreads, the same time frame rules apply. Focus on short-term options that expire in two to three weeks or less.
- Time is on your side, as you want all of the options to expire worthless.

Quick Strategy Guide

Strategy	Trade Legs	Risk Graph
Long Call	Buy call option	Long Stock Risk Graph
Short Call	Sell call option	Long Call

(*continued*)

Strategy	Trade Legs	Risk Graph
Long Put	Buy put option	 Short Call Profit or Loss 0 Stock Price at Expiration
Protective Put	Buy stock Buy put	 Long Put Profit or Loss 0 Stock Price at Expiration
Covered Call	Buy stock Sell call	 Protective Put Profit or Loss 0 Stock Price at Expiration
Short Put	Sell put	 Covered Call Profit or Loss + 0 − Stock Price at Expiration
Long Call Spread	Buy call Sell call at higher strike	 Collar Profit or Loss + 0 − Stock Price at Expiration

Strategy	Trade Legs	Risk Graph
Long Put Spread	Sell put Buy put at lower strike	
Short Call Spread	Sell call Buy call at higher strike	
Short Put Spread	Sell put Buy put at lower strike	
Call Calendar Spread	Buy call Sell shorter-dated call	
Put Calendar Spread	Buy put Sell shorter-dated put	

(*continued*)

Strategy	Trade Legs	Risk Graph
Call Butterfly	Buy 1 call Sell 2 more higher strikes Buy 1 call at higher strike	 Call Calendar Spread
Put Butterfly	Buy 1 put Sell 2 more lower strikes Buy 1 put at lower strike	 Put Calendar Spread
Iron Butterfly	Buy 1 call Sell 1 lower strike call Sell 1 put (same strike as call) Buy 1 lower strike put	 Long Call Butterfly
Long Call Condor	Buy call Sell higher strike call Sell next-higher strike call Buy next-higher strike call	 Long Put Butterfly

Strategy	Trade Legs	Risk Graph
Long Put Condor	Buy put Sell lower strike put Sell next-lower strike put Buy next-lower strike put	
Iron Condor	Buy call Sell next-lower strike call Sell put at next-lower strike Buy put at next-lower strike	
Collar	Buy stock Sell call Buy put	

APPENDIX C

Charts and Volatility Studies

Y ou have heard it many times: A picture is worth a thousand words. When trading, the adage rings true. At a glance, a chart can show price trends and the highs or lows of a security over a period of days or even years. When this is combined with probabilities (Chapter 9), it is a powerful tool. Meanwhile, because volatility is an important component of options prices, volatility studies can help determine whether options premiums are relatively rich or cheap compared to past levels. This appendix covers just the basics of both stock charting and volatility studies. A brief discussion of volume is included as well.

Stock Charts 101

Stocks, bonds, commodities, or other tradable assets often move in trends. During periods when prices are moving higher, uptrends appear on the chart and are often characterized as a series of higher lows and higher highs. Lines can be drawn on the chart to highlight the trend, as seen in Figure C-1.

A downtrend is a period of time when prices are moving lower. When this happens, trend lines can be drawn along the top of the trend, as in Figure C-2. Therefore, while uptrends are characterized by a series of higher highs, downtrends occur when the security makes a series of lower lows.

Trend lines can sometimes be drawn along the series of lower lows in a downtrend. When lines are drawn along the tops and bottoms of downtrends (or uptrends) it forms a trading channel and looks something like Figure C-2.

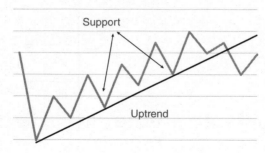

Figure C-1   Uptrend

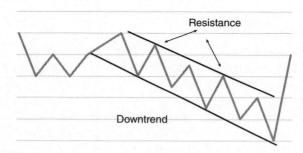

Figure C-2   Downtrend

Figures C-1 and C-2 show how trend lines during uptrends and downtrends can seem to serve as areas of support or resistance. A support level is a price where the underlying security stops falling and begins to move higher. Resistance is the opposite. If a security is having difficulty breaking through a level, it is said to be facing resistance.

Support and resistance don't just appear in uptrends and downtrends. A stock might also find support or resistance at a round number like $100 per share or a currency pair at an even number, such as if the euro reaches parity against the U.S. dollar.

In addition, as in Figure C-3, support sometimes has an uncanny way of becoming a resistance area, and vice versa. This is more likely to occur at a price point for a security that attracts a lot of interest among investors, perhaps a round number like $100 per share or 1.0 for a currency pair.

Moving averages (MA) can be useful when analyzing trends as well. Plotted using charting software, an MA is simply the average of the security's price over a previous period of days. Commonly used

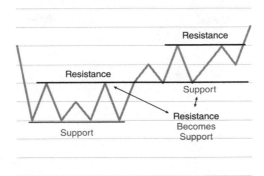

Figure C-3   Support and Resistance

moving averages include nine-day, fifty-day, and two-hundred-day. For instance, the fifty-day moving average for Walmart (WMT) along with a downtrend line and an uptrend line are included in Figure C-4.

Moving averages can sometimes seem to serve as support and resistance as well. Notice on Figure C-4 when Walmart was in a downtrend, the fifty-day moving average was moving lower but was above the upper end of the trading channel (resistance)—that is, until the stock changed trend. Once that happened, the MA was below the stock (support) and moving higher.

In addition to moving averages, hundreds (if not thousands) of technical indicators have been developed in recent years. In fact, there are more than a dozen different types of MAs alone. Each uses a slightly different formula to compute the average. The list is too expansive and well beyond the scope of this book, but technical indicators (or studies) are widely available today through stock charting websites and trading platforms.

Ultimately, these tools and indicators are valuable in helping to see past trends and identify potential price targets for the underlying security, but never has one been developed that can reliably predict the future. Just as markets change, so does the reliability of technical indicators.

Time Frames

It's easy to change the chart's time fame, and doing so can reveal interesting differences between short-term and long-term trends.

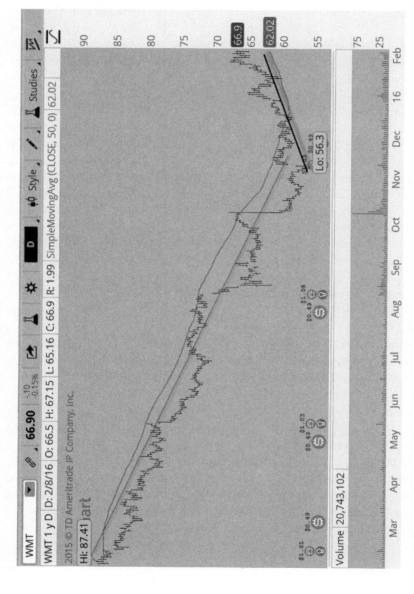

Figure C-4   Walmart Daily Chart with Trend Lines and Fifty-Day MA

Time frames can vary from short-term periods, where each bar represents one minute, to very long ones, where each bar represents a month. For example, Figure C-5 shows the daily chart of the S&P 500 Index and the fact that it was clearly in a downtrend at the time.

Yet, while the daily chart of the S&P 500 is in a downtrend, the monthly chart (Figure C-6) tells a different tale, because the index is moving higher. Although the short-term trend is down, in the bigger picture, it is in a rather serious uptrend.

What's the best time frame to watch? The answer might depend on your investment objectives and trading style. On the one hand, an investor with a longer-term buy-and-hold philosophy with an occasional covered call thrown in the mix is more likely to be interested in trends on the weekly or monthly charts. On the other hand, a day trader aggressively buying calls on volatile stocks will probably be more focused on intraday charts and keying off of short-term support/resistance levels. Two common time frames are fifty-day and two-hundred-day moving averages.

Volume and Volatility

The Chicago Board Options Exchange (CBOE) Volatility Index (VIX) is arguably the most widely watched barometer of market volatility. The index tracks the expected (or implied) volatility in a strip of very short-term options on the S&P 500 Index. Figure C-7 shows how VIX has moved higher or lower over time, with notable spikes that occurred during market turbulence.

Just as the S&P 500 has a measure of implied volatility (IV) reflected in VIX, each optionable security has a level of IV that can be charted using software. It shows the average implied volatility across a class of options and not the IV of a specific put or call, which will vary from one contract to the next. Figure C-8, for instance, shows the daily chart of Procter & Gamble (PG) along with, at the bottom, the thirty-day implied volatility. It is roughly 21 percent and seems to be approximately in the middle of the one-year range.

As the term suggests, implied volatility is a measure that is priced into options and *implied* by the current prices. It often differs from the actual (or real) volatility of the underlying security.

Historical (or statistical) volatility (HV) is a better gauge of the security's past levels of volatility. Expressed as a percentage and computed as the annualized standard deviation over a period of days,

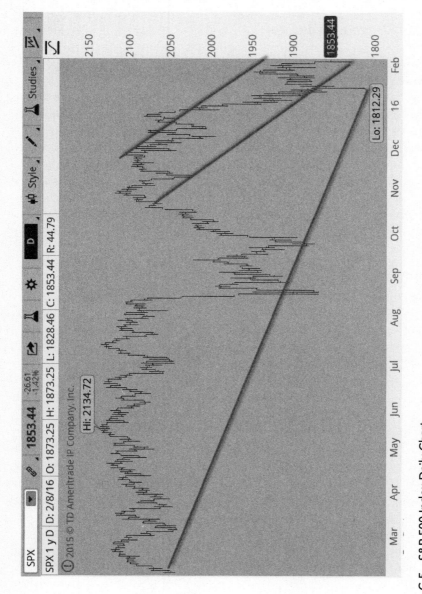

Figure C-5   S&P 500 Index Daily Chart

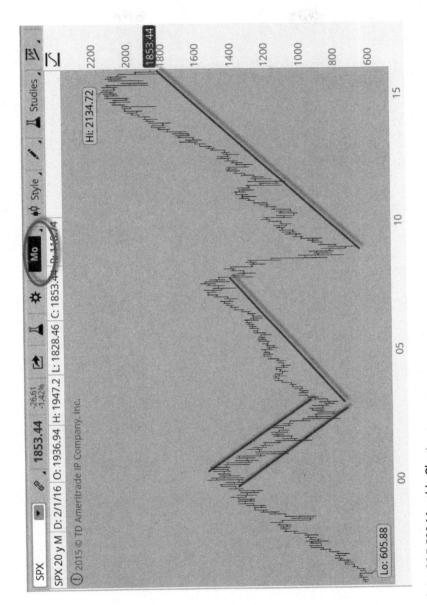

Figure C-6 S&P 500 Monthly Chart

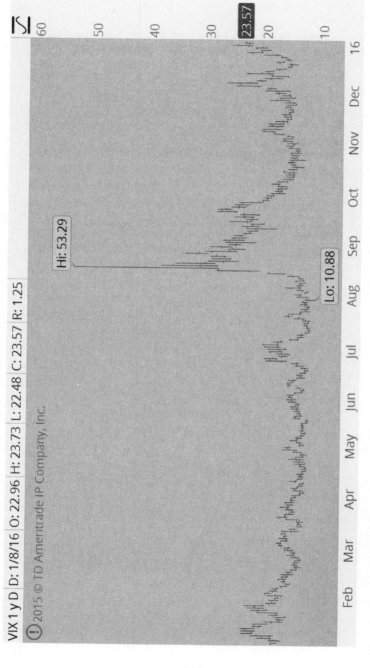

Figure C-7 CBOE Volatility Index

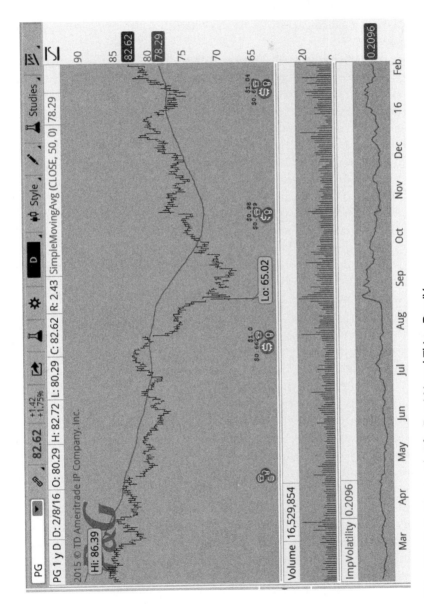

Figure C-8 P&G Daily Chart with Fifty-Day MA and Thirty-Day IV

273

HV is typically computed using closing prices. For instance, Figure C-9 shows the thirty-day HV of P&G on the same daily chart as Figure C-8. Notice that it is near 19 percent. Therefore, the volatility, as measured by closing prices, is a bit less than the implied volatility of 21 percent.

The thirty-day HV in Figure C-9 moves similar to the IV in Figure C-8, but not exactly the same because historical volatility reflects past volatility. Implied volatility is a measure of expected volatility and is heavily influenced by investor perceptions. When the two differ significantly, it is considered to be a sign that the options market is expecting the underlying to see higher (or lower) volatility in the future compared to what has existed in the past.

If IV is much higher than historical volatility, many investors would consider the options rich. If implied volatility is very low compared to HV, then many investors would consider the options cheap. In this case, HV and IV of P&G don't seem different enough to draw any significant conclusions. Both appear to be in a normal range, and that is confirmed by Figure C-10, which shows that the implied volatility in P&G is in the middle (fifty-first percentile) of the fifty-two-week range. HV is in the fifty-sixth percentile.

Volume and volatility often go hand in hand. Just as every underlying security has a unique level of IV, every instrument has a level of volume. Often measured in days, volume of a stock or exchange-traded fund (ETF) is the number of shares that changed hands. The volume for futures and options is measured in contracts.

Volume is greater for some instruments compared to others. The amount of trading activity reflects the investor interest in the security, and that can change over time. In addition, volume often spikes when a security sees an increase in volatility, and volume slows during periods of slow market action.

Notice from figures C-8 and C-9 that volume in P&G shares saw a notable increase when shares fell to lows of $65.02. This was a sign of extreme trading activity and a fast-moving stock. That period of heightened volatility eventually set the table for a substantial rebound in the stock, but only after it had suffered rather notable percentage losses.

Trend lines, moving averages, and volume are basic charting concepts. Technical analysis goes well beyond that to include a wide array of tools and indicators that traders use to make sense of market moves

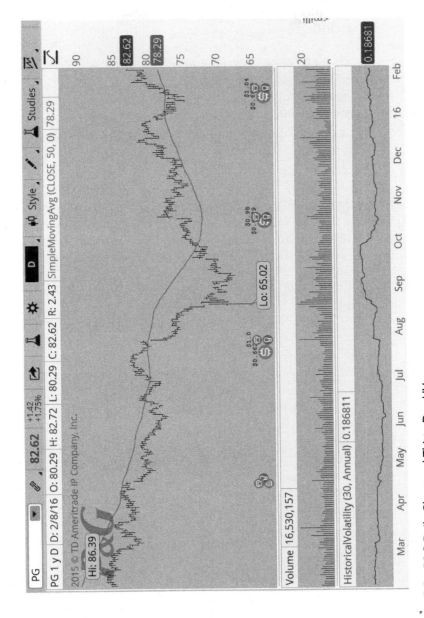

Figure C-9   P&G Daily Chart and Thirty-Day HV

⌄ Today's Options Statistics	
52 week IV High:	0.298
52 week IV Low:	0.119
Current IV Percent...	51%
52 week HV High:	0.286
52 week HV Low:	0.09
Current HV Perce...	56%
Implied Volatility:	20.96%
VWAP:	81.801

Figure C-10   Options Statistics Example Including HV/IV Percentiles
Source: TOS

and attempt to anticipate the future. However, while the tools are useful, none are magic bullets, and no indicator is infallible.

Lastly, volatility is an important concept, not just for technical analysts but also for options traders, because it can have a very powerful effect on the premiums of puts and calls. The primary reason is that the greater the volatility, the higher the probability of the options moving ITM.

Glossary

American-style option A put or call options contract that can be exercised at any time prior to expiration. Stock options, options on exchange-traded funds (ETFs), and some index options settle American-style.

arbitrage Buying (or selling) a security in one market or on one exchange and selling (or buying) it on another where a temporary difference in price exists. Arbitrage is an attempt to score a risk-free profit.

ask The best price that a security or commodity is offered for sale.

assignment When an option seller or writer receives an exercise notice, assignment has occurred. When assigned, writers must deliver the underlying (shares or cash) per the terms of the contract.

at-the-money (ATM) option When the strike price of the option and the market price of the underlying stock are the same, the contract is at the money.

automatic exercise Beginning in June 2008, the Options Clearing Corporation (OCC) adopted a rule that all options that are a penny or more in the money (ITM) at expiration are to be exercised at expiration. Therefore, ITM options with intrinsic value of $0.01 or more are automatically exercised at expiration. This is to ensure that options holders don't inadvertently leave money on the table by allowing ITM options to expire.

back-month options Options with the most distant expirations within a class of options.

bear call spread A strategy that involves selling a call and buying a call at a higher strike within the same expiration month.

bear put spread Buying a put and selling a lower strike put within the same expiration.

bearish A negative (or pessimistic) outlook for a security or market.

beta A measure of a stock's volatility relative to the broader market. High-beta stocks are seeing higher volatility than the broader market.

bid The price that the market is willing to pay for a security.

bid-ask spread Computing the bid-ask spread is simply the current ask price for a security minus the bid price. More actively traded stocks and options typically have smaller spreads compared to less actively traded ones.

block trade A large institutional trade consisting of, for instance, one thousand options contracts or ten thousand shares of stock.

borrow fee Also known as *stock loan fee*, this is the rate that brokerage firms charge customers to borrow shares for the purpose of short selling.

box spread A strategy that gets its name from the fact that it is created using two spreads (bull call and bear put) that form a rectangular box shape on an options chain. It is generally an attempt to score a risk-free profit and is also called an *alligator spread* due to the fact that transaction costs are likely to eat up any potential temporary arbitrage opportunities when they do exist.

breakeven The price of the underlying at expiration where, excluding transaction costs, an options strategy shows no profits or losses.

bullish A positive (or optimistic) outlook for a security or market.

butterfly spread An options strategy that involves selling (or buying) two options and also buying (or selling) one higher strike and one lower strike option within the same expiration month. The middle strikes are said to be the body of the butterfly, and the other two strikes are called the wings.

buy-to-close A transaction that offsets an opening position that was initiated by a seller. For example, to close a position in short calls, an investor buys-to-close the same number of call contracts.

buy-to-open A transaction that initiates a new long position in an options contract.

calendar spread Created with either puts or calls, it's a spread strategy that involves selling (or buying) an option in one expiration and buying (or selling) another option at a different expiration and the same strike price.

call option An agreement between two parties to buy and sell an underlying security at a fixed price through a set expiration period. The owner of a call option has the right to buy the underlying asset at the strike price of the option through the expiration. Call sellers (or writers) have the obligation to sell the underlying per the terms of the contract.

cash-secured put An options strategy that involves selling puts while sufficient cash is deposited in the investor's account to buy the underlying if assignment occurs.

cash settlement A type of options contract that involves the delivery of cash upon exercise (or assignment). Options on indexes like the S&P 500 Index are cash-settled.

chains Tables that list prices and other information about an options class. Options chains typically include the last trading price, the bid and ask prices, and trading volume for all puts and calls for an underlying security. The chains are often sorted by expiration month, with calls appearing on one side and puts on the other.

closing purchase Buying an options contract to offset an open short position.

closing sale An order to offset an open long position in an option.

collar Selling calls and buying puts against an existing or new stock position. One put is bought and one call sold for every one hundred shares. The strategy is a combination of the protective put and covered call with limited downside risk and capped upside potential.

condor An options strategy that involves buying an option, selling a higher strike, selling an even higher strike, and buying an even higher strike. The strikes are equidistant apart and within the same expiration term.

conversion Primarily a professional strategy, an options play that involves a call and a put at the same strike and same expiration month. It is created by purchasing stock and puts while selling calls. Or, it can be viewed as long stock and synthetic short (long puts, short calls) and is typically initiated as an arbitrage play when the synthetic appears mispriced relative to the underlying.

cost basis The value of an asset at the time of purchase and used for tax purposes to calculate capital gains or losses. For a stock, cost basis is merely the purchase price but is adjusted for events such as stock splits and dividends as well.

covered call Selling calls against a new or existing position in the underlying. In the equities market, one call is sold for every one hundred shares of stock. The strategy lowers the effective cost of the stock but also limits the potential upside.

credit Income into an account from selling options premium. The short put is an example of a credit strategy.

credit spread Any options play where the premium received from selling one leg of the spread is greater than the premium paid for the other part of the spread. The result is a net credit.

day trader An investor buying and selling during the trading day but not holding positions overnight.

debit An amount of money deducted from an account when purchasing options. Buying calls is an example of a debit transaction.

debit spread Any options play where the premium received from selling one leg of the spread is less than the premium paid for the other part of the spread. The result is a debit in the account.

deep option Deep in-the-money (ITM) options have substantial intrinsic value. For example, a call is deep ITM if the strike price is well below the current price of the underlying. However, an option is deep out of the money (OTM) if the strike is very distant from the underlying and there is no intrinsic value. A put is deep OTM, for instance, if the strike is well below the underlying price.

delivery The exchange of cash or shares from one party to another to satisfy exercise/assignment on an options or futures contract.

delta The expected change in the value of an option based on one-point moves in the underlying instrument. Calls have positive deltas, and puts have negative deltas.

delta neutral An options strategy where the combined deltas of all positions in the underlying and the options are equal to or close to zero. For instance, buying one hundred shares and two −0.5 delta puts results in a delta-neutral position, because one hundred shares of stock have a delta of 1.0. This is usually temporary, because when the options move, the deltas are changing as well, which is why many traders talk of a range of deltas that they consider delta neutral.

derivative An instrument that has value derived from another instrument. An equity option is a derivative because its value is linked to the performance of an underlying stock. Examples of other derivatives include futures, forward contracts, and swaps.

diagonal spread Created with either puts or calls, a strategy that involves selling (or buying) an options contract and buying (or selling) one with a later expiration date and a higher or lower strike price. It can be considered a combination of vertical and calendar spreads.

diversification An attempt to reduce the risk of a portfolio by allocating investments across an array of securities, sectors, strategies, or assets.

dividend A payment from a corporation to its shareholders. Many companies pay dividends quarterly, and others might offer special dividends on occasion. Some companies pay no dividends at all.

downtrend A formation or line on a chart when the security is falling in price.

end-of-month option An options contract that has an expiration that falls on the last business day of the calendar month.

European-style option An options contract that can only be exercised at expiration. Many indexes, such as the S&P 500 Index, have options that are European-style.

exchange Venues where stocks and options trade. While the New York Stock Exchange is the best-known among the stock exchanges, more than a dozen options exchanges are trading puts and calls today. Many of them are all electronic.

exchange-traded fund (ETF) A type of security that is listed on a major exchange and can be bought or sold like shares of stock. However, rather than representing ownership in one company, an ETF can hold shares of many different companies or other assets, including gold, bonds, or commodities.

ex-dividend date The cutoff date when new stock buyers are no longer entitled to an upcoming dividend. Only shareholders on record prior to the ex-dividend date collect the dividend.

exercise Carrying out the terms of an options contract by the option's owner. In the equities market, a call buyer exercises the contract by instructing his brokerage firm to buy (or call) the stock according to the terms of the option. One hundred shares are purchased for every one call option. Exercising a put involves selling the underlying. Also see *automatic-exercise*.

exercise price The price for buying or selling the underlying asset on exercise/assignment, as stipulated by the options contract. It is also called the *strike price*.

exercise settlement value The settlement value is computed at expiration for index products and, for purposes of exercise and assignment, will determine which options are in the money (ITM) or out of the money (OTM) at expiration. Because settlement values are sometimes computed Friday morning, the last day to trade these index options is on a Thursday before expiration Friday.

expiration cycle The available expirations for a class of options, such as March, June, September, and December. More active contracts typically have standard monthly cycles and weekly expirations as well.

expiration date The date that an options contract, and the right to exercise it, cease to exist.

extrinsic value The value of the options contract beyond its intrinsic value. Extrinsic value is also called an option's *time value*. Out-of-the-money (OTM) options consist only of extrinsic value. In-the-money (ITM) options can consist of both intrinsic and time value.

fill A term used by traders to refer to the execution of a buy or sell order. After the order is executed, it has been filled.

flex options A type of option that is customized to meet the requests of specific investors. Originally created on index products, flex options on equities and exchange-traded funds (ETFs) exist today as well but are typically the domain of institutional rather than individual investors.

float How many shares a company currently has outstanding.

forward contract An agreement between two parties to buy or sell an asset at a set price at a certain future date.

front-month The contracts that are next to expire within a class of options or futures.

fundamental analysis Research into a company, industry, or economy. Fundamental analysis of a stock, for instance, looks into factors such as profits, sales, management, and product development.

futures contract An agreement to buy or sell underlying assets, such as a commodity, bond, or shares of stock at a fixed priced but to be delivered and paid for at a later point in time.

futures options Puts and calls listed on futures contracts.

gamma Delta's sensitivity to changes in the price of the underlying security.

Greeks, the Delta, vega, theta, gamma, and rho are used to measure the sensitivity of options premiums to changes in variables such as time, volatility, interest rates, and movements in the price of the underlying. Collectively, these measures are known as the Greeks.

hard-to-borrow (HTB) A stock is HTB if it's difficult for brokerage firms to lend it to investors for the purpose of short selling.

hedge A protective position designed to limit risk. A protective put is a type of hedge because the put option is designed to protect against a possible decline in the price of an individual stock.

hedge fund An investment that pools funds from a group of high-net-worth investors and initiates sometimes complex strategies, such as arbitrage, market timing, or long and short portfolios with derivatives.

historical volatility (HV) Also called *actual* or *realized volatility*, HV is computed as the annualized standard deviation of prices of a security over a specific period of past trading days, such as twenty, thirty, or ninety days.

horizontal spread A spread with options that have different expiration months. A call calendar spread is a horizontal spread because the investor is buying a call at one strike and selling a call at the same strike but a different expiration month.

implied volatility (IV) The level of volatility embedded in an option's price. Computed using an options-pricing model, IV is constantly changing and will vary from one contract to the next.

index Also known as an *average*, an index is proxy for the performance of a group of stocks within a market, sector, or industry group. The Dow Jones Industrial Average, the S&P 500 Index, and the NASDAQ Composite are examples of indexes that track the performance of the US stock market.

index effect The reaction in the shares of a company after it has been announced that the stock will be included or removed from an index such as the S&P 500 or the Dow Jones Industrial Average.

industry The primary business activity of an individual company. Examples include semiconductors, oil drillers, regional banking, and biotechnology.

in-the-money (ITM) option An options contracts that has intrinsic value. A put option is ITM if the strike price is above the current price of the underlying. A call option is ITM if the market price of the underlying security is above the strike price of the option.

intrinsic value Intrinsic value is tangible value of an in-the-money (ITM) option and is determined by the relationship of the underlying price to the strike price of the option. The intrinsic value of an ITM call option, as an example, is equal to the price of the underlying security minus the strike price. The intrinsic value of an ITM put option is the strike minus the price of the underlying asset. The total value of an ITM option is its intrinsic value plus time value. Out-of-the-money options (OTM) and at-the-money (ATM) options have no intrinsic value.

iron butterfly A type of spread strategy that simultaneously sells a call spread and sells a put spread. The short puts and calls are at the same strike to form the body of the fly. The long puts and calls make up the wings.

iron condor An options strategy that involves the sale of a put and the purchase of a lower strike put, along with the sale of a call and the purchase of a higher strike call. The play is a combination of a short call spread and a short put spread where the strike prices of the calls are higher than those of the puts. All strikes are equidistant apart and in the same expiration term.

LEAPS Long-term Equity Anticipation Securities, or LEAPS, are calls and puts with an expiration of more than nine months when listed.

leg One side of an options spread, straddle, or other strategy. For instance, long call spread consists of two legs: (1) long calls and (2) short calls at a higher strike.

legging Opening an options spread or other complex strategy by purchasing one side of the spread at a time rather than buying or selling the entire position in one transaction. For example, legging into a long call spread would involve buying long calls and then, separately, selling higher strike calls at a different time.

limit order A type of order to buy or sell a security at a specific price or better.

long Purchasing a position in a security in anticipation that the price of the security will increase in value. Going long stock, for example, is a play on an expected move higher in the price of the shares. An investor can also hold long puts in anticipation the options will increase in value if the underlying asset falls in price.

margin Borrowed money to buy or sell investment securities. Or, in the futures market, it is the collateral that is deposited in an account to cover risk of losses.

margin account An account established by a brokerage firm that allows an investor to buy or sell short with borrowed money.

margin call A request from a brokerage to its customer to deposit additional funds in his account after a security (or securities) financed with borrowed money have decreased in value.

market maker A professional dealer in a security or group of securities who buys or sells at specific prices. As the term suggests, it is this person's job to make markets to enable buying and selling by displaying bids and asks.

market order An order to buy or sell a security that does not specify a set price. Instead, it is an order to execute the trade at the next available price.

market timer An investor actively buying and selling securities based on the market outlook. Market timing might be driven by macro events, technical indicators, fundamentals, or a combination of all three.

mean Another way of saying the statistic known as the average. It is computed by summing the values of all observations and dividing that amount by the number of observations.

moneyness Also called *value*, the term describes the relationship between the strike price of the option and the price of the underlying security. An option can be in the money (ITM), at the money (ATM), near the money, or out of the money (OTM).

moving average A chart indicator that is plotted along with the price of the security that shows the average price over a specific number of past days, such as nine, fifty, or two hundred days.

multiplier A number used to compute the actual premium paid (or received) for an options contract. The multiplier for a stock option is one hundred, because one standard contract controls one hundred shares. Therefore, if an option is quoted at $5 a contract, the cost to buy it is $5 × 100, or $500 for one contract.

naked option A short option that is not protected with a position in a long option or the underlying security.

near-the-money option When an option has a strike price near the underlying price, but not exactly equal to it. When the strike price equals the underlying price exactly, the contract is at the money (ATM).

notional value The total value of a position based on the number of options traded and the underlying security's current price. It represents how much the investor might pay (or receive) if exercised (or assigned) on the entire options position.

offer Also called the *ask* or *asking price*, it is the best market price for selling the security and the one that the investor might be expected to pay in order to buy it.

open interest Updated just once per day, open interest is the total number of contracts in an options series that have been opened and not yet closed. Open interest changes as investors open and close positions. Exercising of options and expirations also drive changes in open interest numbers.

options chains See *chains*.

Option Clearing Corporation (OCC) Founded in 1973, the OCC is the clearinghouse that oversees all of the listed options activity in the U.S. markets. In addition to clearing trades for the member exchanges, it also ensures that options contracts are honored, even in cases when individuals or organizations run into financial problems.

options type There are two types of options: puts and calls.

options class All puts or calls on an underlying. For instance, all puts and calls on XYZ Company are considered to be a class of options.

options series All options contracts of a given type with the same strike price and expiration date. An XYZ March 110 call is an options series, as is a ZYX June 100 put.

opportunity risk The potential of not participating in the chance for profits after initiating a limited reward strategy. For instance, a covered call carries opportunity risk because selling call options will cap the upside potential associated with owning the underlying stock.

out-of-the-money (OTM) option An options contract consisting only of time value and no intrinsic value. A call option is OTM when the underlying asset price is below its strike price. A put option is OTM if the strike price is below the underlying asset price.

payoff chart See *risk graph*.

pin risk The risk of the underlying security trading very near (or pinning) to the strike price of the option into the final moments of expiration. When it happens, it can create problems for holders of both long and short options positions, because it adds uncertainty about whether the option is expiring in the money (ITM) or out of the money (OTM), which has implications for exercise and assignment.

portfolio margin (PM) Instituted in 2007, PM is a set of rules that allows margin rates to be set based on the total risk of the portfolio rather than based on traditional strategy-based requirements.

position delta The total delta of a position or portfolio. Because one hundred shares of stock have delta of 1.0, a position consisting of one hundred shares and one −0.5 delta put has a position delta of 0.50.

probabilities A statistical term related to the chance or likelihood of an event happening. For example, an investor might look at the probabilities of stock reaching a certain price level over a period of time to determine if an options contract is likely to be in the money (ITM) or out of the money (OTM) at expiration.

probability of profit The statistical likelihood of an options strategy being profitable by a penny or more at expiration based on a spectrum of possible prices of the underlying security through the life of the options contract.

probability of touching The chances of a stock reaching a certain level over a specific period of time.

put-call parity The relationship between puts and calls with the same expiration term and same strike price. For example, the synthetic equivalent of long stock is long call plus short put at the same strike and expiration. Parity is the idea that the prices of the underlying and the synthetic will be equal, or else a risk-free arbitrage opportunity exists (after taking into account interest rates and dividends).

put/call ratio The number of puts divided by the number of calls traded for a specific security or group of securities. Put/call ratios are typically computed for a trading day and give a sense of whether a name (or market) is seeing relatively high or low levels of put activity relative to call activity.

put option An options contract giving the owner the right to sell (or put) the underlying asset at the strike price through a fixed expiration date. Shorting puts is expressing a willingness to buy the underlying security per the terms of the contract.

quad witch The quadruple witch expiration is a quarterly expiration in March, June, September, and December when a variety of different instruments—including single stock options, futures, futures options, and single stock futures—are expiring simultaneously. Some market watchers contend that the quad witches trigger higher levels of volatility due to all of the buying and selling associated with the expiration.

quarterlys Options with expirations on the last business day of the calendar quarters (March, June, September, and December).

ratio spread A spread strategy that involves buying (or selling) options and selling (or buying) a different number of options at a different strike price or expiration month. Common ratios include 1:2 and 2:3.

resistance A technical analysis term relating to a price level that has served as a barrier or a top for a security on multiple previous occasions.

reversal A strategy that involves selling stock, selling puts, and buying calls with the options at the same strike and expiration month. It can be viewed as short stock and long the synthetic equivalent. Like the conversion, it is not a strategy widely used by individual investors, but rather an arbitrage play by professionals when the synthetic portion seems mispriced.

rho A measure of an option's sensitivity to changes in interest rates.

risk arbitrage Also known as merger arbitrage, the trading strategy is typically initiated by trading desks or hedge funds that attempt to profit from a corporate merger or acquisition. For instance, the arbitrage might involve selling shares of the acquiring company short and buying the shares of the one being acquired to profit from the fact that the prices of the two will converge when the deal is completed. It can result in hefty losses if, for some reason, the deal falls apart.

risk graph Sometimes called a profit/loss line, risk curve, or payoff chart, the risk graph shows the potential profits and losses associated with an investment strategy.

risk-reversal An options strategy that involves the sale (or purchase) of a usually out-of-the-money (OTM) call and the purchase (or sale) of a usually OTM put. As an example, a bullish risk-reversal involves the sale of a put and the purchase of call option.

sector A broad industry group within the equities market such as energy, technology, or health care.

sector rotation Allocating funds from one sector to another based on the outlook for the broader economy and the equities market.

sell-to-close An order to cover a long options position. If long calls, for instance, the investor offsets the position by selling the same call options to close.

sell-to-open An order to open a new short options position. Selling call options to create covered call positions are selling-to-open transactions.

settlement date The date for payment to be made to fulfill the terms (exercise/assignment) of the options contract.

settlement price The price at the end of a trading session at expiration (or in the morning for some index products), which is established by the Options Clearing Corporation (OCC) and used to determine exercise/assignment of options at expiration.

short Selling a position in a stock, options, or futures contract in an attempt to profit from a possible move lower in price. Short stock reflects a bearish view on the shares. However, a short put involves selling puts but is also typically a bullish strategy.

short selling An investment strategy that attempts to profit from a fall in a security's price. In a typical example, an investor borrows stock from a broker, sells it short, and covers the position later by purchasing the stock and returning it to the lender.

skew When two options in the same class have very different levels of implied volatility. A time skew happens when an option in one expiration month has much higher (or lower) implied volatility than a similar strike option in a different expiration. A price skew is when two options in the same expiration term and different strikes have different levels of implied volatility. In most securities, the common skew is for OTM puts to have higher implied volatility than OTM calls.

slippage The difference between the anticipated price and the actual price of the trade at the time it is executed. Slippage typically occurs with market orders during periods of higher volatility

specialist A member of a stock or options exchange with the role of market maker to keep a book on all orders.

standard deviation A statistical measure of price fluctuation that captures how spread out a set of numbers is. It measures the dispersion or deviation from a mean (or average) price.

statistical volatility See *historical volatility.*

stock replacement Swapping a stock position for an options strategy. For example, an investor might liquidate a stock position and replace it with long call options to maintain bullish exposure, but with less capital at risk.

stock split A corporate action taken when a company wants to adjust the price of its common stock. Shares are often split 2-for-1 or 3-of-1 to lower the price and make shares more accessible for individual investors to buy and sell. On the other hand, if share prices have fallen to very low levels, a company might initiate a reverse split to make the stock seem more respectable. Options contracts are also adjusted after a stock split.

stop-order A type of contingency order that becomes a market order when the stock trades, or is bid or offered, through or at a specific price. Often erroneously known as a stop-loss, the order entry technique is sometimes used to exit a position and stem additional losses after an adverse move in the underlying.

straddle A strategy that involves the purchase (or sale in a short straddle) of a call and a put at the same strike and same expiration term.

strangle A call and put on the same underlying asset with the same expiration month and different strike prices most commonly with an OTM put and an OTM call.

strike price See *exercise price.*

suitability A term that refers to whether a security or strategy is appropriate for an investor or a portfolio based on financial resources and previous investing experience.

support A technical analysis term relating to a price level that a security has touched on several occasions but has not dropped below. It reaches that level and moves higher.

swap An agreement between two parties that exchanges cash flows from one party's financial instrument for the cash flow from the other party's. Swaps can be on a variety of different instruments and are typically traded among large financial institutions.

synthetic A strategy involving two or more securities that has the same risk-reward profile as a strategy involving only one security. For instance, the synthetic of long stock position is a short put plus a long call at the same strike and same expiration.

technical analysis The study of stock charts and other price data to analyze past price trends of a security or market and make estimates about possible moves in the future.

theta A measure of a put's or call's sensitivity to time decay.

time decay The negative impact to options prices due to the passage of time.

time value See *extrinsic value.*

trading pit A physical location at one of the exchanges where a crowd of traders gathers to buy or sell a particular security.

transaction costs The commissions or other fees charged by brokerage firms to buy and sell stocks, options, or other investments.

triple witch day The monthly expiration in March, June, September, and December when stock options, futures, and futures options are expiring. It is sometimes called the quadruple witch because single stock futures also expire on these quarterly expirations.

uncovered option See *naked option.*

underlying instrument Also called the *underlying asset* or *underlying security*, it is the security from which a derivative is written on and is to be delivered in the event of exercise or assignment. The underlying for one equity option is typically one hundred shares.

uptrend A technical analysis term relating to a period of rising prices that can be seen on a chart and highlighted with an upward-sloping line.

vega A measure of an option's sensitivity to changes in the volatility of the underlying asset.

vertical spread A strategy where the long and short options within the spread have the same underlying asset and expiration months but different strike prices.

VIX CBOE (Chicago Board Options Exchange) Volatility Index (VIX) is a measure of the implied volatility priced into a strip of options on the S&P 500 Index (SPX). It is sometimes called the market's fear gauge, because it tends to spike during periods of market volatility and when S&P 500 Index options premiums become more expensive due to higher demand for portfolio protection.

volatility The speed of movement associated with the price fluctuation of a security. Fast-moving markets have high volatility. Slow markets are characterized by low volatility.

volatility crush A sudden drop in the implied volatility of an options contract or a group of options. A crush can occur after an important event, such as a corporate earnings report or an economic report, has passed.

volatility skew See *skew*.

volume The number of shares or contracts traded in a stock, futures, or options contract.

wasting assets Investment securities such as stock options that lose value over time.

weeklys Options typically listed on Thursday and expiring the following Friday. Weekly options have very short durations and are listed on the most actively traded stocks, exchange-traded funds (ETFs), and indexes.

writer An options seller.

Index

Note: Page references followed by f and t indicate an illustrated figure and table, respectively.